BIRD OWNER'S
HOME HEALTH AND CARE HANDBOOK

Bird Owner's HOME HEALTH and CARE Handbook

by
GARY A. GALLERSTEIN, D.V.M.

FIRST EDITION
Third Printing
1985

HOWELL BOOK HOUSE Inc.
230 Park Avenue, New York, N.Y. 10169

Library of Congress Cataloging in Publication Data

Gallerstein, Gary A., 1952-
  Bird owner's home health and care handbook.

  Bibliography: p. 283
  Includes index.
  1. Cage-birds. 2. Cage-birds—Diseases. I. Title.
SF461.G34 1984   636.6'86   84-9049
ISBN 0-87605-820-9

To

My Father and Mother, Frank and Sally
*for their support and encouragement
through all my years*

My Wife, Nancy

Love Always

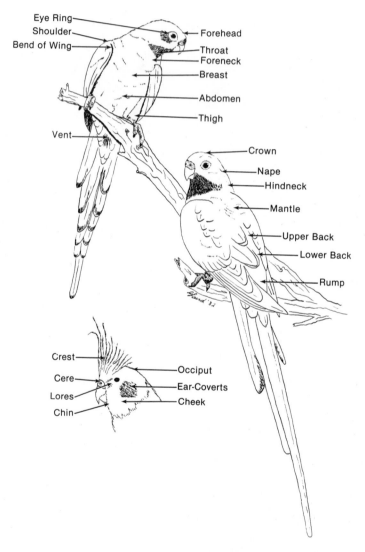

Eye Ring — Forehead
Shoulder —
Bend of Wing — Throat
Foreneck
Breast
Abdomen
Thigh
Vent —
Crown
Nape
Hindneck
Mantle
Upper Back
Lower Back
Rump
Crest —
Occiput
Cere —
Ear-Coverts
Lores —
Cheek
Chin —

Topographical anatomy of birds.

Contents

About the Author   11
Acknowledgments   13
Introduction   15
History of Bird Keeping   17

Chapter 1—Tips on Buying a New Bird—Page 19

Choice of Species, 19; Where to Purchase Birds, 20; Health Before Wealth, 20; Temperament and Trainability, 23; Cost versus Supply and Demand, 23; Buying the Bird, 23.

Chapter 2—Your New Bird: The Do's and Don'ts—Page 25

Bringing Your Bird Home, 25; Stress, 25.

Chapter 3—Feeding for Health, Vitality and Longevity—Page 29

Factors Influencing Choice of Foods, 29; Factors Affecting Energy Requirement, 31; Carbohydrates, 31; Proteins, 32; Vitamins, 32; Minerals, 35; Iodine, 35; Essential Vitamins in Bird Feeding, 36; Grit, 37; Water, 37; Average Daily Water Intake for Birds, 37; Other Liquids, 37; Essential Minerals in Bird Feeding, 38; Diet: Balance Through Variety, 41; Vegetables and Greens, 41; Fruits, 43; Table Foods, 43; Pelleted Foods, 43; Summarizing the Complete Parrot Diet, 45; Diet for Mynah Birds, 45; Diet For Lories and Lorikeets, 45; San Diego Zoo's Recipes For Bird Diets (Finches and Canaries, Small Parrots, Large Parrots, Mynah Birds, Lories), 45; Advice For Feeding the Finicky Eater, 47.

Chapter 4—Creating a Happy Environment—Page 49

Housing, 49; Toys, 50; Flying Exercise, 50; Safety Checklist Prior to Liftoff, 50; What You Can Do, 50; Companionship, 52; Cats and Dogs, 52; Music and Television, 53; Traveling *With* Your Bird (By Car, By Air, By Bus or Train), 53; Traveling *Without* Your Bird, 54.

Chapter 5—Home Sweet Home—Page 55

Cage Design, 55; Cage Paint, 57; Cage Paper, 57; Cage Location, 57; Cage Covers, 59; Perches, 59; T-Stands, 60; Food and Water Cups, 60; Playpens, 60; Toys, 60; Flight Cages, 63; Temperature and Humidity, 63; Cleaning and Disinfecting, 64; Summary of Disinfectant Characteristics, 65.

Chapter 6—Feathers, Feet 'n' Beaks, Too!—Page 67

General Health and Grooming Care, 67; Feathers, 67; Molt, 68; Recommendations During the Molt, 68; Wing Trimming, 68; Bathing, 72; Beaks, 72; Nails, 74; Bleeding—Beaks and Nails, 78.

Chapter 7—How to Restrain Your Bird—Page 79

Chapter 8—Basic Anatomy and Physiology—Page 83

Eyes, 83; *Home Physical*, 85; Ears, 86; *Home Physical*, 86; Integument (Skin), 86; *Home Physical*, 88; Musculoskeletal System, 88; *Home Physical*, 88; Respiratory System; 89; *Home Physical*, 90; The Vitals, 91; Cardiovascular System, 91; Blood Volume, 91; *Home Physical*, 92; Lymphatic System, 92; *Home Physical*, 92; Digestive System, 92; *Home Physical*, 94; Urinary System, 94; *Home Physical*, 94; Reproductive System, 96; *Home Physical*, 96; Nervous System, 96; *Home Physical*, 101; Endocrine System, 101; *Home Physical*, 101.

SPECIAL COLOR FEATURE—Comparison of Normal Droppings from Healthy Birds with Those of Birds suffering various illnesses (from *Diseases of Cage and Aviary Birds* by M.L. Petrak, D.V.M., 2nd Edition 1982, Lea & Febiger, publisher.) Pages 97 through 100.

Chapter 9—Spotting a Sick Bird—Page 103

Early Warning Signs of a Sick Bird, 103; How to Conduct an Examination, 104; Interpretation of Abnormal Droppings, 107; Food Intake Affects Droppings, 107; Normal Appearance of Droppings, 107; Interpretation of Abnormal Droppings— *Diarrhea*, 108; *Common Causes of Diarrhea*, 108; *Constipation*, 109; More Types of Abnormal Droppings—Some Common Changes and Causes, 109; General Guide to Normal Number of Droppings, 110.

Chapter 10—Spills, Thrills 'n' Oops!—Page 111

INDEX OF SIGNS, 112, 113; Handling Sick and Injured Birds, 113; Transporting the Sick or Injured Bird, 113; Emergencies, 113; Shock, 115; Bleeding, 116; *First Aid For Minor Skin Wounds*, 116; *First Aid For Bleeding Beaks or Nails*, 119; *First Aid For Bleeding Feathers*, 119; Broken Bones, 119; *First Aid For Broken Bones*, 121; *Veterinary Care*, 121; Leg Bands, 123; Burns, 123; *First Aid For Burns*, 123; *Veterinary Care*, 123; Convulsions (Seizures), 124; *First Aid For Convulsions*, 124; *Veterinary Care*, 124; Heatstroke, 124; *First Aid For Heatstroke*, 125; *Veterinary Care*, 125; Poisoning, 125; Common Household Poisons, 126; Common Poisonous Plants, 126; *First Aid For Poisoning*, 128; *Veterinary Care*, 128; Lead Poisoning, 129; *First Aid For Lead Poisoning*, 129; Teflon Poisoning, 129; Insecticide Poisoning, 129; How to Prevent Poisoning In Your Bird, 130.

Chapter 11—Aches, Pains 'n' Problems—Page 131

Beak Disorders, 131; Beak Deformities, 131; Mite Infestation, 131; Trauma—Fractures, 133; Cere Disorders, 133; Brown Hypertrophy, 133; Inflammations, 133; Eye Disorders, 133; Conjunctivitis, 134; Trauma, 134; Corneal Ulcers, 134; *First Aid For Eye Problems*, 134; *Veterinary Care*, 136; Respiratory System Disorders, 136; Respiratory Infections, 136; Some Other Common Respiratory Problems, 137; *First Aid For Respiratory Infections*, 138; *Veterinary Care*, 138; Digestive Disorders, 138; The Mouth, 138; *Veterinary Care*, 138; Pox Infection, 139; Regurgitation—A Sign of Affection? Or Disease?, 139; *First Aid For Regurgitation*, 139; *Veterinary Care*, 141; Crop Disorders, 141; Crop Impaction, 141; *First Aid For Crop Impaction*, 141; *Veterinary Care*, 142; Sour Crop, 142; *First Aid For Sour Crop*, 142; *Veterinary Care*, 142; Proventriculus and

Gizzard Disorders, 142; Intestinal Disorders, 143; *First Aid For Simple Diarrhea,* 143; *Veterinary Care,* 143; Constipation, 143; Cloaca Disorders, 145; Cloaca Prolapse, 145; *Veterinary Care,* 145; Liver Disorders, 145; Pancreatic Disorders, 145; Lumps 'n' Bumps, 146; Abscesses, 146; Hematomas, 146; Tumors, 149; Hernias, 149; Feather Cysts, 149; Subcutaneous Emphysema, 149; Gout, 149; Obesity, 150; Kidney Disorders, 150; Feather Disorders, 150; Abnormal Molt, 150; French Molt, 151; Feather Picking, 151; Parasites, 154; Skin Parasites, 155; Scaly Face or Scaly Leg Mite, 155; Feather Mites, 156; Fleas and Ticks, 157; Respiratory System Parasites, 157; Gapeworms, 157; Air Sac Mites, 158; Digestive System Parasites, 158; Roundworms, 158; Capillaria, 159; Tapeworms, 159; Giardia, 160; Trichomonas, 160.

Chapter 12—Diseases—"The Biggies"—Page 163

Psittacosis, 163; Newcastle Disease, 164; Pacheco's Disease, 165; Important Points to Remember, 165.

Chapter 13—Veterinarians: When to Seek Professional Help—Page 167

Evaluating the Doctor, 168; Evaluating the Hospital and Staff, 168; The Complete Exam, 168; Veterinarians and Their Fees, 170; Going to the Veterinarian—What to Bring, 173; Diagnostic Testing, 173; Blood Tests, 173, Urinalysis, 176; Radiology, 176; Tissue Biopsies, 176; Bacteriology (Culture and Sensitivity), 176; Fecal Exam, 176; Endoscopy, 176; Post-Mortem Examination, 180; Therapy, 180; Surgery, 180; General Instructions For Bringing Your Bird Home From the Hospital, 181.

Chapter 14—Home Medical Care—Page 183

Basic Requirements For All Sick Birds, 183; Warmth, 183; Rest and Relaxation, 185; Water, 185; Amounts of Fluids to Give, 185; Food, 185; Various Feeding Methods For Sick Birds, 185; Tube Feeding Technique, 187; Frequency of Tube Feeding, 188; Tube Feeding Recipes, 188; Medications, 189; Antibiotics, 189; Administering Medication, 190; Home Emergency Kit, 191.

Chapter 15—Bird Breeding, Co-author Betty Byers—Page 193

Matchmaker, Matchmaker, 193; Sexing Your Bird or *"Gee, it laid an egg. I thought it was a boy!"*, 194; Management, 196; Additional Routines, 197; Housing, 197; Site Selection, 198; Housing Construction, 198; Design Considerations, 198; Construction Materials, 198; Flooring Materials, 200; Roofing Materials, 200; Nest Boxes, 200; Egg Laying, 200; Egg Incubation, 200; Determining Egg Fertility, 201; Egg Hatching, 201; Newly-Hatched Chicks, 201; Common Misconceptions About Breeding, 203; Hand-feeding, 203; Caring For Young Chicks, 204; Housing, 204; Heat, 204; Feeding, 204; Feeding Frequency, 207; Weighing, 207; Hand Feeding Recipes, 207; *San Diego Zoo's Hand Feeding Formula,* 207; Weaning, 208; Reproductive Problems, 208; Egg Laying Problems, 209; Egg Binding, 209; *First Aid for Egg Binding,* 209; *Veterinary Care,* 209.

Chapter 16—Rules For Transporting Birds—Page 211

Bringing Pet Birds Into The United States (Quarantine Regulations), 211; Special Rules For Bringing Pet Birds Into the United States, 211; What is a Pet Bird?, 211; Importing a Pet Bird, 211; Why All the Rules?, 212; Ports of Entry For Personally Owned Pet Birds, 213; The Quarantine Period, 213; Special Exceptions, 213; Other U.S. Agencies Involved

With Bird Imports, 214; Two Serious Threats to Birds *(Exotic Newcastle Disease, Smuggling)*, 215; Author's Recommendation, 215.

Chapter 17—Taming and Training Birds by Steve Martin—Page 217

Introduction, 217; Professional Parrot Trainers, 218; Biting, 218; Taming, 219; Getting Your Bird to Eat Out of Your Hand, 221; Taming Summary, 221; Discipline, 222; Emotional Discipline, 222; Squirt Bottles, 222; Training, 223; Behaviors, 224; Bridging Stimulus, 224; Training Summary, 225; Training Sessions, 225; Getting Your Bird to Stay On Your Hand, 225; Behaviors to Teach Your Bird, 227; *Waving*, 227; *Kiss*, 227; *Nod Head "Yes"*, 228; *Shake Head "No"*, 229; *Eagle*, 229; *Potty Training*, 230; Talking: Why Do Birds Talk, 230; Talking On Cue, 231; Most Commonly-Asked Questions on Taming and Training, 232.

Chapter 18—Wild Birds: Attracting Them to Your Yard, Co-author Ron Ridgway, D.V.M.—Page 237

Food Preferences, 237; Supplementary Foods, 237; Some Additional Recommendations, 238; The Food Preferences of Wild Birds, 238; Feeders, 239; Feeding Stations, 239; Feeding Tables, 239; Feeders, 241; Guidelines for Placement of Feeders, 241; Bird Baths, 241; Additional Considerations, 242; Nesting, 242; Injured and Orphaned Wild Birds: How to Care For Them, 243; How to Handle an Injured Bird, 243; How to Care For an Injured Bird, 244; How to Care For an Orphaned Bird, 244; *Basic Rules to Follow*, 245; Immediate Care, 245; Housing and Feeding of Orphaned Birds, 245; Feeding Technique, 246; Birds of Prey, 246; Oil-Damaged Birds: Their Care and Treatment, 249; Immediate Care, 249; Removal of Oil or Grease, 249.

Appendix A—Everything You Always Wanted to Know About . . .
        by Betty Byers (a Species Guide)   251
        Canaries, 251
        Finches, 253
        Budgerigars, 256
        Lovebirds, 257
        Cockatiels, 259
        Conures, 261
        African Grey Parrots, 263
        Amazon Parrots, 264
        Cockatoos, 267
        Macaws, 270
        Lories and Lorikeets, 272
        Mynahs, 275
Appendix B—Security and Your Bird   277
Appendix C—National and Foreign Bird Organizations   278
Appendix D—Magazines of Interest to Bird Owners   281
Appendix E—Metric Conversion Table   282

Bibliography—Page 283

Bird Information, 283; Bird Disease, 284; Bird Care, 285; Bird Breeding, 285; Wild Birds, 285; Nutrition, 285; Miscellaneous, 286.

General Index—Page 287

About the Author

In recent years, as the interest in keeping and raising exotic birds has continued to grow nationwide, it has created a corresponding need for more knowledgeable and sophisticated medical care of these birds. Not too long ago, the treatment of sick birds was the almost-exclusive province of the owner, or whenever possible an aviculturist. When birds did become seriously ill, little could be done and it usually resulted in their loss.

Today, the owner as healer is giving way to the owner as helper to the veterinarian who can provide the important health care to our beloved and very valuable birds. Dr. Gary Gallerstein, author of *The Bird Owner's Home Health and Care Handbook,* is a recognized specialist in the field of avian medicine and has made major contributions to the knowledge and expertise in this rapidly expanding area of veterinary medicine. Dr. Gallerstein, though young by medical standards, maintains a high level of enthusiasm, combined with hard work and dedication to the ideals of the highly respected avian practitioner.

Born in Los Angeles, California, Dr. Gallerstein was raised in the beautiful city of San Diego and attended San Diego State University as an undergraduate majoring in zoology. He continued his undergraduate studies at the University of California, Davis, and the following year was admitted to the UCD School of Veterinary Medicine, where he earned his Bachelor of Science degree in Veterinary Science and his Doctor of Veterinary Medicine degree in 1978.

Dr. Gallerstein has enjoyed working with a variety of animals over the years. His work with horses, livestock, zoo animals, laboratory animals, dogs, cats, and of course birds in both medical and non-medical contexts, has given him an exceptionally diverse pool of experience. His interest in avian medicine has continued to grow over the past several years.

Upon graduating from veterinary school, Dr. Gallerstein accepted a position in a large practice in San Francisco. It was here, that he developed his special interest in avian medicine. After eighteen months in this internship-like setting he returned to San Diego. The warm climate in Southern California is very conducive to bird keeping and consequently there are large numbers of hobbyists and breeders in the area. As co-owner of a very successful practice which became the primary avian referral practice in San Diego, he was able to further develop and fine-tune his medical skills. In June of 1984, Dr. Gallerstein moved his practice to Escondido, a beautiful

community thirty miles north of San Diego. There, his Acacia Animal
Hospital has become a well-known avian referral practice.

As *The Bird Owner's Home Health and Care Handbook* goes to press,
Dr. Gallerstein is on the Board of Directors of the Association of Avian
Veterinarians. This national association is dedicated to furthering the
knowledge of the care and treatment of pet birds. His other professional
memberships include: American Veterinary Medical Association, American
Animal Hospital Association, California Veterinary Medical Association,
San Diego County Veterinary Medical Association, American Association of
Avian Pathologists and he is also on the Board of Directors of the Veterinary
Pet Insurance Company.

Memberships outside his profession, but related to animals include: San
Diego Zoological Association, San Diego Turtle and Tortoise Society,
American Federation of Aviculture, and a number of local bird clubs in
Southern California. Quite understandably, Dr. Gallerstein is in high demand
by avicultural and veterinary groups in his area to speak at meetings and
seminars.

Away from his profession, Dr. Gallerstein is an avid jogger, sailor and
woodworker. He and his wife Nancy had their first child, Laura Brook, born
in June 1983.

Gary A. Gallerstein, D.V.M.

Acknowledgments

It is difficult to thank all the people that have helped in the conception and development of this book. What began as a series of informational handouts for our clients, has through an over-two-year ripening period, evolved into a real book. I had not planned on becoming a writer—it just happened, and I have found that I enjoy it very much.

This book is a reality, in large part, due to the help of many friends and colleagues:

Dr. Ron Ridgway, my former partner in San Diego, is due thanks for his many suggestions during the writing of this book. His many years of "hands on" experience with treating birds has taught me a great deal. Thanks also, for co-authoring the **Wild Birds** section with me. His interest and sincere encouragement have added considerably to the finished product.

Dr. Chuck Galvin, a recognized pioneer in the field of avian medicine, for helping to teach me the intricacies involved in treating and caring for birds, and for critical reading of the manuscript.

Dr. Steve Schuchman, private practitioner, Castro Valley, California for his helpful suggestions in the critical reading of the manuscript.

Dr. Murray Fowler, professor, University of California, Davis—School of Veterinary Medicine for his valuable instruction during my years at Davis and for his critical reading of the manuscript.

Steve Martin, professional bird trainer, for his excellent section on **Taming and Training.** Deirdre Ballou, Senior Animal Trainer, San Diego Zoo, for her assistance to Steve in the writing of this section.

Betty Byers, aviculturist, for unselfishly giving of her time. Her valuable writing contributions and numerous suggestions have greatly helped in the final outcome of this book. Debbie Laird, for her superb drawings and dedication to her work. Tony Costanza for his fine camera work.

Connie Houk for her typing of the final draft. One must never forget the very person, who at the whisk of her fingers, could change these very words. I greatly appreciated her dependability and dedication to the manuscript.

Mr. Elsworth Howell and Mr. Seymour Weiss of Howell Book House, for their dedication and desire to make this the best book possible.

Finally, to my wife Nancy for her understanding and support during the growth and development of this book. There were a few too many times my thoughts were on my writing or that I would fall asleep in the early evening after having risen early before work to write.

— GARY GALLERSTEIN

To The Reader:

This book is meant to be a guide for the proper care and management of birds in both health and illness.

Above all, when it comes to health problems I hope you will be able to detect early warning signs of disease before they become life-threatening.

The first aid and home medical care recommendations are generally safe and simple methods of treatment. However, they are *not* going to work in every case. The disease process is very complex and it is always strongly recommended that a veterinarian be consulted before any treatment is begun. Remember too, your fine feathered friend is fragile and even the act of restraint and administering the medication can be hazardous to its health.

Introduction

Welcome to the wild and wonderful world of birds. Birds are increasing in popularity faster than any other pet. Why? Our growing mobile society and our shrinking living spaces have increased the need for pets that require minimal space and that are easy to care for. Birds fill the bill admirably. In addition, their magnificent kaleidoscope of colors is unsurpassed in the animal kingdom. They can be affectionate, loving and comical companions. The unparalleled ability by certain species to mimic human speech allows you to personalize your new pet. Nowhere else can you find a pet that offers all this, and depending on species, can live a lifetime—your lifetime!

Few people have grown up with birds, and as a result know little about taking care of them. As a veterinarian engaged in private practice and all aspects of bird care, I meet new bird owners every day and time after time a pattern emerges: inexperienced, well meaning people believing they were doing the right thing, when in fact, they were doing things all wrong, resulting in unnecessary illness and sometimes even the death of their much-loved pet. To complicate matters even more, there is a great deal of incorrect and misunderstood information being liberally passed around about birds.

Most first-time pet bird owners are frantically running themselves ragged; hoping, trying and praying that all is being done correctly. If you haven't already, you will quickly realize that caring for a bird is a whole lot different than raising the 'ol dog or cat. Most new pet bird owners want and need to learn more about birds to help prevent problems and to know how to manage them if they arise.

It is for these reasons that this book on all aspects of bird care has been written. This book is written for the new bird owner and serious bird fancier who cares enough to learn how to provide his bird or birds with a happy and healthy environment. Most everything you will need to know about purchasing a bird, those first few weeks after purchase, feeding, housing, companionship, general health, disease prevention and recognition, as well as, disease treatment and emergency first aid care are covered.

There is also a short chapter on bird breeding. It is my sincerest hope that in the years to come all pet birds will have been bred in captivity and the need to import birds will be eliminated. Captive-bred birds not only make superior pets but more importantly, wild birds have enough environmental pressures already placed on their very existence that it will be great to look forward to the day that bird importation can be a thing of the past.

15

Every day bird fanciers, breeders, pet dealers and veterinarians are gaining new insights for better, more efficient bird care. In the years to come we can look forward to more new and even better ideas to help improve the overall health of our birds.

Remember, love alone is not going to create that happy and healthy environment we all want for our fine feathered friends.

History of Bird Keeping

Bird keeping has a history that dates back thousands of years. Sonia Roberts, in her book *Birdkeeping and Bird Cages—A History,* states that birds were probably the first pets kept strictly for pleasure and their beauty.

The Chinese were probably the first aviculturists. They were breeding pheasants before the Europeans had discovered the wheel. The sport of falconry first began in China around 2000 B.C.

One of the first recorded accounts of birdkeeping was in 1500 B.C. when Queen Hathepsut of Egypt was collecting hawks and falcons for display in the royal zoo. There were no hieroglyphics depicting parrots back then since they were probably unknown to these people.

The Chinese of 600 B.C. were using cormorants to catch fish. They would use a thread tied around the neck preventing the fish from being swallowed. Simple but ingenious.

Alexander the Great was one of our most famous and pioneering bird fanciers. The peacocks he saw in India while on his voyages fascinated him so that he collected them and shipped many back to his native homeland. The Alexandrine parakeet, named for the great warrior, became the most popular caged bird in the Roman Empire. Pet birds even accompanied many warriors on their conquests of foreign lands.

Aristotle was one of the first to write about and publicize the fascinating world of birds. His descriptions were based on many of the birds that Alexander the Great brought back from the Far East. Psittace, a pet bird that Aristotle frequently wrote about, formed the basis of the scientific name for the parrot family—Psittacines.

The first parrot was seen in England in 1504 and since then their popularity has grown astronomically. It has been said that over half the population of England own birds. The English are the true pioneers in the field of aviculture; their influence on bird keeping and bird breeding has been great. They have done a great deal to increase our knowledge and capability in these areas.

In 1894, the Avicultural Society of England was formed, the first of its kind. A similar society, The Avicultural Society of America, was founded in the United States in 1927. The United States saw an explosion of pet birds beginning in the 1950s with the budgie and since this time birds have become one of America's most sought-after pets.

Bird clubs and societies are rapidly growing. Who would have ever thought of pet shops specializing in birds. Birds are appearing in advertisements and as designs on clothes. It seems as if a bird mania is sweeping our country.

1

Tips on Buying a New Bird

Owning a bird is a big investment in both time and money. The price paid for a bird is important, but other factors such as health and temperament are even more so. Over the years, the original price paid will seem increasingly insignificant as your bird provides the love and companionship that you had always desired from a pet.

As an inexperienced person looking to purchase a bird, do not go out and buy the first one you see. Shop around, look at lots of birds, and talk with as many knowledgeable people as possible before you settle on that one special feathered friend.

Choice of Species

Remember there are over 8700 species of birds living today: every size, color, shape and personality imaginable. Fortunately for us, those species that have become popular are much fewer in number, making our choice much easier.

BUYING A BIRD SHOULD NEVER BE DONE ON WHIM OR IMPULSE.

Consider the following when buying a bird:

WHY DO YOU WANT A BIRD?

- Companionship
- For the children (The bird may well be with you long after the children leave.)
- Hobby—Breeding and/or exhibition
- Sport—falconry, homing pigeons

Consider the following:
- Initial cost
- Feeding and housing requirements
- Time and attention required
- Neighbors and noise
- Children and other pets

19

Many first-time bird owners want to go out and buy the big, beautiful macaws and cockatoos before fully realizing the extra care that is involved with these birds. Don't be too ambitious. Misunderstanding and poor management often become frustrating and expensive. These strikingly majestic birds do not necessarily make the most desirable pet for the neophyte bird owner. Remember, budgerigars, cockatiels, and the larger Amazon parrots make excellent pets that may be better suited for the first-time bird owner.

Where to Purchase Birds

Birds can be obtained from pet shops, breeders, private dealers and individuals. For the inexperienced buyer, it is best to deal with someone in the business. These people are usually experienced, have a reputation to protect, and will often offer some type of guarantee should a problem occur within a reasonable period of time. Ask your friends, veterinarian, and others involved with birds about the reputation of the seller.

Buying from an individual may be quite risky. Often these birds are sold because of an unfavorable and aggressive disposition or illness. Think a moment, if you had an affectionate and loving bird, especially one that talks, would you sell it?

NEVER buy birds at auctions or swap meets. The health and previous history of these birds are unknown and they may be plagued with problems. In areas located near the Mexican border smuggled birds are an especially common problem and caution must be exercised whenever buying from an unknown individual. Many of these birds harbor diseases which can be transmitted to humans or other birds. (See sections on Psittacosis and Newcastle disease in Chapter 12.)

Health Before Wealth

Health must be a prime consideration when selecting a bird. Carefully observe the following:

1. The area where the birds are kept should be clean and sanitary.
2. Your bird should appear bright and alert; its feathers smooth and held close to its body; its eyes clear and open wide. (See Early Warning Signs of a Sick Bird in Chapter 9.)
3. It should be eating and drinking water. The food should be fresh and the water cups clean.
4. The droppings should appear normal. See the section on "Interpretation of Abnormal Droppings" in Chapter 9.
5. Observe the birds in nearby cages. Sick birds should never be kept close to healthy ones.

The bird should appear bright and alert. The area where the birds are kept should be clean and sanitary. —*Tony Costanza*

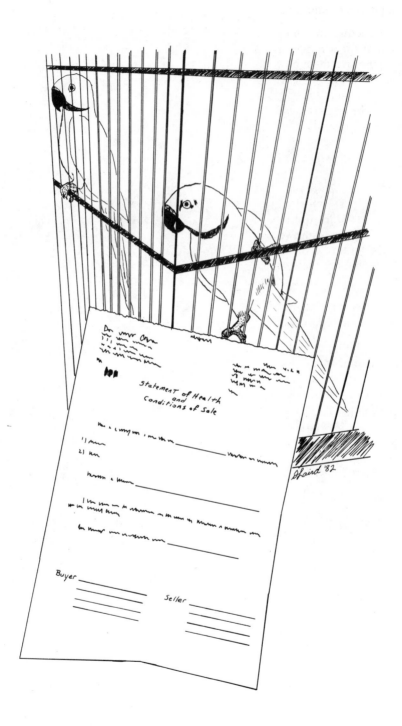

Temperament and Trainability

Selecting an intelligent bird with a good disposition is absolutely essential for a happy life-long companionship. In their temporary state of being for sale, most birds are very stressed. It may be difficult to assess a bird's potential for gentleness and trainability. Birds are naturally wary of strangers, so don't expect too much at first.

Many birds, especially those recently imported, are not people-oriented and frighten easily. On the other hand, birds hand raised in this country are usually more trusting of people from the start. When buying a bird look for a young one. It will usually become more trusting of people and so prove easier to train.

Talking ability is difficult to assess. In a strange environment, it is uncommon for most birds to talk. Even when brought home, most birds will not begin talking until they feel totally safe and secure in their new home and with you. As a result, you must often accept the seller's word and it is here that his reputation becomes very important.

Remember that many parrots do not talk, but still have other endearing qualities, such as a comical, affectionate personality and make superb companions.

Cost versus Supply and Demand

A number of factors will determine the asking price for a bird. We have already spoken of two of these, health and temperament. Availability is another important factor.

For finches, budgerigars, cockatiels and lovebirds, that are commonly bred in the United States, the prices are relatively low. For many of the larger birds such as Amazons, cockatoos and macaws that must be imported, the price is going to be higher. Many of these species are even no longer being imported or domestic breeding attempts have failed and will cause the prices to be even higher.

Buying the Bird

Consider these factors:

1. Will you be able to find the seller tomorrow or next week should problems occur?
2. Is there a health guarantee? How about returns or exchanges?
3. Verification of age and birthplace. (This is not always possible.)
4. Will you get a written bill of sale?

A pet shop can guarantee your bird will talk. They cannot guarantee it will live a long, healthy life. KNOW your seller. Be sure he is reputable and knowledgeable about birds. Give time and thought when selecting a bird— you will be glad of it for many years to come. Be especially careful when buying a so-called "bargain bird." The BEST bargain is a healthy bird with a good temperament, NOT its cost.

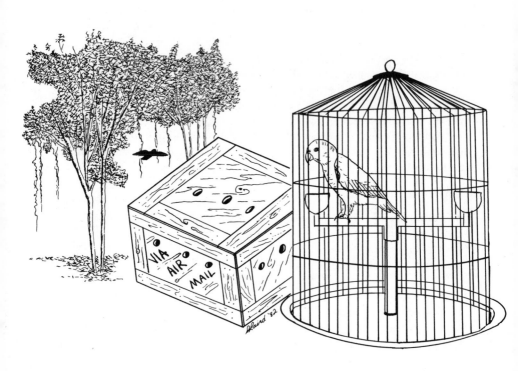

2

Your New Bird:
The Do's and Don'ts

Bringing Your Bird Home

When introduced into a new environment, birds, like people, require an adjustment period. This is the time when your bird is becoming accustomed to its new home and its new friend—you. It is also a period of tremendous stress for any bird.

Now let's think about your bird: where it came from, where it has been, and where it is now. Wow! Your new bird has probably experienced a lot of traveling in a very short period of time. This is hard on any living creature, especially one as small as a cage bird. It is the most turbulent and stressful period in your bird's life. This is the time when many disasters occur and when many can be avoided.

Stress

In our hectic life we are confronted with some type of stress almost every day. It can cause high blood pressure, heart disease, and stomach ulcers, among other things. We know, all too well, many of the things that bring about stress. But few of us realize the other serious affects it can have. Stop and think. When are you most likely to become ill? Isn't it when you have been working very hard and/or when you are most stressed? In this regard, animals are the same. In an animal as small as a pet bird, the effects are multiplied.

Causes of Stress in Birds

- New home/New owners
- Temperature extremes (less than 60°, greater than 90° F)
- Overcrowding
- Too much darkness (greater than 15 hours a day)
- Too much daylight (greater than 15 hours a day)
- Poor caging
- Loud noises
- Disease

Rest and relaxation are vital necessities for your new companion. Isolate the newly acquired from other birds for at least 30 days. —*Tony Costanza*

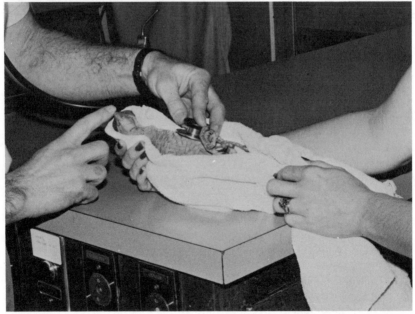

Have your new bird examined by a veterinarian who is familiar with avian medicine.   —*Tony Costanza*

- Breeding
- Molting
- Harassment from other animals, including man
- Poor nutrition

Overwhelmingly, the most common time for birds to become ill or injured is within the first few months of new ownership. This is the time of greatest stress. Stress lowers resistance and increases susceptibility to all types of disease. Therefore, stress must always be kept to a minimum.

With this in mind, what follows is a list of recommendations to use as a guide for the first few weeks of new bird ownership.

1. Have your new bird examined immediately by a veterinarian knowledgeable in avian medicine. Blood tests, radiographs or stool analysis may be recommended as part of the examination. Consider this cheap insurance for the health of your bird. (Fig. 2-2)
2. Isolate your new bird from other birds for at least 30 days. Keep them apart in separate rooms whenever possible. Should your new bird be harboring any disease, this will help avoid exposing your other birds.
3. Rest and relaxation is essential for your new companion. Quiet time is very important. DO NOT spend lots of time with the bird. Avoid having all the neighbors coming over and peering into the cage.
4. A cage of proper size, placed in the corner of the room, is important. See Chapter 5—"Home Sweet Home."
5. Maintain a higher than normal temperature for your bird; 80° F is ideal during this period. Try a portable heater or heat lamp to save on energy costs.
6. Birds are susceptible to colds; avoid drafts. If you are in doubt, light a candle near the cage. If the flame flickers there is a draft and the cage should be moved.
7. For the first week, feed your bird the same food that it has been used to eating. Then, if necessary, over the next few weeks alter the diet. Abrupt dietary changes should be avoided.
8. Do not add grit to the bird's diet the first few weeks. Due to the stress and anxiety, overeating of grit may occur and cause serious problems.
9. You may want to clip the wings to prevent your bird flying away or flying into objects that can injure it.
10. Insure 10-12 hours a night of total quiet and darkness. If needed, use a cage cover, towel or blanket to block out sounds and light.
11. This is a period of major adjustment, so don't attempt to train or tame your bird. You must allow it sufficient time to become comfortable in its new surroundings.
12. Unless your bird is tame and seeks human companionship, avoid excessive handling during this stage.
13. Keep your new bird confined to the cage and avoid free flight in the house.
14. Watch for and AVOID these dangers:
    - Paint fumes, insecticides and other poisons
    - Windows—opened or direct sunlight striking the cage which can cause sunstroke

- Leg bands (have them removed, but keep track of the number)
- Fans - drafts
- Smoke
- Lead in paints, caulking in stained glass windows, drapery weights, or toys
- Spoiled foods, moldy grains, unwashed fruits and vegetables
- Long toe nails and beaks
- Cage - Sharp edges
- Other household pets and inquisitive children

15. Learn everything you can about birds—sources of information can be obtained from your veterinarian and pet shops. There are many bird clubs, magazines and books, some of which are listed in the appendix of this book, to help you.

16. Remember, the major causes of illness are poor nutrition, lack of cleanliness, exposure to sick birds and, of course, STRESS.

17. Train yourself to be observant. Watch for signs of illness and seek veterinary care immediately if they should appear.

PREVENTION IS ALWAYS BETTER THAN CURE

3

Feeding for Health,
Vitality and Longevity

Good nutrition is the single most important factor that contributes to the health, vitality and longevity of our birds.

Most of us realize the importance of a good diet for ourselves. Why should birds be any different? They have the same basic requirements that we do, as do all mammals. The criteria for a well-balanced, nutritionally complete diet is the proper combination of proteins, carbohydrates, fats, vitamins, minerals, and, of course, water.

Pet birds live under artificial, man-made conditions. They are not able to forage for food as in the wild state, so it is up to us to see that the proper food is being provided and eaten. Unfortunately, little is actually known about the true and exacting food requirements of all species. However, through many years of captivity; with feeding trials, observations from the wild state, and some of the current research, we are able to draw many conclusions regarding the optimal diet for pet birds.

In birds, the rate at which life-sustaining chemical reactions occur in the body is among the fastest of all animals. The energy needed to generate these high-speed chemical reactions, known as METABOLISM, requires relatively large amounts of the correct types of food. Therefore, any lack of proper nutrients or decreased food intake will be noticed in birds very quickly. The importance of a well-balanced, nutritionally complete diet cannot be over-emphasized.

FACTORS INFLUENCING CHOICE OF FOODS

Environment:
Young birds are more easily taught to eat a variety of foods.

Adult-captured birds often are set in their eating habits and may be difficult to change.

29

Food Appearance:
Birds have keen eyesight and few tastebuds. Therefore, texture, color, and preparation of food is important, while food smell is not.

FACTORS AFFECTING ENERGY REQUIREMENT

Stage of Life:
Age—A young, growing bird requires more food on a per weight basis than a mature specimen living in a stress-free environment.

Molting period—increases the requirements

Temperature:
Increased requirement in cold weather

Activity Level:
Cage confinement vs. flying and exercise

Reproductive Stage:
Additional food is required by hens during egg laying and feeding young

CARBOHYDRATES are the body's fuel, the quick energy sources needed to power all the chemical reactions occurring in the body. Starch and sugar are the simple components of carbohydrates and, under normal conditions, maintain the blood glucose level. Cellulose, an indigestible carbohydrate found in green vegetables, supplies the "bulk" commonly known as fiber, which helps to both maintain normal intestinal function and prevent constipation.

Good Carbohydrate Sources:
Fresh fruits and vegetables

Grass and cereal seeds are highest
   Examples: Millet, canary, wheat, oats, rice, milo,
             corn, buckwheat

NOTE: Oil seeds are low in carbohydrates.

FATS are the most concentrated energy source, providing more than twice as much energy per unit than either proteins or carbohydrates. They help to insulate and store food for the body and are necessary for the normal utilization of the fat-soluble vitamins (A, D, E, K).

Good Fat Sources:
Nuts, oils, fats and linseed

Oil seeds are the highest

Examples: Rape, flax, niger, sunflower, poppy, hemp, sesame, peanuts

NOTE: Cereal and grass seeds are low in fats.

Since most of our pet birds live a rather sedentary life, over zealous supplementation of these foods will cause an overweight condition. Fat in birds will usually collect in the chest area.

It is thought by some experts that certain species of birds are unable to tolerate milk and, if given, can cause diarrhea. More research is needed in this area and it would be wise to avoid its use or, if tried, use sparingly.

PROTEINS are essential for the health and maintenance of all the body's tissues, as well as for normal growth, reproduction, and resistance to infection. Protein is composed of *Amino Acids,* some of which are termed ESSENTIAL and must be supplied in adequate amounts in the diet. Proteins which contain these essential amino acids in the optimum quantities are said to be of **High Biological Value** since they are of the greatest value to the body.

Good Protein Sources:

Eggs—cooked only (Raw egg white binds *biotin,* an important B vitamin, and prevents its absorbtion from the gut.)

Muscle meat, milk, fish meal, beans, yeast, nuts, insects and mealworms.

Oil seeds are highest in protein among seed varieties.

NOTE: Cereal and grass seeds, fruits and vegetables are low in protein.

VITAMINS are the "little guys," needed in only very small amounts, but are essential for normal development, growth and maintenance of good health. Without them, the utilization of protein, carbohydrates and fat would be impossible. During periods of added stress, molting, reproduction, sickness, and antibiotic therapy, the requirements are even higher.

Birds require approximately 13 essential vitamins and appear to only be able to partially manufacture three of these—Vitamins C, D, and Niacin. The diet, then, is responsible for supplying the majority. As has already been mentioned, birds have a rapid metabolism and this, coupled with their selective eating habits, make vitamin supplementation essential.

Good Vitamin Sources:

A balanced diet, including seeds, fresh fruits and vegetables will provide a good supply of vitamins.

NOTE: To insure an adequate vitamin supply, all birds should be given a daily multi-vitamin supplement. Vitamins can be added to the food or water.

Sunflower seeds form a large portion of many hookbill diets, but should always be provided in balance with other varieties of seeds.
—Tony Costanza

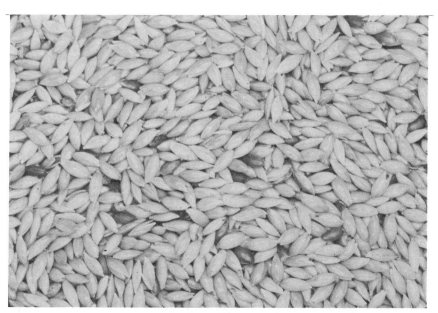

Canary seed is very important to the food requirements of many psittacine and passerine birds. *—Tony Costanza*

The size of grit selected is important and depends on the size of the bird.   *—Tony Costanza*

Ground oyster shells can be a good mineral supplement that is especially high in calcium.
—Tony Costanza

Cuttlebone provides some valuable minerals and helps maintain the shape and condition of the beak. It is best suited for the smaller hookbills such as budgies, lovebirds and cockatiels.   *—Tony Costanza*

Avoid human vitamin preparations! People require Vitamin D_2, whereas birds can only utilize the Vitamin D_3 form. Although it may not seem important at first, it is! Use vitamins made expressly for birds.

MINERALS play a crucial role in the maintenance and strength of bone, acid-base balance and water distribution throughout the body. They are also vital in the enzyme systems and egg production—normal body function and good health is impossible without them. A good diet containing seeds, fresh fruits and vegetables will supply most of the necessary minerals; however, supplementation is still recommended, especially for calcium since seeds contain only minute amounts. During egg production and egg laying calcium supplementation is essential to prevent deficiency problems.

To insure the necessary minerals, try some of the following:

- Cooked eggs
- Cuttlebone (soft side towards bird)—excellent and also helps control beak growth for the smaller birds.
- Dry dog, cat or monkey food (ground or chipped, depending on size of bird)
- Fish or bone meals
- Fresh branches and twigs (edible trees such as apple, cherry, elm, oak and eucalyptus)
- Mineral mixture blocks
- Ground oyster shells
- Insects

Iodine

Many seeds are deficient in iodine and in areas with a very low iodine content in the drinking water, iodine should be supplemented. Check with your veterinarian. Iodine is essential for normal thyroid gland function and budgerigars appear to be particularly susceptible to this deficiency. Good sources include finely ground oyster shell or cod liver oil. Also a diluted iodine preparation, such as Lugol's solution, can be used according to your veterinarian's directions.

ESSENTIAL VITAMINS IN BIRD FEEDING

Vitamin	Primary Importance	Common Deficiency Symptoms	Major Natural Sources
A	Vision, growth and healing of tissue—commonly, mucus membranes, skin and bone	Poor eyesight and other eye problems, mouth and throat lesions	Fish oils, egg yolk, some fruits and vegetables. Absent in seeds. Sweet potatoes are highest vegetable source; liver is highest animal source.
B complex	Essential for metabolic reactions, nerve and muscle functions, and red blood cell production.	Leg paralysis, poor appetite, impaired egg hatchability and chick survival, anemia, poor growth and bone abnormality.	Cereal grain and seeds, meat, brewer's yeast, leafy plants, beans.
C	Tissue growth and healing, red blood cell formation	Scurvy, possibly in fruit and nectar eating birds	Citrus fruits, green leafy plants; synthesized by most birds.
D	Healthy bone, calcium utilization; normal growth and feather structure	Rickets ("soft bone"), soft shells and egg binding	Fish livers, egg yolk, absent in bird seed and plants. Sunlight activates production of Vitamin D in the body.
E	Anti-oxident—prevents degeneration of fatty acids, Vitamin A & D, Increases fertility and blood circulation.	Poor fertility and egg hatchability, muscle and nervous disorders, glandular enlargement	Seeds and grains, leafy plants and vegetable oils, eggs. Animal products are poor sources.
K	Blood clotting, liver functions	Bleeding problems	Green leafy vegetables, egg yolk and fishmeal. Synthesized by bacteria in the intestine.

Grit

Since birds do not have teeth, a gizzard, the muscular stomach, grinds up the food into an easily digestible form. Grit collects in the gizzard and aids in this grinding process. Grit can also help suppy some necessary minerals since it is typically composed of calcium, charcoal, iron, magnesium and iodine.

Avian veterinarians and other bird experts do not all agree that grit is essential in the diet. It definitely does not need to be added on a daily basis. In the wild, grit (along with minerals) is obtained in the form of small pebbles from the soil. The size grit selected is important and dependent on the size of the bird. The smaller or finer grit is designed for finches, canaries, parakeets and the like. Medium to coarse grit is for the Amazon parrots, macaws, and cockatoos.

Overeating grit can cause serious problems. Grit remains in the gizzard for a long period of time and, therefore, only small amounts are needed in the diet. *Add only a pinch to the food a few times weekly.* A separate grit dish is not necessary, and for good hygiene do not feed it off the cage floor.

Water

Water is essential for all forms of life. Every cell is dependent on water for its very existence. Water functions to transport nutrients and help regulate body temperature. The body is composed of about 80% water.

Animals can survive without food longer than if they are without water. It has been stated that small birds, like canaries and finches, that are provided only a seed diet will die in about 48 hours if they have no access to water. A constant readily available source of water is essential. Be sure the container is clean and that the water is provided fresh daily. By not placing the food and water cups directly beneath a perch there will be less chance for fecal contamination.

AVERAGE DAILY WATER INTAKE FOR BIRDS

Finch	2.5 mls (1/2 tsp)
Canary	3-4 mls
Budgerigar	5 mls (1 tsp)
Cockatiel	10-15 mls (2-3 tsp)
Parrot	25-45 mls (2-3 tbsp)

Other Liquids

Various fruit juices can be offered to pet birds. Remember that the "new" color may be viewed as suspicious by your bird and it may not drink it right away. Be sure to always change the liquids daily and rinse the cup.

ESSENTIAL MINERALS IN BIRD FEEDING

Mineral	Primary Importance	Common Deficiency Symptoms	Major Natural Sources
Calcium	Development and function of bone and muscle; blood coagulation, nerve impulse transmission, egg production	Rickets—bone and joint problems, soft egg shell, egg binding, seizures.	Green leafy vegetables, meat and bone meal. Seeds are a poor source.
Chloride	Regulation of body fluids, acid-base balance, digestive stomach acids	Poor digestion, upset in body fluid and acid-base balance	Fish and meat products, salt
Cobalt	Component of Vitamin B$_{12}$	Anemia and weakness, appetite loss	Most foods
Copper	Component of red blood cells, many enzymes and feather pigments	Anemia, poor growth, abnormal feather coloring	Seeds and most other foods
Iodine	Regulator of metabolism as part of thyroid hormone	Thyroid gland enlargement (goiter), weakness, poor reproduction	Most foods, fish and fish oils
Iron	Hemoglobin in red blood cells, transport of oxygen; components of enzymes	Anemia and impaired oxygen transport; generalized weakness	Green leafy vegetables, bone marrow. Widely distributed cereal grains are poor
Magnesium	Bone formation and normal metabolism. Activates enzymes.	Bone disease, improper metabolism of carbohydrates, seizures.	Most foods; seeds and vegetables. Animal products are poor source.
Manganese	Enzyme activator and bone formation.	Bone disease, leg problems, egg problems.	Most foods, seed and vegetables. Animal products are poor sources.
Phosphorus	Closely associated with calcium for normal development and function of bone.	Bone and joint problems, muscle weakness, slow healing.	Milk, cereal grains, fishmeal and meat products containing bone.

ESSENTIAL MINERALS IN BIRD FEEDING (cont'd)

Potassium	Regulation of body fluids, nerve and muscle function, carbohydrate metabolism	Retarded growth and weakness seizure.	Plants
Selenium	Closely linked with Vitamin E metabolism	Muscle disease—muscular dystrophy, slow healing	Plants
Sodium	Regulation of body fluids, acid-base balance	Dehydration, acid-base upset, poor egg production	Animal and fish products, salt. Vegetables are low in sodium.
Sulphur	Constituent of proteins, insulin, thiamine and biotin	Associated with protein deficiencies	Protein diets
Zinc	Normal metabolism and component of many enzymes	Poor metabolism, retarded growth, poor feathering and bone abnormalities.	Widely distributed, yeast, cereal grains.

The seeds shown above, in correct proportion, are all important to providing good nutrition for pet birds. They are: top left—red millet; top right—white millet; middle left— hemp; middle right—oats; lower left—safflower; lower right—niger.
       —*Tony Costanza*

Diet: Balance Through Variety

This section pertains to members of the parrot family. Diets of other popular birds are mentioned later in the chapter.

Seeds

Seeds form the foundation of a good diet for birds. A variety of seed types is essential and many dealers offer seed mixes specially formulated for different types and sizes of parrots. The fresher the seeds, the higher the nutritional value. Purchasing seeds from a supplier that sells large quantities of food and has a rapid turnover in inventory will help insure freshness.

- Seeds should form about 75% of the diet.
- Supplemental seed mixes are also available. They can serve important functions during certain periods of the life cycle. Included here are foods for molting, singing (canaries), conditioning, and coloration.
- Nutritional value of seeds not only depends on freshness, but also the way they have been grown and handled since harvesting.
- Seeds lack sufficient amounts of Vitamin A, calcium, and iodine.
- Oil from cod-liver or fatty acids have been commonly recommended additives to bird seeds for a variety of reasons. For the average pet bird owner, this practice is not suggested. These oils will turn the seeds rancid within 24 hours. Also, an oil-coated beak can mat and destroy the insulating properties of the feathers through the normal preening process.
- Since birds shell their seeds, the empty hulls often collect on top of the whole seeds. Don't be fooled. Be sure to discard these hulls daily and add more seeds.
- "Webby" seeds is a term denoting insects in the seeds and the webs they often spin. The insects are not harmful and are actually very nutritious for the birds.
- Seed storage: To insure freshness and to avoid contamination always store seeds in an airtight container. Excess amounts of seeds can be stored in a freezer.

Vegetables and Greens

These are an integral part of a good diet and are commonly overlooked. Table vegetables are excellent. Iceberg lettuce has minimal nutritional value and should be used sparingly. Experiment with several types of greens until you find the ones your bird most prefers.

Most all vegetables and greens are acceptable, but the following seem to be especially favored:

Spinach	Celery	Alfalfa
Broccoli	Carrots and tops	Endive

In addition to the seed varieties illustrated on page 40, those shown here belong in the diet of the well-nourished pet. They are: top left—rape; top right—pine nuts; middle left—white corn; middle right—wheat; lower left—pumpkin; lower right—buckwheat.   *—Tony Costanza*

Cabbage	Corn on the cob	Dandelions
Sweet potato	Zucchini	Lettuce
Beets and tops	Pea pods	Chard

A variety of dehydrated greens are now widely available. They are very nutritious and can be mixed with the seeds.

- Raw vegetables are preferred to cooked. Before serving, wash the vegetables to rinse off any insecticide residues as these could prove fatal.
- Freshness is essential. Remove any uneaten portions at the end of the day.
- Vegetables and greens are rarely the cause of diarrhea. The droppings often become more watery due to the higher water content of these foods. The stools will also become softer and greener in color.

Fruits

These are another valuable addition to the diet. Birds prefer all different types, so experiment until you discover the combinations that your bird likes best.

Try some of the following by cutting up and placing them in a food dish or attached to the wall of the cage where they are easily accessible.

Bananas	Pears	Grapefruit
Grapes	Oranges	Plums
Cherries	Pumpkin	Apples
Peaches	Dates	Raisins
Pomegranate	Papaya	

- Be sure to wash fruit thoroughly before serving.
- Feed only the freshest produce.
- Dried fruits are also very good.
- Always remove uneaten portions at the end of the day.
- Fruits are very high in water content which will result in wet droppings.

Table Foods

As an occasional treat, table foods are acceptable. Avoid foods which contain heavy seasonings, excessive sugar or chemicals. Ideally, the food should be pure and simple. Begin by offering only small amounts. Many foods spoil rapidly and unless eaten immediately should be discarded.

Pelleted Foods

Pelleted foods are now commercially available for birds. They make a good supplement to the basic seed, fruit and vegetable diet. However, at this time they are not recommended as a sole food source.

Vegetables are a valuable addition to the diet.

Fruits are another valuable addition to the diet.

SUMMARIZING THE COMPLETE PARROT DIET

Fresh seed mix	75% of diet
Fresh fruits and vegetables	20% of diet
Cooked eggs, bread, nuts, insects, etc.	5% of diet
Vitamins and mineral supplements	
Fresh water	

Diet for Mynah Birds

Unlike parrots, these birds do not eat seeds. Most popular and convenient are the pelleted foods specially formulated for mynahs. Pelleted food is nutritious but should not be considered a complete diet. Other types of foods still need to be given. Fruits, chopped vegetables, cooked eggs, chopped meat, softened dog food and insects are ideal additions to the basic ration. Many kinds of insects are part of the mynah bird diet in the wild, and every effort should be made to obtain a few for daily feeding. Food larger than pea size is difficult to swallow and should not be fed as it could cause choking. Fresh water must always be available and vitamins provided daily.

Diet for Lories and Lorikeets

The diet for this family of birds is among the most specialized. It consists primarily of fruits, nectar and pollen. These birds have evolved a brush-like tongue ideally suited for eating these types of foods. Fresh or canned fruit cocktail, softened mynah pellets, finely diced vegetables and condensed or evaporated milk can be added to their diet. Corn syrup or Karo™ syrup added to the food makes for a readily available energy source. These foods should be mixed together and fed in a soupy consistency. Fresh water and daily vitamins are always essential.

SAN DIEGO ZOO'S RECIPES FOR BIRD DIETS

The following diets are used daily at the San Diego Zoo. They are good basic formulations that along with the daily addition of vitamins will form a complete and nutritious diet. If desired, other seeds, fruits and vegetables can also be added to these mixes.

Actually, the exact proportions of seeds in a mixture are not that important. Birds will often have certain favorite seeds and will eat these and leave the others.

For the owner of from one to a few birds it is usually not cost efficient to purchase individual seeds and mix them yourself. Most pet shops offer packaged seed mixes that are good and nutritious.

Finch and Canary Diet—San Diego Zoo

Basic mix consists of the following in equal proportions:
Canary millet

Niger
Proso millet
Small yellow millet

Daily additions to diet may include:
Diced apples
Diced spinach
Ground whole wheat bread
Spray millet

Small Parrot Diet—San Diego Zoo

(For Budgerigars, Love Birds, Cockatiels, Small Conures)

Basic mix consists of the following in equal proportions:

Canary millet	Oat groats
White proso millet	Safflower
Hemp	Oyster shells
Niger	

Daily additions to the diet may include:

Apples	Raisins
Carrots	Spinach
Celery	Sweet Potatoes
Corn-on-the-cob	Whole wheat bread

NOTE: Dried fruits are given periodically.

Large Parrot Diet—San Diego Zoo

(Large Conures, Amazon Parrots, African Greys, Cockatoos, Macaws)

Basic mix consists of the following in equal proportions:

Canary millet	Safflower
White proso millet	Hemp
Niger	Oat groats
Sunflower	Oyster shells
Peanuts	

Daily additions to the diet may include (sliced):

Apples	Oranges
Carrots	Papaya
Celery	Raisins
Corn-on-the-cob	Spinach
Grapes	Sweet Potatoes
Whole wheat bread	

NOTE: Almonds, other similar nuts and dried fruits are given periodically. For the large Macaws, Brazil, hazel, and filbert nuts are given periodically.

Mynah Bird Diet—San Diego Zoo

Mynah pellets are always available.

Daily additions to the diet may include (sliced):

Apples	Papaya
Bananas	Pears
Grapes	Raisins
Raw, ground hamburger	Spinach
Tomatoes	

Lory Diet—San Diego Zoo*

4-5 apples
2-4 leaves of lettuce, spinach, chard, etc.
1½ oz. carrots
3 oz. raisins
1 oz. trout chow
5 oz. sugar
3-5 oz. cooked rice, wheat, and millet
1 piece coconut (includes milk and meat)
1 teaspoon Lory Premix™

*This diet has been reduced proportionately for feeding a small number of birds.

Place these ingredients into a large blender. Add water as needed for a consistency that is similar to applesauce. This recipe makes approximately ½ gallon and can be frozen until needed.

Lory Premix is available from:
Zeigler Brothers
P.O. Box 95
Gardners, PA 17324

Advice for Feeding the Finicky Eater

Many birds become fussy about the food they eat. Poor eating habits are one of the chief causes of nutritional problems, and owners are usually helpless in correcting this dilemma. Birds will often eat only one or two types of seeds (usually sunflower seeds or peanuts), or they totally avoid fruits and vegetables. Sound familiar? It's a common problem. To make matters worse, once established, it's a difficult habit to break.

Birds depend more on the visual recognition of foods rather than the smell or taste. Until they become familiar with the appearance of a food, they will be reluctant to try anything new. Therefore, you must be persistent. If your bird doesn't accept a new food immediately, don't give up. Keep offering it, but be sure it is always fresh.

Avoid abrupt changes in diet. Never starve your bird into eating new foods. Here are some suggestions to try:

1. For the fussy seed eaters, try removing most, but not all, of the one or two types of seeds that your bird seems only to be eating.
2. Take out the preferred foods at night. DO NOT put them back in first thing in the morning. If necessary, add them later in the day.
3. Mix new foods in with the regular food.
4. Place new foods near a favorite toy or at the end of the perch.
5. Sweeten new foods with a small amount of molasses or brown sugar.
6. Try hand feeding new food, but don't get him too dependent on this method. Also try offering the food as a "game" or "reward."
7. Feed in favorite areas outside the cage.
8. Try feeding new foods in different forms; i.e., chopped vs. whole. Try warming the food.
9. Use your imagination—where there's a will, there's a way.

ALWAYS BE SURE THE FOOD STAYS FRESH AND IS FREQUENTLY CHANGED WHILE YOUR BIRD IS BECOMING ACCUSTOMED TO ITS LOOK AND SMELL.

GOOD LUCK!!! REMEMBER: PERSISTENCE PAYS OFF.

4

Creating a Happy Environment

Humans are social animals. The need to feel secure and wanted, to have friends, is at the very center of a healthy and happy existence. So it is with most birds, too. These needs and others must be fulfilled if you and your bird are going to develop that very special relationship. Remember you are isolating your bird from its peers and even removing its primary means of defense—the freedom to fly away.

If your new bird is going to live a long, happy and healthy life, YOU must provide all its basic needs. The fear of captivity must be removed. Allow it time to become adjusted to its new home. Move slowly, talk gently, and don't expect too much too quickly. It will require some time before your bird begins to feel like a family member.

Birds help bring fulfillment to our lives, love and a smile to our faces. In exchange for this, we provide shelter, food and security for them. A mutual trust will soon grow between the two of you. You will become your bird's best friend, perhaps its only friend.

Like humans, birds are emotional living creatures. They have good days and bad days. With time, you will become finely tuned to your bird's behavioral patterns. You will know when it is happy or sad, healthy or sick. This is very important since signs of illness must be spotted early.

Remember, birds are very much individuals with their own personalities and each behaves differently under varying conditions.

As Rosemary Low states in her book, *Parrots: Their Care and Breeding*, there are four qualities needed to care for birds well:

1. A basic knowledge of their requirements,
2. An observant eye to detect when something is wrong,
3. A love of birds,
4. Imagination.

Housing

You will need to convert the cold metal cage into a warm, loving home. It is important to provide for the essentials of life, as well as creating a comfortable and secure environment. Most tame pet birds prefer living in a busy room of the house such as the living room or den where there is a lot of activity. Good caging "sets the stage" for all future interactions. (See Chapter 5, HOME SWEET HOME for more on this important subject.)

Toys

Wild birds are in a normally stimulus-rich environment with constant challenges and dangers that require their full attention. Having to scavenge for food is also very time-consuming. Boredom is never a problem. This is not the case for caged birds. Attention needs to be directed towards making their new surroundings exciting and interesting. Toys are of great benefit. They are a must for kids of all ages. Birds too! Many toys can also function as a form of exercise. (See the section on toys in Chapter 5 for more information.)

Flying Exercise

Many birds enjoy flying around the house. Like jogging for people, the mental and physical benefits are plentiful. It's great exercise and recreation, but use caution. There are many dangers involved.

SAFETY CHECKLIST PRIOR TO LIFTOFF

- Windows and drapes are closed.
- Doors are closed and locked—no unexpected visitors.
- All other pets, particularly dogs and cats, are kept away.
- Children—can injure or be injured.
- Cover mirrors.
- The kitchen can be especially dangerous. Cover pots and turn the stove off.
- Avoid exposure to heat, fire, fans, hot coffee, oil and boiling water.
- Be aware of which house plants are poisonous.

WHAT YOU CAN DO

- Remain quiet.
- Do not attempt to chase or catch the bird.
- Leave the cage door open.
- When exhaustion sets in and landing occurs, offer a finger for perching.
- Warn guests—swooping loose birds can be very frightening.
- Many birds, especially the larger ones, love to chew and gnaw. In a very short time they can destroy beautiful furniture or ingest toxic material. Watch them closely.

NOTE: Obviously a bird's wings cannot be trimmed if full flight is desired. New birds and those actively engaged in training should have their wings trimmed. Otherwise, free-flying around the house especially for the smaller birds such as parakeets and cockatiels will be fun for all and

psychologically uplifting as well. (See Wing Trimming in Chapter 6, FEATHERS, FEET 'N' BEAKS, TOO.)

Companionship

It's nice to have company—to share life's experiences together. Like the "Betcha can't eat just one" commercials, many people who start out with one bird soon manage to acquire another feathered friend. Most birds will also enjoy the companionship of another bird.

Then the question is, "Do we put them in the same cage?"

The answer is not without some thought and careful planning. One bird is going to prove more dominant than the other and this could lead to problems. Birds in training should always be kept separate as distractions would constantly occur to the detriment of the lessons.

Before moving birds in together and risking potential injury, consider the following:

- The younger the birds, the greater the chance of successful mixing.
- The species should be the same, so keep canaries with canaries, budgies with budgies and so forth.
- Finches, canaries, budgies and lovebirds generally do well together. The larger parrots, such as Amazons, cockatoos and macaws, do not generally mix well and much more thought and planning must be given.
- Let the birds get to know each other from separate cages at first. Over a short period of time begin to move the cages together.
- The first actual encounter should be outside of the cage. Carefully observe the birds' behavior and be prepared to separate them.
- Use as large a cage as possible and initially leave them together for only short periods. You might try opening both cage doors and placing the birds opposite each other.
- NEVER LEAVE THE AREA until you are convinced the birds will be completely compatible.

Cats and Dogs

When birds are kept in the same household with cats and dogs, extra time and thought must go into planning for the birds' safety. In some instances these pets mix well and in many others it can lead to serious, if not fatal, injury—most often for the bird.

In too many instances owners believed they had a fool-proof system for keeping their pets separated when all of a sudden to their horror they realized they didn't. Always proceed cautiously and with common sense when first placing pets together. Be sure the animals will mix well or do not leave them near each other. Be especially careful of cats since they can often get to what was thought to be an inaccessible location for the cage and bird.

Music and Television

Many birds greatly enjoy the background noise and it can even prove an aid to teaching talking and singing. Also try records or tapes of bird sounds. BIRDS, LIKE ALL OF US, NEED TO LIVE AN ACTIVE AND STIMULATING LIFE FOR OPTIMUM HEALTH. An important goal is to keep boredom to a minimum and their time well occupied.

TRAVELING *WITH* YOUR BIRD

Birds generally travel well.

By Car

It is best to keep your bird in its regular cage and to bring along a cage cover and its favorite toys. If the cage is too large, find a smaller one that will fit comfortably in your car, but still gives your bird the freedom to stand up, turn around and, ideally, flap its wings. Be sure to bring along the home water supply or fresh bottled water, and the regular diet since abrupt changes can cause loose droppings and other problems.

If you must leave the bird unattended in the car on a warm day, ALWAYS park in the shade and leave a window partially open. The inside temperature will be several degrees higher than outside and overheating can occur rapidly. An indoor plant sprayer filled with cool water and used on warm days to spray the bird periodically is an excellent way to help avoid overheating and encourage preening as well.

By Air

Birds are accepted on most flights. Always check with the airlines well in advance to find out their rules and regulations since they do vary between carriers. Generally speaking, one pet is allowed in the cabin on each flight and *must* be kept beneath the seat. Reservations must be made and there will be an extra charge. Larger birds may have to travel in the baggage compartment. Here a cage cover is a must since the temperature is variable and can become quite cool.

The traveling crate must be sturdy and large enough to allow the bird to stand up and turn around. It must also meet airline regulations for size. Fresh water and food is essential. However, since water may spill, additional fruits and vegetables, if eaten, will help lessen the bird's need for another water source. Try indoor/outdoor carpeting on the floor and even the walls for padding and warmth. Be sure to include a perch.

By Bus or Train

Forget it. No pets are allowed.

- Health Certificates are usually required by airlines when traveling into foreign countries. Check with your veterinarian and travel agent. A health certificate helps to insure the good health of the animal and verifies examination by an accredited veterinarian just prior to departure.

- Quarantining of your pet is required by many foreign countries, and even Hawaii. It can last from one day to six months or longer. It may be necessary to make reservations in advance.
- Sedation or motion sickness medication should not be used.
- Some hotels and motels may not accept pets. Ascertain the policy where you will be staying and plan your trip accordingly.

TRAVELING *WITHOUT* YOUR BIRD

Whenever possible, always keep your bird in its home setting. Any change in location is stressful, especially in a bird already saddened by the absence of its owner. Find a reliable person knowledgeable about birds to house-sit and bird-sit. Or, at the very least, have them come by twice daily to check and see that all is well. Consider having the stereo or TV turned on a few hours every day to simulate human companionship. A taped recording of your voice may even be helpful.

Occasionally you may have friends willing to keep the bird at their home during your trip. If boarding becomes necessary, choose a facility that is clean, quiet, and kept warm and, of course, familiar with birds. Ask your veterinarian or local bird club for a recommendation. Reservations a few weeks in advance are always advised, especially during the holiday season.

- In case of emergencies, always leave a number where you can be reached or that of a close friend or relative.
- Written care instructions are a must. Detail your bird's particular habits, its likes and dislikes.
- Always supply your bird's regular diet and treats that it enjoys.
- Be sure to leave the name, address and phone number of your veterinarian.
- Remember it is a major responsibility to ask someone to care for your bird.

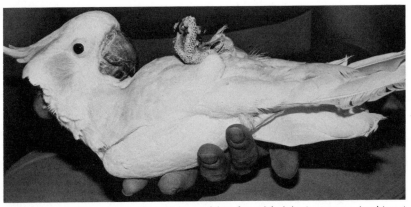

This is normally a very vulnerable position for a bird, but once mutual trust becomes well established it is possible with time and training.
—*Tony Costanza*

5

Home Sweet Home

The cage is your bird's home—a place to lounge and a place to live. Providing good shelter is basic to the happy and healthy existence you are striving to create. Mental and physical health is dependent on the feeling of security and comfort that proper caging affords.

Most pet birds are housed in cages. Other choices include flight cages or aviaries. Although these certainly provide room for flight and exercise, the additional expense and space requirements do become a factor. Training and close personal contact also become very difficult. Both of these types of shelters are very acceptable and each has its own advantages and disadvantages.

For pet birds, caging is the most practical and popular. Most birds still possess their native instincts and are accustomed to free flight and the security that it brings. This type of open environment cannot even pretend to be simulated, however, the goals need to be the same—safety, security, and comfort.

Remember, an artificial environment is being created. The IDEAL CAGE should supply the following:

1. "Room to Stretch"—wings should be able to be outstretched and flapped without touching the sides. The cage should be as large as possible.
2. Perches arranged to avoid ruffling the tail feathers.
3. A cage door large enough to allow easy access.
4. A removable bottom tray for easier clean-up.
5. Readily accessible food and water dishes.
6. No sharp or rough edges.

Cage Design

Cages are made in all shapes and sizes. Unfortunately, many are designed for eye appeal rather than for function and comfort. Here are some important guidelines to keep in mind when shopping for a cage.

- A rectangular shape is much preferred. More movement and even some flying may become possible.

55

- Cages that are tall and cylindrical in shape are not as functional as rectangular ones. Birds naturally move from side to side, not from floor to ceiling.
- The bar spacing needs to be narrow enough to prevent the bird from poking its head through and creating a potentially dangerous problem.
- The cage door fastener must be sturdy and allow for a lock to be used. The larger birds are especially clever and can learn quickly how to open the cage door.
- Cages should be made out of metal. The bamboo and wicker cages are totally impractical. Cleaning and sterilization of these is impossible.
- Ornamental cages may be pleasing to the eye but, again, not very practical—cleaning is more difficult.
- Cage simplicity is best for the bird, more practical, and less expensive for you.

Cage Paint

Never use cages painted with lead-base paints. Lead poisoning occurs in birds and can be fatal. This is rarely a problem with cages manufactured in the United States. Anodized finishes, where the color is applied electronically, are ideal and are usually found on the more expensive cages. Some of the very large cages are painted a flat black color with no finishing coat. These should also be avoided since the color rubs off easily and can soil the bird.

If you have one of these cages, or if the bargain is too good to pass up, don't despair. The paint can be easily removed by having the cage dipped professionally into a large vat containing hot acid which will rapidly remove the paint without damaging the cage. Be sure the new paint is non-toxic and durable enough to stand up against a constant thrashing by the bird's beak.

Cage Paper

For ease of cleaning, paper should be placed on the floor of the cage, and changed daily. Simply place several layers of paper down and just pull the top sheet off each day. Newspaper is readily available and works quite well. It may, however, discolor the feathers. Paper towels or computer paper are also very good to use.

When discarding the top sheet, take a second to look at the quantity, color and consistency of the droppings. This is an excellent indicator of a bird's health. (See "Interpretation of Abnormal Droppings" in Chapter 9.)

Cat litter, wood shavings or dried corn should never be used on the cage floor. Birds may think of these things as food and if eaten will cause serious problems. Daily cleaning also becomes very difficult.

Cage Location

Most birds are social animals. They like lots of attention and a feeling of involvement in the activities around them. The more tame a bird, the more

Cages are available in a variety of sizes and shapes. Many pet shops carry a wide assortment and can offer helpful advice in making selections.
—*Tony Costanza*

The T-Stand is an excellent adjunct to the right cage, but not a substitute for it. —*Tony Costanza*

attention it craves. Therefore, it is best to place the cage in areas of high use, such as the living room or family room.

Place the cage in the corner of the room, backed by a solid wall for that added dimension of security. If the cage is not too large, keep it at eye level, but always up off the floor. Avoid placing it too close to heating and air conditioning vents, drafts, or direct sunlight.

Cage Covers

Birds are sensitive to light and sleep best in darkness. By covering the cage at night with a cover made for this purpose, especially for the small birds, you are darkening their environment and providing added warmth and greater security. This may be especially helpful in the care of sick birds.

Try a cage cover for quieting a noisy, boisterous bird. It may work well!

Perches

Pet birds spend most of their lives—awake and asleep—standing on perches. When they walk, they use a "jumping" type of motion moving from one side to the other. Many birds even use their feet when eating. All of these factors exert special stress on the feet.

In order to condition, strengthen and exercise the feet, a variety of shapes, sizes and textures of perches should be used. There are many choices including:

Hard Perches: (Wood and certain plastics)—Wood is by far the most commonly used material. Wooden perches can be purchased at most pet shops or wooden dowels can be obtained at lumber stores and cut to size.

Branches are excellent and provide "natural padding", flexibility and tapering widths. Peeling the bark can become a game, as well as a source of nutrition. Branches from edible trees such as maple, ash, eucalyptus, and fruit and nut trees are safest. Clean the branches first and do not use any containing insecticides or excessive sap.

Be very careful with most plastics as they can shatter and cause serious health problems. The PVC tubing used for plumbing and electrical work makes safe and durable perches. Lightly sanding the surface assures better traction and so less slippage.

Soft Perches:—Unless foot problems arise, soft perches are usually best avoided. Fabric, carpet or rubber perch coverings should not be used since, once again, birds may eat this material and develop serious problems.

Sandpaper-covered perches are also available. However, they do little to keep the nails short and can cause foot problems. It is best to avoid their use altogether.

Shapes:—Round, oval rectangular, square, and flat: all of these shapes have been tried and used successfully. Varying the shapes alters the weight-bearing areas of the foot and helps condition all parts of the feet.

Always have at least two perches available in the cage. They should be of varying thicknesses and placed at slightly different heights. Three or four are ideal but avoid overcrowding. Cleanliness is important, so clean the perches periodically. Soap and water followed by a light sanding works well. Replace perches that become damaged from chewing or are heavily soiled.

T-Stands

These are excellent for display or change of scenery for the larger parrots. They do not provide the necessities of a good caging environment and, therefore, should be used only during the day as desired. Be sure food and water are easily available. Many of these T-stands come with food and water cups affixed to the ends of the perch and a large sheet of metal below to catch the droppings.

Food and Water Cups

These should be placed in convenient locations near the perches. Never place them directly below the perches as contamination from droppings will become a problem. The cup material needs to be strong, durable, and non-toxic. They should be cleaned weekly. Most cups can be safely washed in the dishwasher.

Playpens

Playpens are an ideal addition to your bird's environment. They are as the name implies, an assortment of wooden swings, ladders, and other simple amusements. They can even be connected to the cage with a series of ladders, or dowels. Most pet shops sell them or you can handcraft one yourself.

Toys

Toys not only make life more enjoyable, they help satisfy the bird's normal instinct for chewing. They can function as a form of exercise as well as helping to maintain the beak and nails at their proper length. Many different types are available. Most of them, however, have been designed for smaller birds, such as budgies. For the larger parrots, with their destructive beaks, few strong and durable toys are available. With a spark of creative imagination coupled with a few simple hand tools, many wonderful toys can be quickly and easily fashioned.

- Swings hung from the cage ceiling are always a favorite. They can be made using two metal rods and a wooden dowel.
- A dumbbell made from two wooden blocks connected by a wooden dowel makes an excellent chew toy.
- Small wooden sewing thread spools (if you can still find them), without the thread, make good playthings.
- Mirrors are always popular with birds. For small birds, pet shops

Food and water cups are manufactured in a variety of sizes, shapes and materials. Many pet shops carry an assortment and can offer advice in making selections.
—*Tony Costanza*

A playpen offers additional exercise opportunities for the pet bird.
—*Tony Costanza*

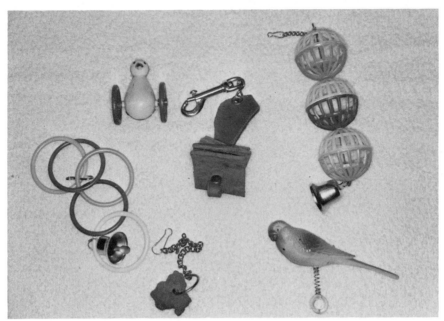

Some of the toys available for budgerigars and other smaller birds.
—*Tony Costanza*

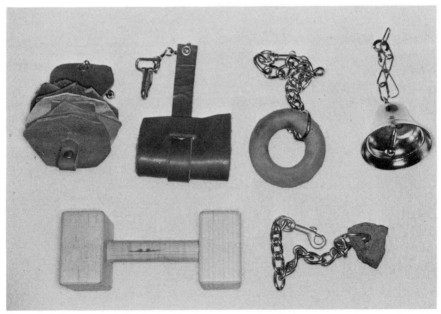

Some of the toys available for the larger parrots. These are much more durable and better able to withstand the abuse from their powerful beaks.
—*Tony Costanza*

usually have an ample assortment. Mirrors for larger birds can prove very dangerous and certain precautions must be taken. Use either a polished aluminum or stainless steel mirror which will still give a good reflection.

- Metal cowbells attached to a metal chain make fine play things. The ringing sound is enjoyed by most birds.
- Lava rocks suspended by a chain are sold in many pet shops. They are fun to play with and help keep the beak and nails down to a reasonable length.
- Rawhide chews for dogs are another favorite.
- Try cutting heavy leather into small squares and stacking them on a chain suspended from the cage ceiling.
  CAUTION: When using chains, be sure the links have a large enough diameter to prevent beaks and feet from getting caught. Also, do not use any toys that contain lead.

There are no general rules regarding types of toys for your bird. Select ones that are safe and durable. Obviously, parrots must have stronger toys than budgies. Wood must be free of paint and chemicals. Toys made of fabrics, soft rubber, brittle plastic or string can create a real danger for a bird from becoming tangled somewhere on the body or being ingested.

Never overcrowd the cage with toys. There must be sufficient room for the bird's comfort. Remember: a cage is like a house; time, work and love make it into a home.

Flight Cages

The design and construction of these special cages are discussed in Chapter 15, "Bird Breeding."

Temperature and Humidity

Most parrots are from tropical environments where the temperature is always warm and the humidity is usually high. Few areas in the Northern Hemisphere can duplicate these conditions. Fortunately for us, most birds will still thrive in conditions different from their natural habitats.

Many birds are kept in outdoor aviaries year 'round without any noticeable problems. Most pet birds are kept indoors with relatively little temperature variation. Birds should be kept warm, 68°-75° F is ideal. However, most will still do fine in the 60°-90° F range. Any greater temperature extremes may cause problems. It is very important that temperature changes be made GRADUALLY. Abrupt temperature changes can be disastrous for a bird.

The higher the humidity the better, but it is not as critical as the temperature. In a very dry environment more frequent spraying or bathing is recommended.

Cleaning and Disinfecting

For the benefit of you, your bird and your home, it is essential that the necessary steps be taken to control infection and contamination. This, sadly, is a frequently forgotten area of care and yet, critically important for everyone's health.

A bird's health, both mental and physical, is largely dependent on its environment. Birds are very clean animals and do much better when their home is clean and free of contamination. Since birds' fecal matter has no odor, it can be easily overlooked when general house cleaning is done. Keeping the bird's quarters clean and disinfected will help decrease the possibility of transmitting disease.

To disinfect means to destroy infective agents, namely bacteria, viruses, and fungii. Nonporous materials such as metal, plastics, glass, masonite, tile and cement are easily disinfected. Porous material such as wood, bamboo and wicker are impossible to sterilize. Therefore, their use for caging material is not recommended.

It is a good idea to thoroughly clean the cage and all its contents weekly with mild soap, hot water, and a strong scrub brush. Every two weeks use disinfectant. FIRST, before scrubbing, soak all the items in a disinfecting solution for thirty minutes. A large garbage can works well for this. Afterward, use a heavy duty scrub brush and go over the cage and its contents, then rinse. Allow to dry, preferably in the sun where possible, because it is also a good disinfectant. For the large cages, the soaking procedure will probably have to be abandoned. Start right in with the scrubbing.

REMEMBER: The cage paper should be changed daily.

There are many excellent disinfectants available today. They are classified according to their chemical composition and the substances they contain. Each group has certain properties in common and this is helpful in determining the effectiveness of the various disinfectants. The table herein lists the major disinfectant classifications and summarizes the general properties of each group.

The following are a few of the many good disinfectants available at grocery stores, through your veterinarian, or janitorial supply. This is by no means a complete listing, but rather, is meant to be a helpful guide to some of the more commonly used disinfectants. There are many other equally good disinfectants available.

LYSOL™, Manufactured by Lehn & Fials Products, Div. of Sterling Drug Inc.
  Dilution: 4 oz. per gallon water.
  An excellent all-purpose disinfectant.
ONE-STROKE ENVIRON™, Manufactured by Vestal.
  Dilution: 1/2 oz. per gallon water.
  Official disinfectant of the USDA.
CHLOROX™, Manufactuced by the Chlorox Co.
  Dilution: 6 oz. per gallon water.

SUMMARY OF DISINFECTANT CHARACTERISTICS

Revised from *Zoo and Wild Animal Medicine* (p. 25)
Edited by Dr. M.E. Fowler (Permission granted)

DISINFECTANT	KILLS BACTERIA	KILLS VIRUSES	KILLS FUNGI	KILLS ALGAE	INACTIVATED IN ORGANIC MATERIAL	INACTIVATED BY HARD WATER	STABILITY IN SOLUTION	TOXICITY	COMMENTS
Common Detergents (*Tide, All, etc.*)	+/−	—	—	+	—	+	+	Minimal	Poor disinfectants
Phenolics (*Lysol, One-Stroke Environ*)	++	+	?	—	—	+	+	Minimal—irritating to skin	Excellent disinfectants
Quaternary NH₄ Compounds (*Roccal-D*)	++	+/−	?	++	—	+	+	Minimal	Better disinfectants are available
Chlorine Compounds (*Chlorox, bleaches*)	++	+	+	++	—	+/−	+	Minimal—may be irritating to skin	Excellent and inexpensive
Chlorhexidine (*Nolvasan*)	+/−	—	?	+	—	+	+	Minimal	Better disinfectants are available
("Tamed" iodines, Betadine, Weladol, etc.)	++	+	?	+/−	—	+	+	Minimal	Excellent but more expensive
Lye (*NaOH*)	+	+	+	—	+/−	—	—	DANGEROUS—Use extreme caution	NOT for general use
Quicklime	+	+	+	+/−	—	—		DANGEROUS—Use extreme caution	NOT for general use
Formalin	+	+	?	+	—	+	+	Irritating	NOT for general use

++ / Highly Effective   + / Effective   — / Not effective   ? / Questionable effectiveness

Inexpensive. May be corrosive to bare metal. Great for concrete flooring. Most all chlorine bleaches are equally effective.

BETADINE™, Manufactured by Purdue-Frederick, Inc.

Dilution: 3/4 oz. per gallon water.

Available through your veterinarian. Safe for hands and non-corrosive. Many similar products available under different brand names, such as Weladol®, Prepdodyne®, and Betadyne®.

- Follow manufacturer's recommendations carefully.
- Gloves are recommended for some of the disinfectants.
- Be sure to rinse cage well and dry out well before putting bird back into it. No strong odors should be present.

Filing a bird's beak with an emery board.

6

Feathers, Feet 'n' Beaks, Too!

GENERAL HEALTH and GROOMING CARE

Birds are very particular about their cleanliness. Their natural instincts for self-grooming are strong. In much the same way that cats groom themselves, birds preen themselves. They will spend many hours every day methodically preening their feathers. As a veterinarian treating birds, one quickly realizes the importance of evaluating the overall appearance of a bird. Simply standing back and observing is paramount in any exam. A healthy bird will appear very alert, the feathers will gleam and lie smoothly in neat rows. A sick bird, on the other hand, will appear depressed, the feathers scruffy and unkempt.

Feathers

Birds have been called *glorified reptiles.* Indeed, aside from their feathers and other adaptations associated with flight, they are very similar to their reptilian ancestors. The feathers have evolved from the reptile's scales.

Feathers not only impart the beautiful rainbow of colors to birds, but play several other important roles necessary for survival. The ability to fly away quickly allows birds to escape from danger and permits them to forage over large areas for food, making them one of the most successful animals on earth!

The outer colorful layer of feathers covering most of the body and wings are referred to as the *contours.* The *flight feathers* are found on the wings and tail. These feathers provide protection against the elements, and in the bird's natural habitat, the coloration blends well with the surroundings, acting as camouflage. Sexual attraction and waterproofing are also important functions of these feathers.

The underneath layer, or *down feathers,* provides the insulation for temperature regulation. Part of these greyish-white feathers will slowly disintegrate, producing the "powdery dust" which often resembles dandruff and is perfectly normal. It is this "dust" that may cause allergies in people.

The feathers are lubricated by natural oils that the bird secretes from a special gland at the base of the tail called the *preen* or *uropygial* gland. These oils help give the feathers their water-repellency and durability, and the beak evenly distributes these oils over its feathers when preening. Preening, a form of self-grooming, is important and should be encouraged. Some species of birds lack this specialized gland.

Molt

This is the shedding or loss of "old" feathers with the replacement of new ones. The old feathers will be pushed out by the growth of the new feathers. Classically, most wild birds molt once yearly. It is very sudden, with a loss of many feathers, leaving the bird virtually defenseless and flightless for a few weeks. However, most pet birds do not show this pattern of molting. A slow, continuous molt, where only a few feathers at a time are lost and flight is still possible, seems to be the rule. In large part, this is due to the nonfluctuating temperatures and lighting that we have in our homes. The new feathers begin growing in immediately and take from six to eight weeks to complete their growth. Immature feathers, referred to as *pin* or *blood feathers,* grow out in a keratin sheath. Preening removes the keratin sheath allowing the feather to open up. These sheaths have a large blood supply in them and if damaged will bleed excessively and must be removed immediately. The feather must be pulled out firmly from its base and pressure applied to the skin opening until the bleeding stops. This can take several minutes.

RECOMMENDATIONS DURING THE MOLT

- Eliminate all stressful situations (allow rest and relaxation).
- Keep temperature 75°-80° F; avoid sudden fluctuations.
- Diet must be the best, and should include high protein and mineral supplements.
- Preening should be encouraged. Light misting of the feathers will help (see BATHING).
- Baths are delightful and invigorating. Avoid allowing your bird to become chilled.

Wing Trimming

This is a much-practiced ritual to prevent pet birds from flying away or flying into objects and injuring themselves. Taming and training birds will also be made easier resulting in fewer distractions. However, by trimming, an important form of exercise and excitement is lost and the bird's ability to escape dangers, such as other pets and kids, vanishes. Many a "trimmed" bird has flown away either due to improper trimming or the owner forgetting that new feathers will eventually grow back. There are many wild parrots flying free these days much to the dismay of their previous owners.

Cutting feathers is preferable to plucking them out. The cut feathers will have to molt out requiring extra time (as opposed to new feathers growing back in six to eight weeks after plucking.)

Appearance of the three common types of feathers found on birds.

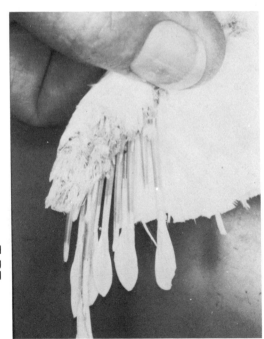

Blood feathers should not be cut during wing trimming or bleeding will result.

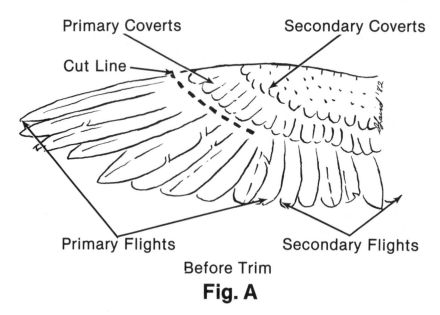

Before Trim

Fig. A

Dotted line shows proper location for wing trim.

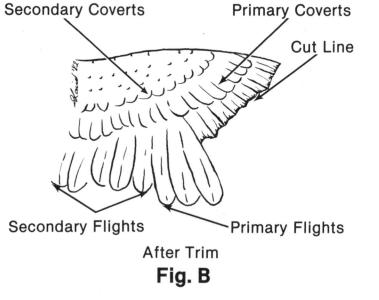

After Trim

Fig. B

Appearance of wing following trimming.

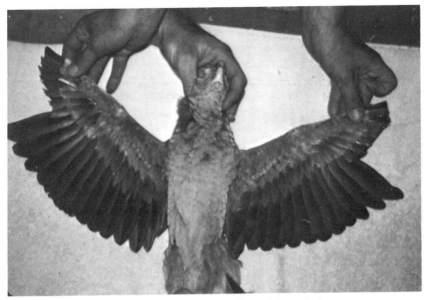

Properly trimmed wings viewed from below.

The same bird viewed from above.

There is more than one way to trim the feathers. Not any single method will work in every instance. Some birds seem to have an uncanny ability to fly regardless of the method used. The preferred technique is to cut the outer five to eight primary flight feathers on BOTH wings. Cut them even with the length of the row of primary covert feathers. This technique is also safest since it still allows birds to have a controlled glide down to the ground. When only one wing is trimmed, their balance is poor and "crash-landings" can occur. It is best to avoid cutting any blood feathers. Wait for the feather to grow out, then cut it.

Trimming is not difficult, but have your veterinarian or an experienced bird fancier show you how the first time. Remember, many trimmed birds can still fly so don't take safety for granted.

Bathing

Bathing is a natural and excellent way to aid in grooming and encourage preening. In the wild, birds bathe when it rains or are often observed splashing around in the wet grass or leaves. Experiment with the various methods until you find the one that suits both of you best.

When possible, bathe your bird during the warmest time of the day and allow it plenty of time to dry out before it cools down. A good wetting of the feathers should be done at least twice weekly and some birds may even enjoy it daily.

Here are some suggested methods:

- *Water Bowl*—size dependent on the bird
- *Plant Mister/Shower*—ideal method for larger birds
- *Water Faucet*—must be careful the hot water doesn't get turned on accidentally.
- *Wet Lettuce Leaves*—Especially liked by budgerigars and other small birds.
- How about a shower companion?

There are commercially available bathing solutions that may be purchased at local pet stores. However, fresh water is as good or better than these other solutions. NEVER use soap as it can destroy the protective coating on the feathers.

Beaks

The correct length and shape of the beak is essential to the overall health of your bird. Beaks are not only used to catch and prepare food for swallowing, but also for climbing, singing and talking, defense, preening, feeding the young, and of course, for giving affection.

The beak is composed of hollow bone, on the inside are the sinuses and the outer covering is a thin layer of horn-like material called keratin. There is a

On a warm day, birds can be showered from an outdoor water source.

A hand-held water sprayer is a good way of showering your bird. Use a fine mist and not a stream of water. Do not use a bottle that has previously contained household cleaning solutions.   *—Tony Costanza*

blood and nerve supply present. The beak grows from its base and not from the tip. Average growth for parakeet beaks is said to be approximately 1/4" per month or 3" per year. The lower beak grows somewhat slower than this.

Often the outermost layer of keratin begins to flake or peel. This is a normal process of shedding the oldest layers and does not indicate a health problem. A light sanding with a fine sand paper or emery board will help remove these old layers.

The normal "hinge-like" action of the lower beak usually maintains the proper length and shape of the upper beak. If, for any reason, the normal alignment of the upper and lower beak is distorted, overgrowth will occur. These birds can usually lead a normal life, however, their beaks will have to be trimmed periodically.

Birds should be encouraged to chew as a means of maintaining and conditioning the beak. The following items are especially helpful:

Branches	Bones	Cuttlebone
Mineral Blocks	Lava Rock	Grit Mixture

A healthy bird with a normal-shaped beak rarely needs to have its beak trimmed. If it does become necessary to trim a bird's beak, proper restraint and complete control of the head is absolutely essential. The process usually requires two people to complete the job, especially on the larger birds. One person holds the bird in a towel as described in Chapter 7, "How To Restrain Your Bird." You must then carefully grasp the head from behind and slide the fingers over to one side of it. Move the fingers so that the index and middle fingers are resting on the top of the upper beak. The thumb of the same hand is placed under the lower beak and the beak is held closed. The upper beak should come to a dull rounded point and extend below the junction where both beaks meet. Since each species varies as to normal beak shape and length, refer to pictures of the species you own in general bird books and magazines to learn what is correct. Your veterinarian and knowledgeable aviculturists may also be able to advise you. Do all of this BEFORE attempting to trim the beak on your own.

Human fingernail or toenail clippers, depending on your bird's size, generally work well and are preferable to scissors. Finer sculpturing can be achieved with an emery board or nail file. Care must be exercised to avoid splitting or cracking the beak. If the beak is cut too short, bleeding will occur. Be sure to protect the tongue during all trimming operations.

Trimming a beak is difficult and practice is required to do a good job without getting bitten. Remember, if the trimming is done incorrectly it may interfere with the bird's ability to eat. It is best to let someone with experience do the trimming, or at least, show you how it is done the first time.

Nails

In birds, as in other animals, the toenails grow continuously. Normal activity is often sufficient to maintain the proper length. However, some birds

The normal shape and length of the beak is essential to normal activity among birds. The budgerigar (top), Finsch's Amazon (middle) and green-wing macaw (bottom) shown here all exhibit what is right for their respective species and genera.   —*Tony Costanza*

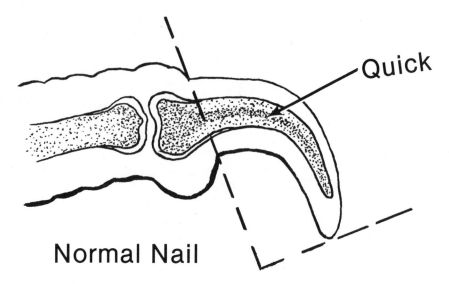

Normal Nail

Cross-section of normal nail. Notice that the claw curves down and forms a full right-angle of approximately 90 degrees.

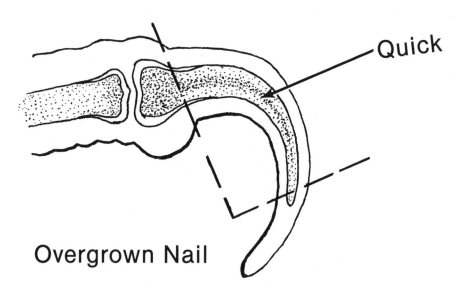

Overgrown Nail

Cross-section of overgrown nail. Notice that the proportion of quick to overall length of nail is decreased.

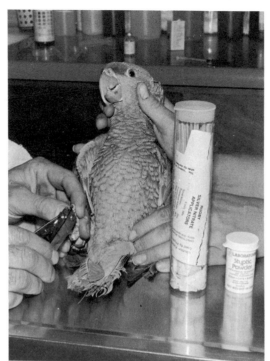

A procedure for trimming the nails on a small or medium sized bird. Some type of powder should be readily available if bleeding should occur. Styptic powders are available at many pet shops.

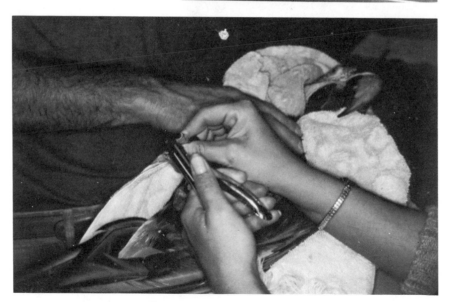

Trimming a macaw's nails.
—*Tony Costanza*

still need to have their nails trimmed periodically. Overgrown nails make perching difficult and can cause serious foot problems.

A normal claw will turn down and complete a full right angle. The *quick* is the living portion of the nail containing the blood and nerve supply and extends from between 2/3 and 3/4 of the length of the nail. In overgrown or deformed nails these proportions will change. The quick can be seen in light colored nails, but unfortunately, is hidden in darker nails.

Use human nail clippers for small birds. Dog nail clippers may be used on the larger birds. Often just cutting off the sharp tips of the nails is sufficient, for if the quick is exposed, bleeding will result.

Once again, it is best to have someone with experience demonstrate the proper method. If too much nail is cut, not only will bleeding occur, but it may also become painful for the bird to bear weight on the foot.

Bleeding—Beaks and Nails

Unfortunately, it is not uncommon for nails and beaks to start bleeding while they are being trimmed. Since birds have only small amounts of blood to begin with, any loss, however small, is significant. With a little experience and the proper supplies, it is usually easy to control the bleeding. Always have the necessary supplies within easy reach. See the section "First Aid for Bleeding Beaks and Nails" in Chapter 10 before beginning.)

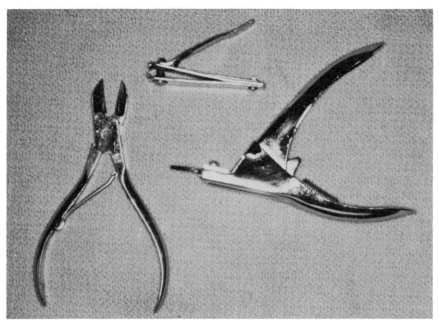

Depending on the size of the bird any of the instruments here can be used to trim nails or beaks. Clockwise from top: human nail cutter, guillotine nail cutters (made for dogs) and cuticle nippers.

7

How to Restrain Your Bird

From time to time you will need to catch and restrain your bird. This could be for trimming the nails, beak, or wing, giving an examination or administering treatment.

Your main concerns should be avoiding injury to yourself and preventing injury to your bird. Birds have fragile bones that can break easily. So be gentle. Breathing in birds is totally dependent on their being able to fully expand the chest wall. So never rest your hand on a bird's chest or squeeze its body too tightly.

Before catching the bird, plan ahead. All tools and medications needed should be handy and ready to go. To minimize stress and over-heating, ALWAYS HOLD YOUR BIRD FOR AS SHORT A TIME AS POSSIBLE.

In general, gloves are not needed once the towel method is perfected. Towels are less cumbersome and can completely "wrap-up" the bird. For birds that can fly, work in a small closed-off room just in case of escape. If your bird gets loose, sometimes a net can be helpful to catch it again.

Respect the beak! The larger parrots can and will inflict severe injury if given the opportunity. Even the budgerigar's bite may hurt. The nails may scratch or prick the skin, but it's the beak you want to watch out for.

To capture a bird in its cage, remove the perches and toys that the bird can hide behind. For the smaller birds (finches, canaries, budgerigars, and cockatiels), use a thin cloth or paper towel. Approach the bird slowly and grasp it from behind with the cloth and in one smooth motion scoop it up. Then position the bird in the cloth resting in the palm of your hand. Use the cupped hand and place the thumb on one side of the head and the other fingers on the opposite side. The bird should be loosely cradled in your palm. The other hand is free for the treatment or helping with added restraint.

For excitable birds, it's often easier to catch them in the dark. Take note of the bird's location and have someone turn off the lights. The bird will usually stay where it is. At this point drop a towel over the bird and gently scoop it up. Then turn the lights back on.

The larger parrots require a little more skill. Since it's the beak that can crush and injure fingers, always grab the head first and then let go of the head last when turning the bird free. Approach the bird slowly from behind and

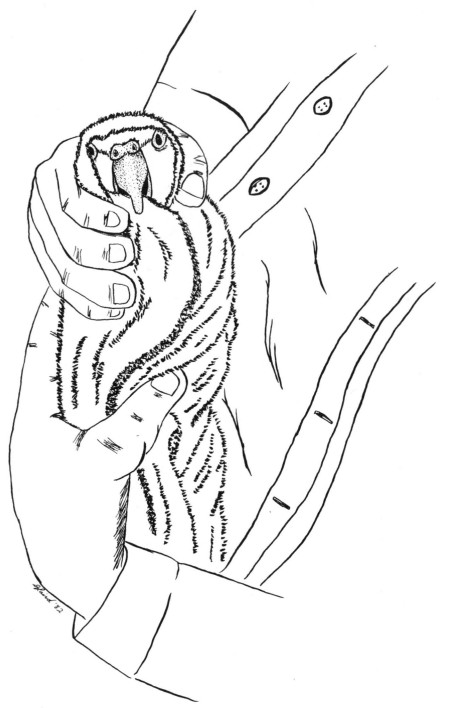

Proper method of restraining large bird with
towel. Note the position of the hands.

throw the towel over it. Then, in one "fell swoop," grasp the bird's head firmly. Use the cupped hand and place the thumb on one side of the head and the other fingers on the opposite side. For better control, especially for the larger birds, try sliding your index finger over the top of the head. With the other hand wrap the towel completely around the body and then scoop it up. Keep this hand resting gently over the upper part of the legs and if needed, the bird can be cradled between your forearm and abdomen. This is no time to be timid so don't hesitate in your actions. Uncover the head and be sure not to hamper breathing. Let the bird chew on the towel as this helps to keep its mind occupied. Often a second person may be needed for assistance with actual treatment.

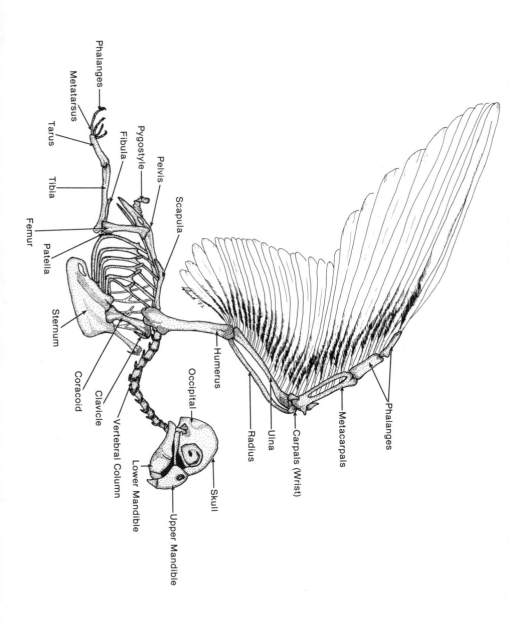

Phalanges
Metatarsus
Tarus
Tibia
Femur
Patella
Pygostyle
Fibula
Pelvis
Scapula
Sternum
Coracoid
Clavicle
Vertebral Column
Lower Mandible
Occipital
Upper Mandible
Skull
Humerus
Radius
Ulna
Carpals (Wrist)
Metacarpals
Phalanges

General skeletal anatomy of parrots.

8

Basic Anatomy and Physiology

"It is only through understanding the normal, can you better understand the abnormal." Our professors in veterinary school literally drilled this concept into our heads.

It is with this thought in mind that this chapter has been written. It is difficult to summarize this most incredibly complex and fascinating structure that gives life. It is meant as an overview of the major organs of the body and how they work. It is not meant to be an in-depth report on the subject. Little, if any, background in the sciences should be needed to understand and appreciate what follows.

First of all, remember that a bird's body is very similar to all other animals', including man's. The body in its most basic form is composed of millions and millions of cells, all invisible to the naked eye. These are the actual workhorses carrying out all the various reactions needed to sustain life. Tissues and organs are groups of similar cells with specialized functions, such as the heart which contracts to pump the blood throughout the body. A system such as the cardiovascular system is a collection of organs. Namely, the heart, blood and vessels all working together to nourish, supply energy and remove wastes from the cells. The systems, respiratory, digestive, cardio-vascular and all others must all be integrated with each other to work toward that most noble of goals—survival.

Since most birds do have a unique physical modification, namely their ability for flight, certain changes have evolved that make this type of existence much simpler. These changes include excellent vision, a very efficient breathing system, rapid energy production, powerful flight muscles, feathers, lightness and, of course, wings.

LET'S TALK BASICS

Special Senses

Eyes

The birds' eyes are very large compared to the size of their heads. Their vision is the sharpest and keenest of all animals—and for good reason. While

83

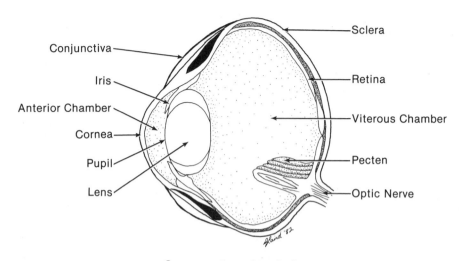

Cross-section of eyeball.

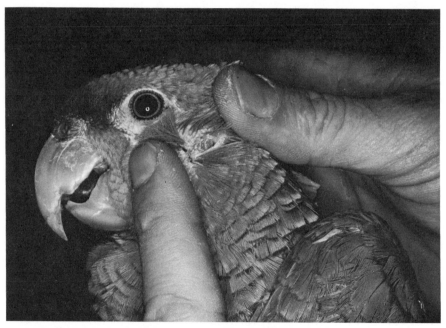

The view of an ear through parted feathers.

flying, vision becomes their most important sense. Their vision is much more developed than their senses of smell or taste. Colors are even detectable.

When looking at the eyes you'll first see the *eyelids*. In addition to an upper and lower eyelid, birds, like dogs and cats, have an extra or third eyelid called the *nictitating membrane*. It can be seen sweeping horizontally across the eye beginning at the inner corner. The lids all help to protect the eyeballs, remove foreign particles, and spread *lacrimal fluid* (tears) across the eye to keep it lubricated.

The *conjunctiva* is the glistening pink membrane lining the inside of the eyelids. It also attaches to the outer rim of the eyeball. It acts as a barrier to disease and helps keep the eye moist.

The *cornea* is the clear, transparent outer covering of the eyeball. When the cornea is damaged it will usually appear cloudy in color and lose some or all of its transparency.

The *sclera* or "white of the eyes" is the fibrous covering beginning at the outer edge of the cornea and continuing around the entire eye. It maintains the eye's rigid circular shape.

The *anterior chamber* is the space between the cornea and the *iris* and is filled with a thick transparent fluid.

The *iris* not only determines one's eye color, but also, very importantly, it regulates the amount of light entering the eye. It constricts the *pupils* when it is light and dilates them when it is dark.

The *lens* is the transparent body immediately behind the iris. It is changing shape constantly in order to focus the light rays perfectly onto the retina. *Cataracts* result from an opacity of the lens and, depending on their severity, will cause various degrees of impaired vision. These are most often seen in older parrots.

Behind the lens is the *vitreous chamber* containing a colorless, jelly-like fluid which holds the retina smoothly in place.

The *retina* is the thin membrane lining the inside of the back wall. The eye is like a camera. Light rays entering the eye are bent and focused onto the retina while passing through the various layers just discussed. The *rods and cones* in the retina are the light sensitive cells converting the messages to electrical impulses and sending them to the brain via the *optic nerve,* for interpretation. This all happens in less than a 2000th of a second!

Home Physical:

- The eyelids should be open wide, appear smooth and clean. They should not be swollen, crusted or pasted closed. The feathers surrounding the eye should lie flat and not be "caked" together.
- The conjunctiva should be pink and glistening, not red, swollen, or inflamed.
- The cornea should appear clear and transparent.
- The pupils should both be the same size and shape. Their size should vary with the amount of light entering the eye. Excitement usually

causes the pupils to be more dilated than what would be normal for the amount of incoming light.
- The eye should not be bulging from its socket. This can suggest an abscess or pocket of infection behind the eye.
- Both eyes should always have the same appearance and shape. If they do not, then there could be a problem.

Ears

As in most animals, the ears are the organ of hearing and balance. Both are well developed in birds.

A bird's ears appear hidden from view because the ear flaps or pinna are absent. Look closely at the area behind and slightly below the eyes, part the feathers, and you'll find the ears.

The *external ear canal* is a short tubular duct that collects and funnels the incoming sound waves. As these waves reach the end of the canal, the *tympanic membrane* or ear drum begins vibrating. This, in turn, puts the *columella* or *stapes bone* in motion. This bone connects to the *oval window,* which separates the middle and inner ear portions. When it begins vibrating, fluid in the inner ear is set in motion (similar to that of a breaking ocean wave). These waves then trigger the *auditory nerve* to relay the message to the brain for interpretation. It's amazing to realize that through this chain reaction, sound waves must travel through air, bone and fluid.

Above the inner ear are the *semicircular canals* which contain fluid. Moving the head or flying about moves this fluid around which, once again, stimulates a nerve that sends messages to the brain. The brain senses the change in head position or pull of gravity and instantaneously directs the body's muscles to correct and balance itself, thus giving birds their excellent sense of balance and ability to avoid numerous potential mishaps.

Ear problems are actually uncommon in pet birds.

Home Physical:

- Your bird should be sensitive to noises.
- Balance should be very good. Birds fall off perches *usually* because they are too weak to stand or have just had a convulsion and not just because they lose their balance and slip off.
- There should not be any swelling or discharge from the ears. Watch for any loss or abnormal parting of the feathers around the ear.

Integument (Skin)

The bird's skin is thinner than that of other animals. Thin skin means less weight. Most of the warmth and protection is provided by the feathers.

There are no sweat glands in the skin. As with dogs, birds pant to blow off excess heat.

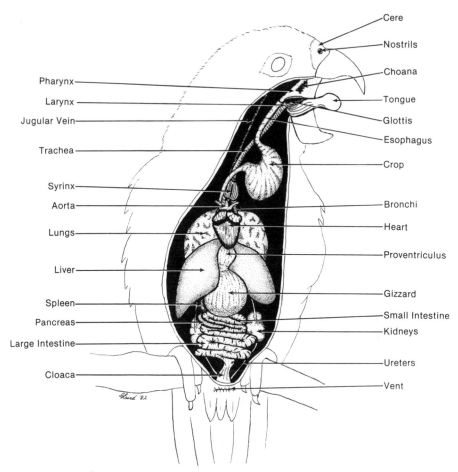

General location and names of major internal organs.

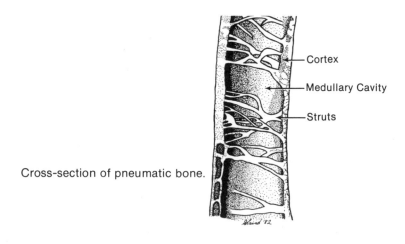

Cross-section of pneumatic bone.

Home Physical:

- The skin should lie smooth and appear almost the same color over the entire body.
- Watch for wounds, cuts and bruises. An area of wet or matted feathers may indicate an injury.
- Any swellings or bumps are abnormal.

MUSCULOSKELETAL SYSTEM

We all know that the muscles and bones protect, support and move the body. But that's not all they do. The muscles also play vital roles in swallowing, circulation of blood, respiration, defecation, egg laying and much more. The bones are also intimately involved in blood cell production and in the regulation of the levels of calcium and phosphorus in the body. The inner core of bone, referred to as *marrow,* produces the blood cells.

The evolution of flight has also caused many changes in the architectural framework of the bones and muscles. Here are a few of the more important and obvious adaptations:

- Many of the bones are hollow. These *pneumatic bones* contain air sacs which act like reservoirs for air and communicate with the lungs for breathing.
- *Skull*—There is a marked reduction in the number of bones and this gives added strength and power to the beak.
- *Neck bones* of the spine are elongated and have freely moving vertebrae. This allows for the great flexibility and rotation of the head that aids in preening and feeding.
- The *sternum* or breastbone is massive and along with the powerful pectoral muscles, enables birds to develop the great force necessary to flap their wings.
- The *wing bones* have been specially evolved for flight. These bones have become fewer in number and strengthened.
- *Toes*—in passerines (canaries, finches, mynahs) one toe points backward and three toes point forward. In psittacines (parrots), two toes point backward and two toes point forward. The arrangement of the toes gives birds better balance for perching. It also allows great agility for picking up food with their feet.

Hidden from view is the makeup of the bones themselves. They are very lightweight, but thin walls. As a result, these bones are very fragile. Like snapping a toothpick, fractures can easily occur. Always handle birds carefully. They ARE delicate creatures.

Home Physical:

- Thinness or weight loss; this is most evident around the breast area.

The normally full and rounded chest muscles will appear more "pointed" and the breastbone becomes more prominent.

- The joints should flex easily and not give evidence of pain or appear swollen.
- The wings should both be held at equal heights and right alongside the body. An injured wing will "droop" and lie slightly away from the body.
- Both legs should bear equal weight when standing. The legs should also appear similar to each other. If they do not, it could indicate a problem.
- Examine the toes for any deformities. Look for missing nails or curled toes. Overgrown nails can cause leg problems.
- Watch for any lumps 'n bumps—abnormal growths.
- Back problems are rare except in cases of trauma, i.e., an unplanned collision with a wall.

RESPIRATORY SYSTEM

Respiration is important because it supplies life-giving oxygen to every cell in the body. Oxygen provides the fuel for cells to produce energy and carry out all their important functions—and there are many. One of the waste products of this metabolism is carbon dioxide. It is expelled during the expiratory phase of respiration. The continuous supply of oxygen to the cells is critically important. The need for oxygen in birds is especially great because of their rapid metabolic rate and for doing what they do best—fly.

Birds' mechanism for breathing is strikingly different from mammals'. It has evolved into a lightweight and remarkably efficient system. It is very sophisticated and allows birds to perform athletic feats at altitudes at which most mammals would have trouble just staying alive.

The *nostrils* are the paired openings just above and behind the base of the beak. This area is called the *cere*. The *sinuses* are found inside the upper beak and skull. Acting like a mini-filter, humidifier and heater, the sinuses remove many of the impurities, as well as, warm and moisturize the incoming air.

The *choana* or slit-like opening along the roof of the mouth lets the air pass into the *pharynx* which is the hallway for air and food often referred to as the throat. Food from here will enter the esophagus while the air passes into the *larynx* which is located immediately below the esophagus. The larynx in birds is only a passageway for the air and does not produce sound as it does in mammals. From the larynx, the *trachea* or windpipe, and the *bronchi* funnel the air into the lungs. The lungs of birds are small and compact, and it is here where the actual exchange of gasses, oxygen and carbon dioxide occurs.

The *syrinx,* or voice box, is located at the far end of the trachea just before it divides into the right and left bronchi. Sound is produced as the syrinx changes shape causing a turbulence in the air flow thus producing noise.

Unique to birds are their *air sacs*. These are transparent membranes, like balloons, located in hollow bones and body spaces that function to supply fresh air continuously through the lungs during the entire breathing cycle.

In mammals, the diaphragm, which separates the chest cavity from the abdominal cavity, plays a vital role in breathing. The rudimentary diaphragm in birds is not necessary for breathing. It is the continuous changes in the size of the chest wall during inspiration and expiration that forces air to move in and out of the lungs.

The respiratory system is susceptible to injury and infection. Colds in birds come on quickly and can become life-threatening early in the course of the disease. Prompt attention is always necessary. With the large surface area of the air sacs, it makes them particularly susceptible to air-borne diseases and toxic fumes. Anesthesia must always be handled with great care to avoid serious problems.

Home Physical:

- First, from a short distance, observe the nature of the breathing. Respirations should flow easily and appear smooth. Problems to watch for include: open mouth breathing, panting at rest and the excessive bobbing up and down of the tail.
- Listen for strange sounds. Sneezing can be pronounced like an "achoo" or it can be as subtle as a soft "click." Coughing can also occur.
- After exercise, any heavy breathing should return to normal within about 90 seconds.
- The nostrils should both be open and the area around them clean. There should be no swelling, redness or discharge. With a cold, one or both nostrils are commonly plugged.
- If the sinuses become congested they commonly cause the areas around the eyes to swell or become puffy.
- If the mouth can be examined, pay particular attention to the roof. If white "cheese-like" material is noticed this can be indicative of a Vitamin A deficiency.
- If the syrinx becomes inflamed talking may cease or hoarseness may occur. Note: This may also result from a pharyngitis or sore throat.
- Infection of the air sacs is difficult to diagnose, but is often a cause of a lingering respiratory problem.

NOTE: ALWAYS USE EXTREME CAUTION WHEN HANDLING BIRDS WITH RESPIRATORY PROBLEMS. KEEP HANDLING TIMES SHORT AND MINIMIZE STRESS.

THE VITALS

Species	Respiratory* Rate	Heart* Rate	Body Temperature (°F)
Canary	60-100	500-1000	Variable for
Budgerigar	65-85	350-550	all birds.
Cockatiel	100-125	350-450	104° - 112°
Parrot	25-40	150-300	
Dog	10-30	60-120	100.5° - 102.5°
Man	12-16	60-80	98.6°

*These are the approximate per minute rates at rest. The rates during flight would be considerably higher.

NOTE: Birds' body temperatures are so variable that it is not recommended that readings be taken. It has usually proven to be of little value. Also, great care must be taken so as not to injure the bird with the thermometer.

CARDIOVASCULAR SYSTEM

Transportation is the circulatory system's chief responsibility. Every single cell is dependent upon an adequately functioning blood supply for its survival. Oxygen and food are carried to the cells, while carbon dioxide and other waste products are removed. In addition to this, other important functions include: transportation and distribution of water, electrolytes, hormones, and antibodies to fight infection. Body temperature is also largely dependent on the distribution of the blood supply.

The basic structure of the cardiovascular system is very similar to that of mammals. The *heart* has four chambers, two *atria* and two *ventricles.* The heart functions to pump the blood in adequate amounts to meet the needs of the cells. Oxygenated blood is pumped into circulation from the left ventricle, through the blood vessels—arteries and capillaries—to the cells. Then unoxygenated blood is removed via other capillaries that converge into veins and travel to the right atrium. This blood is then pumped into the right ventricle, through the lungs to become reoxygenated and is returned to the left atrium to repeat the cycle once again.

The heart rates in birds are markedly faster than in most other animals. This is necessary to meet the bird's high energy requirements. The *pulse* which is a helpful means of determining the heart rate of animals is not practical in birds because their blood vessels are so small that it is difficult to feel them.

Blood Volume

In general, about 8% of body weight coincides with the blood volume. For example, a one-ounce (28.5 grams) Budgie has about 1/11 of an ounce (2.5 milliliters) of blood. While a one-pound Amazon parrot has about 1½ ounces (42 milliliters) of blood. That's the total amount of blood!

It should be obvious that any amount of blood loss, even a few drops, can be life-threatening and demands immediate attention.

Heart disease is only occasionally encountered in birds. Diagnosis is difficult since it can easily be confused with other diseases, most notably, respiratory or liver problems.

Home Physical:

- Any bleeding is abnormal and must be controlled immediately.
- Cyanosis or blue color of the mouth, tongue, or legs is abnormal. This blue color results when the blood is transporting decreased amounts of oxygen.
- Estimating heart rate is difficult because the heart beats very rapidly.
- Birds most prone to circulatory problems include those that are overweight, inactive, old or on a poor diet.

LYMPHATIC SYSTEM

The lymphatic system is part of the larger circulatory system. Similar to the venous return of blood, the *lymphatics* transport *lymphatic fluid* which ultimately is returned to the main blood circulation. This fluid is composed mostly of water and protein, similar to blood plasma. This is blood minus the red blood cells. Along its course the fluid is filtered and any harmful substances are removed. Lymph nodes which perform this filtering process in mammals are less common in birds. Instead, there are networks of tiny vessels which perform this function.

The *Spleen* also filters out harmful substances from the blood stream as well as removing the old, worn-out red blood cells. Changes in the appearance of the spleen, noted on radiographs or a post-mortem, are found in some of the more important diseases of birds.

Home Physical:

- If a lymphatic vessel becomes blocked, the area which it drains will become *edematous* or swollen with fluid. For example, if a lymphatic vessel draining a leg becomes obstructed due to a tumor, the leg will develop a large amount of fluid.
- In general, problems are rare, symptoms are vague and diagnosis is difficult.

DIGESTIVE SYSTEM

As mentioned, energy requirements are very high and the conversion of food into energy must be very rapid. A small bird will eat upwards of 20% of its own body weight daily. It's like a 150-pound person devouring about 30 pounds of food in a single day!

Digestion is the process whereby food is converted into simpler compounds so that it can be absorbed into the blood stream and used for fuel by the cells.

The digestive tract of birds functions similarly to other animals', but there are some important structural differences. The beak and tongue collect the food, the *saliva* lubricates it as it passes through the *pharynx* and into the *esophagus*. Birds do not have teeth. No teeth means less weight and no time wasted chewing. This rapid swallowing means less time eating the food, less time spent on the ground and, hence, less exposure to dangers.

The esophagus, at the base of the neck, bulges out to the left and forms the *crop*. The crop acts as a "storage bin" continuously supplying small amounts of food to the stomach. In pigeons and doves, *crop milk* is produced by both sexes and usually only in female parrots to feed young.

Birds have two stomachs. The forestomach, *proventriculus,* adds the digestive juices to food as it moves into the muscular *gizzard*. It grinds up the food into smaller particles and passes them into the *small intestine*. Here, more digestive juices are added and the food gets absorbed into the blood stream and is distributed throughout the body. The wastes, unusable portions of the food, pass into the *large intestine* and out the body as feces.

The *cloaca* is a shallow, cup-like depression just inside the vent. It is the junction to the outside, the crossroads of some important structures. From the large bowel, feces enter near the bottom of the cloaca. The *ureters,* carrying urine from the kidneys, empty in towards the top of the cloaca. Last, but not least, in females, eggs pass through the cloaca near the top.

The *liver* does many jobs. As Catherine Anthony states:

> ". . . Because of the diversity of its activities, a single liver cell might be likened to a *factory* (it makes many chemical compounds), a *warehouse* (it stores such valuables as glycogen [stored carbohydrate] iron and certain vitamins), a *waste disposal plant* (it excretes bile pigments, urea, and various detoxification products), and a *power plant* (its catabolism [breakdown of products] produces considerable heat)."

The *pancreas,* which is located alongside the small intestine, supplies important enzymes that digest the protein, carbohydrate and fats present in the food. It also secretes the important hormone, insulin, which is intimately involved with regulating blood sugar levels. A lack of sufficient amounts of insulin causes a high blood sugar level resulting in diabetes which is occasionally diagnosed in birds.

In only a few short hours, food swallowed will pass through the entire digestive tract and the waste will be passed out as feces. Birds can only store small amounts of feces; eliminations are therefore more frequent than among other animate forms.

The avian metabolic rate has been referred to many times. Ultimately, it depends on the speed of conversion of food into energy. As Isaac Newton so eloquently said, "For every action, there is an equal and opposite reaction." In this case, the by-product of food being turned into energy is heat. The faster this turnover, the more heat produced and the higher the temperature. For this reason the body temperature of birds is very high compared with other animals.

Home Physical:

- The beak should have a normal appearance and shape. The normal shape and length varies with each species.
- Swallowing of food should be easy. Birds having difficulty will stretch their necks and hold their heads back.
- If swallowing becomes difficult or if talking ceases, the mouth and throat should be examined. The *mucus membranes* lining the mouth and throat should be pink in color, or if pigmented, will appear black. Look for problems such as white creamy-like plaques covering the roof of the mouth. Any odor is abnormal.
- The crop can be felt or seen after a large meal, at the base of the neck on the left side.
- The droppings, in this case the fecal portion, should appear normal. (See Chapter 9 for a complete discussion.)
- The cloaca area should be clean. Any collection of fecal matter or urine should be considered abnormal. This is caused by droppings that are loose and sticky.

URINARY SYSTEM

The *kidneys* are the filtering system for the blood, removing poisonous waste products. They also play a critical role in regulating the balance of water and electrolytes (sodium, potassium, and chlorides).

Bird urine is only part liquid. The white material seen on or around the feces is uric acid, or urates. This portion also forms part of the urine and is produced in the liver and are the end product of protein metabolism. The urine normally consists of only a small amount of liquid. It forms a small ring of wetness around the dropping. The urates should appear semi-dry, pasty and white in color. With disease, as discussed in the next chapter, the appearance of the droppings will often change.

From the kidneys, the *ureters* transport the urine to the cloaca where it is excreted along with the feces. To decrease weight, birds have eliminated the need for a urinary bladder. This also means that they can store only small amounts of urine and must void frequently.

Kidney disease is common in birds. One of the reasons for this is that the blood supply from the intestines and legs passes through the kidneys. The problem arises when an infection of a leg or intestines occurs; this can lead to a secondary kidney infection.

Home Physical:

- The droppings, in this case the urine portion, should appear normal. The normal appearance can vary with species so become familiar with what is normal for your bird. If there is any change from the normal, suspect a problem.

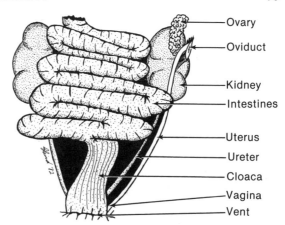

Female reproductive tract.

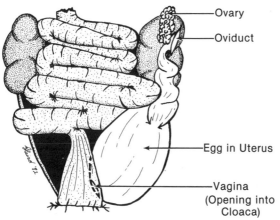

Female reproductive tract with developing egg in uterus.

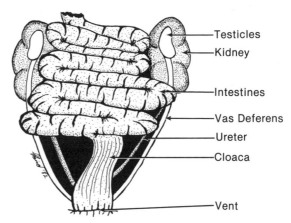

Male reproductive tract.

- The cloaca area should be clean. Any collection of feces or urates around the vent, often matting the surrounding feathers, is abnormal and called a "pasted vent."
- A marked increase in water intake can be associated with kidney disease, diabetes, as well as other diseases. The droppings will also contain more liquid under such circumstances.

REPRODUCTIVE SYSTEM

We all know that birds lay eggs. Over and beyond this few of us understand their unique reproductive system. The most commonly asked question is, "What sex is my bird?" Most notably, unlike mammals, neither sex has external genitals and very few have any other observable sexual differences. This is discussed more fully in Chapter 15, BIRD BREEDING.

Only the left *ovary* in females is fully developed. It produces the female hormones *estrogen* and *progesterone* and releases the *ova*. These ova enter the *oviduct* and it is here that they begin to develop. The *uterus* or shell gland, being an enlarged portion of the oviduct, among other things, adds the hard calcium shell. The final step is passage through the *vagina* and finally out the cloaca.

The *testicles* are paired structures producing the male hormone, *testosterone*. Males in the majority of bird species do not have a penis as with mammals. However, there is a small mound of tissue in the cloaca called the *phallus* which secretes the sperm.

Mating does occur. The male will mount the female from behind and the cloacas will join.

Home Physical:

- Signs of problems are very general and non-specific.
- Watch for any abdominal swelling around the cloaca in females. It may indicate an egg.
- Any piece of tissue seen protruding out the vent is abnormal and can be serious. See CLOACA PROLAPSE on page 145.

NERVOUS SYSTEM

As we've mentioned, the body in its simplest form is made up of millions of tiny cells. These cells working in groups carry out all the important job tasks discussed. This tremendous unifying effort is directed toward the ultimate goal—*SURVIVAL*. All of these varied tasks must be integrated into a smoothly working operation. *Communication* is the key. The *brain,* the body's central computer, coordinates these activities. The *nerves* are the messengers that relay information from every part of the body to and from the brain. These messages are transmitted, interpreted and answered in only minute fractions of a second.

The photographs of normal and abnormal droppings of cage birds (courtesy of Marjorie McMillan) shown on this and the following three pages are reproduced from *Diseases of Cage and Aviary Birds* by M.L. Petrak, D.V.M., 2nd Edition 1982, Lea & Febiger, publisher.

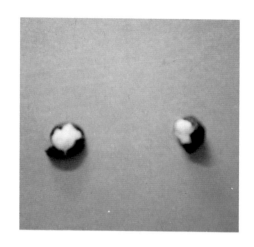

Normal budgerigar droppings.

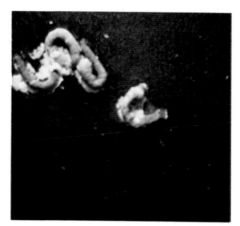

Normal canary droppings.

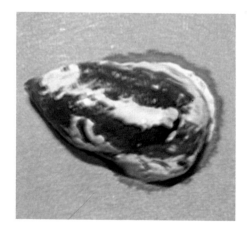

Normal parrot droppings.

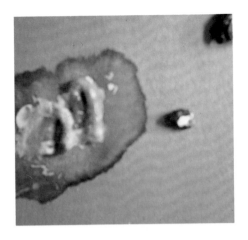

Normal and abnormal budgerigar droppings.

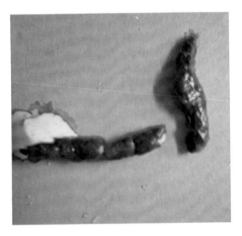

Droppings from dehydrated parrot.

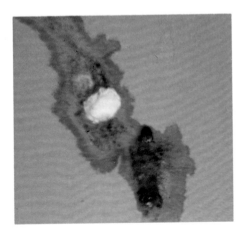

Droppings from a budgerigar with lipidosis.

Droppings from a budgerigar with diabetes mellitus.

Droppings from a budgerigar with possible pancreatic exocrine deficiency.

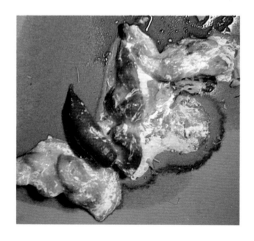

Droppings from an Amazon parrot with possible pancreatic exocrine deficiency.

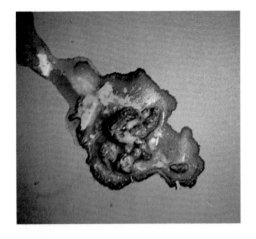

Droppings from an Amazon parrot with hepatitis and pyelonephritis.

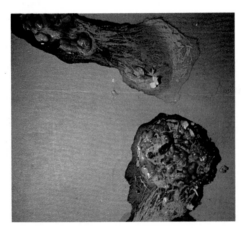

Droppings from an Amazon parrot with hepatitis—cause unknown.

Droppings from a parrot with hemorrhagic enteritis—cultured E. coli.

Brain damage can be hereditary, or the result of trauma, such as an unplanned collision with a window or door. Nerve damage can also result from trauma. For example, a broken bone damaging a surrounding nerve.

Home Physical:

- Problems to watch for include: personality changes, seizures, poor balance, walking in circles, head held in abnormal positions and paralysis (inability to move an affected area).
- The *sciatic nerve* is the main nerve to the legs. Tumors or eggs in the abdominal cavity can injure this nerve causing a paralysis of one or both of the legs.

ENDOCRINE SYSTEM

Similar to the nervous system, the endocrine system communicates with and controls many of the organs in the body. This is accomplished with chemical substances known as hormones. These are secreted from numerous glands and then travel through the blood stream until they reach their specific target area. Hormones are critically important to the normal and healthy functioning of the body. Deficiencies or excesses of hormones cause some of the most profound effects on the body.

Home Physical:

- Sign of problems are very general and non-specific.

9

Spotting a Sick Bird

Birds are generally very hardy. However, like all living creatures, they do occasionally get sick.

The major difference with birds is that their natural instincts for survival often prevent them from showing any outward signs of disease until it becomes well-advanced. Therefore, you need to become like a Sherlock Holmes and train yourself to be observant. A bird that has appeared to have become sick suddenly, many times has been ill for some time. The signs just went unnoticed.

On a day-in and day-out basis, when you live closely with an animal a "oneness" develops with them. Like a shepherd and his flock, your sixth sense will often tell you if there's a problem. If you suspect something is wrong, be concerned because you are probably right.

The knowledge of *your* bird's *normal* behavior is vital. Its actions and appearance will be the first clue that a problem is arising. Learn to develop your senses of sight, touch, hearing and even smell.

Early Warning Signs of a Sick Bird:

- Changes in food or water intake; an increase or decrease in weight. A bird may continue to eat, but still lose weight. Most sick birds lose their appetite.
- Evidence of regurgitation; look for evidence around the face or vomitus adhering to the beak or feathers and it may also be seen around the cage or floor.
- Abnormal droppings; discolored or watery, decreased or increased in number
- Changes in activity or appearance (behavioral changes); remaining on cage floor showing reluctance to perch; listless, decreased activity, less talking or singing, more sleeping, droopy look; "Fluffed-up" feathers ruffled; heavy breathing, wheezing, sneezing, prolonged open-mouth breathing; runny eyes, runny nose; any enlargement or growths
- Feather problems; prolonged molt, feathers ragged; chewing or picking at feathers

- Lameness
- Droopy wing

How to Conduct an Examination

First and most importantly, just stand a short distance from the cage and observe. Try not to startle or frighten your bird. A great deal of information will be gleaned in this way. Ask yourself these questions:

Posture:
Standing up straight or slouched over?
Wings held high and close to the body?
Bearing weight equally on both legs?
Head up? Eyes open wide?
Any abnormal swellings or deformities?

Mental Alertness:
Aware of their surroundings?
Aware of your presence?
A sick bird may initially perk up at the sight of you, but then in a very short time will become listless again.

Breathing:
Is it smooth and easy or labored?
Prolonged open-mouth breathing or tail bobbing?
Any sneezing or coughing?

Balance:
Is the bird perching or resting on the cage floor?
- This is related to the strength of the bird. Rarely do healthy birds fall or slip off a perch.

Feathering:
Note the condition and color. Are they shiny or faded? Are they well-groomed or ragged?
- Sick birds usually stop preening and develop a ragged coat.

Skin:
Any bruising or swellings noted?

Now, walk slowly toward the cage. Less obvious problems can now be detected. Encourage the bird to move. Is it steady on its feet? Is it alert? Look closer at the breathing. Is there any crusting or wetness around the nostrils? Is the breathing noisy?

Look around the cage. This gives lots of clues. Is the bird eating? If so, what kinds of food? Is there any spoiled food? Is the bird drinking water? Is the water fresh?

Look at the cage floor. Are the droppings normal? Are there any feathers or blood on the floor? Is there any regurgitated food?

A seriously ill bird. Note the sleepiness and "fluffed up" appearance.
—Dr. R. Woerpel

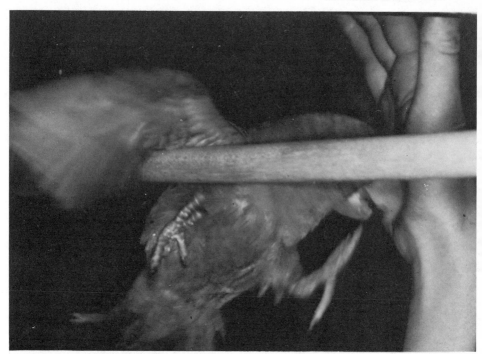

Healthy birds rarely lose their balance or fall off a perch. If this occurs, an underlying problem should be suspected.

This parrot is leaning towards its right side, showing reluctance to bear full weight on its left leg. This can be a subtle indication of an injury to the left leg.

Examine the cage. Are there any missing or chewed objects that may suggest they were eaten? This might suggest a metal poisoning. Is there anything that does not belong in the cage? Is there anything to suggest an attack from a dog or cat, for example?

Interpretation of Abnormal Droppings

Abnormal droppings are one of the first clues we have that a bird is sick. Unfortunately this is an area that owners frequently ignore. Why? It's simple. As an example, consider a similar problem in a dog. When a dog has diarrhea, the condition will be noticed very quickly. The dog will often eliminate in the house, producing that unmistakable foul odor, or at the very least, spotty tracks in the yard. When taken for a walk, diarrhea or constipation would be noted quickly. If there were a problem causing abnormal urinating in the house, it too would be discovered early. No doubt the dog would probably be taken to the veterinarian for treatment—not only because he was ill, but also because he was soiling the home.

Such is not the case with birds. The same problem may go unnoticed for a longer period of time. There is no mess and no foul odors. And yet, these same problems can be far more serious in birds than in other animals. Daily visual examination of the droppings will give you some of the best clues to the overall health of your bird. Cage paper should be changed daily and a mental note made of the number and appearance of the droppings from your bird.

Food Intake Affects Droppings

The number of droppings are a reliable index to the amount of food being eaten. Food eaten in the morning is stored in the crop and slowly but continually passed through the digestive tract. The unusable portions become feces and in only hours will be excreted from the body.

If a bird suddenly stops eating or decreases its intake, (which is common when sick) but still continues to drink water, it will become obvious in a very short time. The number of droppings may remain the same or decrease slightly, but there will be little or no feces present, just the urine. If water intake is also reduced, then the total number of droppings will decrease.

Normal Appearance of Droppings

Unlike mammals, birds urinate and defecate in the same motion at the same time. The feces drop first, immediately followed by the urine.

The feces are tubular in shape, soft, yet hold their form. The color ranges from light green to dark green (almost black). The diet has a major effect on the color and water content of the feces. The more vegetables and fruits eaten, the lighter green and wetter the feces will appear. A predominantly seed diet will cause the feces to be darker and drier. The size of the cloaca will effect the size, shape and frequency of droppings passed. A hen laying eggs will have a relatively large, dilated cloaca causing the feces to be very large and, hence, the droppings to be markedly fewer in number.

Normal feces have little or no odor. Not all droppings will appear identical during any time period and some variation should be considered normal.

As discussed in the last chapter, the urine is a combination of a clear, transparent liquid, and urates which are pasty and white in color. The water content or wetness of the urine depends on the water content of the diet, the total amount of water in the body and very importantly, the normal functioning of the organs, most notably the kidneys and liver. It is primarily the kidney that regulates the urine volume. If the body has more water than it needs, more is excreted causing the urine to contain more water. If the body has less water than is required, it conserves what it has by excreting a drier urine.

Interpretation of Abnormal Droppings

Diarrhea:

When you observe abnormally watery droppings, first determine if the cause is loose, watery feces, watery urine, or both. It is a very common mistake to see wet droppings and immediately diagnose diarrhea, when in actuality, it is a watery urine. For proper diagnosis and treatment the differentiation between the two is important.

If the feces are normally formed, then it is not diarrhea. Conversely, if the feces are runny and lack shape, then diarrhea is present. *In practice, abnormally watery urine is much more common than diarrhea.* The differentiation can become a little trickier when, due to the extra water in the urine, the feces become wet and may run slightly.

Another area that will help to determine if there is a problem is the feathers around the cloaca. If there is matting or staining of these feathers with feces or urates, then a problem is present. The presence of either loose sticky stools or wet urine on the vent or surrounding feathers is called "pasted vent."

Note: Diarrhea IS NOT a disease. It is only a sign of some other disease process in the body.

Common Causes of Diarrhea:

Diet—Poor nutrition, spoiled food, new foods in diet, or lack of fresh water.

Intestinal infection—Bacteria, viral, fungal parasites

Diseases of other organs affecting intestines—Liver, kidney, pancreas

Foreign body swallowed—i.e., string, beads, wood or metal chips

Poisons—Chemicals

Stress—Especially whenever a bird becomes excited, i.e., change in daily routine.

Constipation:

Occasionally birds can become constipated, which results in little or no feces being passed in the droppings. There are several causes for this, all of which can be very serious:

- Intestinal blockage—obstruction
- Grit impaction of gizzard
- Dehydration—insufficient water to help soften feces
- Obesity
- Abdominal tumor
- Retained egg—pressure on the intestines

Note: Don't forget that a bird that is not eating will also at first appear constipated but is not. It's simple: no food being eaten produces no feces.

More Types of Abnormal Droppings
Some Common Changes and Causes

Feces:

Fresh blood (bright red)—Bleeding in large intestine, severe intestinal infection, poisoning, excessive stress.

Mucus in stool—Intestinal infection, poor digestion.

Clay-colored feces (bulky)—Poor digestion.

Passing whole seeds or granular texture—Poor digestion, lack of digestive enzymes, spastic or hypermotile intestines.

Urine:

Excessive liquid—Stress, diseases affecting kidneys, liver and pancreas.

Note: Diets high in fruits and vegetables will also cause this since they contain large concentrations of water.

Bloody—Kidney infection, excessive stress, poisoning; can be seen with lead poisoning.

Yellow-colored—Liver disease. Note: this is similar to icterus or jaundice that causes yellow skin in people with liver diseases.

Green-colored (pea soup)—Liver disease, excessive red blood cell destruction; Psittacosis. Note: This green color is due to the accumulation of bile pigments. Bile is produced in the liver, stored in the gall bladder and used to help digest fats. In the face of a liver infection or obstruction of the bile duct which transports the bile to the intestines, bile builds up in the blood stream and is excreted in the urine.

Sounds complicated? It can be! There are also a number of very different diseases that can display the same general signs. Hopefully, you have been given the tools needed to detect early signs of disease. This is what is most important. The next step is to try to determine what organ or organs are affected. Whenever possible, the specific diagnosis and treatment should be left to a veterinarian.

GENERAL GUIDE TO NORMAL NUMBER OF DROPPINGS*

"Rule of Thumb" to General Health

Condition	Percent Decrease in Volume of Droppings in 24 hours	Budgerigar—Number of Droppings in 24 hours
Normal	Normal Volume	40-60
Mod. Sick	10-25%	30-40
Seriously	25-50%	20-30
Critical	50% or more	Less than 20

*In these instances the fecal portion of the droppings volume is estimated or counted.

Reprinted with permission from Dr. T.S. Lafeber from his book, *Tender Loving Care For Pet Birds* (Dorothy Products, Ltd.).

10

Spills, Thrills, 'n' Oops!

Now that you have a good idea as to when a bird is sick, these next three chapters will discuss some of the more common diseases. The most loved and well-cared-for bird is going to become ill sometime during its life. These chapters are meant as a helpful guide to the diagnosis and general treatment of some common problems affecting birds. They are not meant, however, to substitute for good veterinary care.

The best way to use this section is to become familiar with its contents. In this way, when a problem arises, no time will be wasted having to digest and understand the new material. You will know where to look and a quick review is all that will be necessary. Also, knowing what problems can arise will greatly help in their prevention.

Relatively few signs signal the presence of disease. As we've mentioned, very different diseases will cause the same general signs and often can only be differentiated from one another by specialized diagnostic tests such as blood tests, cultures and sensitivities, and radiographs. Keep this in mind when you attempt to diagnose a problem—especially if it does not respond to the initial treatment. Obtaining an accurate diagnosis and selecting the best treatment can be difficult and requires proper training and experience.

The following pages are an *Index of Signs.* This is an alphabetical listing of the changes or signs that occur when a bird becomes sick and the corresponding pages that discuss the diseases that may be causing the problem. To use this index, first determine what the signs are. For example, loose droppings or loss of appetite—then look these signs up in this index and turn to the page or pages listed. Read about the possible causes and what to do.

If you cannot find the signs that you see or if you are having trouble putting them into words, refer to the *General Index* in the back of the book. Look up the part that is involved, i.e., digestive tract or feathers. Use the General Index whenever you want to read about a general subject, i.e. nutrition or a specific disease, i.e. psittacosis.

INDEX OF SIGNS

Appetite, change of, 103
(seen with most diseases)

Beak,
broken, cracked, deformed, 119,
131-133

Behavior, change of, 103
(seen with most diseases)

Bleeding,
from beak, 78, 119
in droppings, 109, 129, 143
from feathers, 68, 119
from nails, 78, 119
from skin, 88, 116
from wound, 116-119

Bone protruding from wound,
119-121

Breathing difficulty, 90, 113, 115,
136-138, 163

Bugs (see PARASITES)

Bumps (Swellings, growths)
on skin, around eyes, from
feather follicle, 146-150

Burns, 123

Chewing (see FEATHER PICKING)

Constipation, 108, 109, 143

Convulsions, 101, 113, 124, 125,
129, 145, 164, 165

Coughing, 90, 125, 136-138

Cuts (see WOUNDS)

Diarrhea, 108, 115, 125, 138-145,
163-165

Discharge
from eye, 85, 133-136
from nose, 90, 116, 136-138

Drinking (see WATER INTAKE)

Droppings,
abnormal, 97-100, 107-110

Eyes,
discharge from, 85, 103, 133-135
reddened, 85, 134

Feathers,
bleeding, 68, 119
broken, 68, 119
picking, chewing, pulling, 150,
154, 156
parasites, 154

Holding head down,
tilted to one side, 86, 101,
103, 129, 164

Lameness (sore leg), 78, 89, 101,
104, 119-121, 146-150

Listlessness, 103
(seen with most diseases)

Mites (see PARASITES)

Mouth problems, 90, 94, 138,
139, 146

Muscle tremors (twitching), 124,
125, 129, 165

Non-weight-bearing leg (see
LAMENESS)

Obesity, 92, 109, 143, 150

Paralysis of wing or leg, 101,
115, 121, 164

Parasites,
in droppings, 158-161
on feathers, 154, 156, 157
in respiratory tract, 157, 158

Redness,
of eyes, 85, 133-136
of skin, 88, 116-119, 123

Regurgitation, 103, 115, 125,
139-142

Reproductive problems, 96, 208, 209

Seizures (see CONVULSIONS)

Shock, 115, 116, 123-125

Sneezing, 90, 116, 136-138

Straining to pass droppings, 108, 109, 138, 143, 145

Swallowing, difficulty with, 94, 137, 138

Swelling,
    of eyes, 85, 90, 133-136, 146
    of leg, 121, 123, 146-150
    of skin, 146-150
    of vent, 145, 149

Unconsciousness, 113, 115, 124, 125

Vomiting (see REGURGITATION)

Water intake,
    decrease of, 103 (seen with most diseases)
    increase of, 96, 145, 146

Weakness, 103
    (seen with most diseases)

Weight loss, 88, 103
    (seen with most diseases)

Wing,
    hanging low, droopy, 89, 104, 121

Wounds, 88, 116-119

Worms (see PARASITES)

Handling Sick and Injured Birds

Handle the bird as little as is absolutely necessary. Any undue stress can worsen the condition and lead to shock. Injured birds are more prone to bite due to fear and pain. Dim the lights, approach them slowly and offer a reassuring voice.

If restraint is needed, refer to page 79.

Transporting the Sick or Injured Bird

When going to the veterinarian, try to bring your bird in its own cage. Leave only a small amount of water or none at all, in the cup and cover the cage. *Do not clean it,* since examination of the cage and the bird's droppings will help the veterinarian in diagnosing the problem.

If the cage is too large to move, use a cardboard box or other similar container. Be sure there are holes for breathing. Fold up the cage paper and bring it along with you so that the veterinarian can examine the droppings. If any medications were given, bring those too.

Emergencies

An emergency is any condition that is life-threatening or that may result in irreversible damage to your bird. It necessitates immediate treatment.
These signs indicate an Emergency:
    Bleeding
    Coma or loss of consciousness
    Convulsions (seizures)
    Extreme breathing difficulty
    Not perching, staying on floor of cage

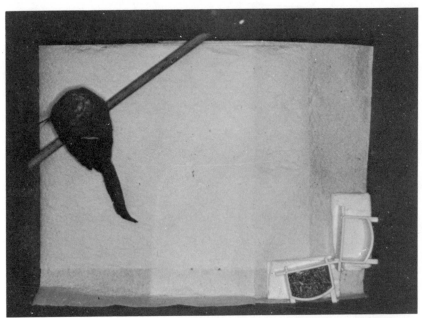

A modified cardboard box is an inexpensive carrier for transporting birds.
—*Tony Costanza*

A variety of manufactured carriers used for transporting birds.
—*Tony Costanza*

Recurrent regurgitation and/or diarrhea

Sudden paralysis

Shock

In many cases, it's difficult to determine if a certain problem is actually an emergency. Follow your instincts and use good common sense as to what is the best course of action. Remember since birds are small their condition can worsen more quickly than that of most other animals.

Most emergencies should be handled by a veterinarian, and should be treated *immediately* regardless of the time of day or night. Most veterinarians do not mind being called upon at an odd hour for a true emergency. But remember that regardless of any emergency fee collected, no veterinarian enjoys being pulled away from family or friends, especially if the problem could have waited until morning. On evenings and weekends, most veterinary hospitals use an answering service or tape recorded message with instructions on what to do in case of an emergency.

Shock

Shock is a term frequently heard, yet, just as frequently misunderstood. It is not a disease, but rather results from some serious problem in the body. Severe injury is one of the most common causes, but bleeding, body-fluid loss as seen in prolonged vomiting or diarrhea, infection, poisoning or breathing difficulties can also cause shock. Physiologically, the cardiovascular system fails to provide adequate oxygen and other nutrients to the cells of the vital organs. It also is unable to remove the waste products. It is an emergency and is life-threatening.

If it is not treated promptly shock may become irreversible resulting in death. Some of the causes of shock in birds are uncontrolled blood loss, trauma, egg binding, severe infection, and continued watery droppings.

The signs are well defined, in humans, dogs and cats. The signs are:

1. Profound weakness and/or unconsciousness, unresponsive to stimulation.
2. Rapid heart rate and breathing rate.
3. Pale or muddy-colored gums.
4. Slow capillary refill time. To test for this, use your finger and press against the gums; a whitening or blanching will result. Lift your finger away and see how long it takes for the color to return. The normal refill time is about 1-2 seconds. Slow capillary refilling is a cause for concern. DO NOT TRY THIS ON BIRDS!
5. Low body temperature.

THESE SIGNS ARE VERY DIFFICULT TO DETERMINE IN BIRDS. IF YOUR BIRD IS LISTLESS, FLUFFED-UP AND BREATHING RAPIDLY, SHOCK SHOULD BE SUSPECTED.

If shock is present, no amount of home treatment will be effective. It is a very difficult and challenging syndrome to treat. The best thing to do is keep your bird warm, cover the cage, minimize handling and transport your bird to your veterinarian immediately. Call ahead so that the hospital staff will be ready to begin treatment the moment you arrive.

The therapy is very sophisticated and includes the following:

- Warmth and oxygen
- Fluids (dextrose and/or lactated Ringers™) to increase the blood volume and help restore circulation to the "starving" cells.
- Corticosteriods
- Antibiotics

There are many other drugs and emergency measures used depending on the patient and the inciting cause. Close monitoring and frequent evaluation of the patient are critical. With birds, handling must always be kept to a minimum making treatment more challenging than normal.

Note: The first aid and home care recommendations are generally safe and simple methods of treatment. Since diseases are very complex and complications do arise, it is always recommended that a veterinarian be consulted before any treatment is initiated. Remember too, our fine feathered friends are fragile and even the act of administering the medication can be hazardous to their health.

Bleeding

Bleeding problems are common in pet birds. Since birds have such small total blood volumes, any bleeding must be controlled immediately. If the cause of the bleeding is not readily apparent, examine your bird carefully. Pay particular attention to any new wounds and broken feathers or nails.

Look carefully around the vent and nostril area. If blood is seen on the cage floor it may be passing in the droppings. Sometimes flecks of blood are seen around the nostrils or on the cage walls. This may be from sneezing out blood resulting from head trauma or a clotting problem causing bleeding into the respiratory tract. The blood clotting problem appears to be caused by a Vitamin K deficiency. It responds to injections of Vitamin K. There is no home treatment for these particular problems and they must receive immediate veterinary attention.

Excessive blood loss can quickly lead to depression, weakness, unconsciousness, breathing difficulties and death. Treatment varies and depends on the cause.

First Aid For Minor Skin Wounds:

Blood loss is usually minimal unless a blood vessel has been severed.

1. STOP THE BLEEDING FIRST!
   Apply direct pressure to the area. Use a sterile gauze pad or clean cloth and apply firm, steady pressure. The pad absorbs blood, allows

Severe bruising occurred when this bird was attacked by a dog. The injury itself may not be life threatening, but the shock occurring secondarily can be. It can occur from minutes to sometimes hours after the injury.

Surgical Repair of a Major Skin Laceration

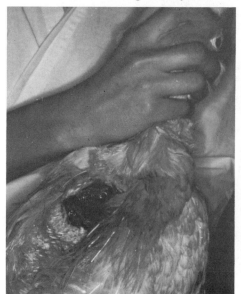

Before surgery

Six months after surgery.

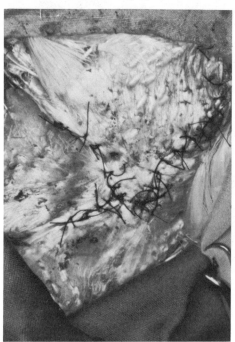

Closed wound following surgery. Special surgical techniques had to be used to pull the skin together.

clotting and prevents contamination. If the bleeding does not stop after a few minutes, seek veterinary attention immediately.

2. Clean the wound and prevent contamination.
Using tweezers, remove any debris such as dirt and feathers. Cleanse the area with hydrogen peroxide or dilute betadine solution. A moistened cotton-tipped applicator (Q-Tip®) can be used to clean and wipe foreign material from the area. Be gentle and do not probe deeply. Blot the area with sterile gauze. An antibiotic spray or powder can be applied.

3. Get veterinary advice if there are any questions or if the bird appears listless.
The wound may require further care such as surgery to close the wound or bandaging for protection.
Antibiotics can be given to control infection.

First Aid For Bleeding Beaks or Nails:

1. Act immediately and handle the bird gently.
2. Apply a styptic powder and pack it into the bleeding area. If this is not available, baking powder, corn starch or even flour will work in an emergency. Direct pressure with your finger or gauze pad may also be tried.
3. As a last resort, the area can be seared with a red-hot needle.
4. Watch the bird for about an hour afterwards to be sure the bleeding has completely stopped.
5. If blood loss appears extensive or the bird is listless, consult your veterinarian immediately.

First Aid For Bleeding Feathers:

1. Act immediately and handle the bird gently.
2. If a feather breaks and begins to bleed, it must always be pulled out completely from its follicle.
   - With firm pressure, gently pull the feather out with tweezers or needle-nose pliers.
3. Once the damaged feather has been removed, blood may be noted coming from the follicle. If this occurs, apply direct pressure to the outside of the follicle for one or two minutes using a gauze pad or clean cloth.
4. Watch the bird for about an hour afterwards to be sure the bleeding has stopped completely.
5. If blood loss appeared extensive or the bird is listless, consult your veterinarian immediately.

Broken Bones

Bird bones are brittle and, like toothpicks, can be easily broken. Pet birds

Surgical Repair of a Broken Leg

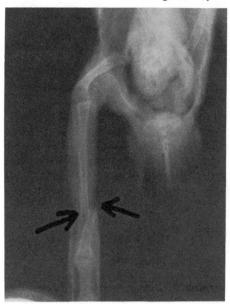

Radiograph showing fracture

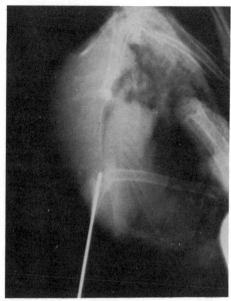

Radiograph showing a metal pin inside the broken bone. The pin helps to rigidly hold the two fragments together in their normal place while the bone is mending.

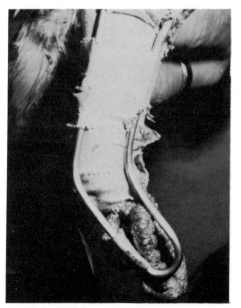

In this particular case, an additional support was necessary. A splint was fashioned from a metal coat hanger.

Four weeks after surgery. The leg has healed well and the bird is once again able to use it.

most commonly fracture a leg, more specifically, the *tibiotarsus* or *tarsometatarsal* bones. Wild birds usually have fractured wing bones secondarily to being shot, hit by cars or flying into electrical wires.

Fractures are usually caused by an accidental injury such as an unplanned collision, attack by another animal or rough handling. Poor nutrition or other diseases can weaken bones and make them more susceptible to fracturing.

Signs to Watch For:

- Sudden onset of bruising or swelling at the affected site
- Difficulty perching and non-weight bearing of affected leg
- Deformity of affected leg or wing
  Crooked leg or wing—held in an awkward position
  Wing is "droopy" or hung lower than the other one
- Loss of function or movement of affected leg or wing.
  Usually the affected leg or wing will just hang limply.

Other Problems That Can Mimic a Fracture:

Luxations (bone slipping out of its joint).
Arthritis (inflammation and pain of a joint).
Muscle, ligament and tendon injuries.

First Aid For Broken Bones:

1. Observe the bird for any other problems that may have resulted from the injury—watch for shock.
2. Confine the bird. If it's out, gently place it back in its own cage or a smaller transport cage.
3. Keep it quiet and provide rest and relaxation. Remove perches.
4. Transport patient to veterinarian.

Do not attempt to handle the bird unnecessarily. Any movement can cause more bruising and damage around the affected area.

Do not attempt to bandage. An improperly applied bandage will often cause more harm than good.

Veterinary Care:

The bird will be evaluated and treated for any other problems that may have resulted from the injury. Radiographs may be recommended to determine the severity of the fracture and its best treatment. The treatment will include applying a rigid splint over the affected area. In some instances, surgery will have to be recommended as the treatment most likely to get the best results.

For fractures to properly heal, the fractured ends must be realigned and rigidly held together. Fractures will heal in about four weeks if properly treated and complications do not occur.

A broken wing has been taped to the body to prevent its movement while the bone is mending.

A splint is being applied to support this broken leg while it is mending.

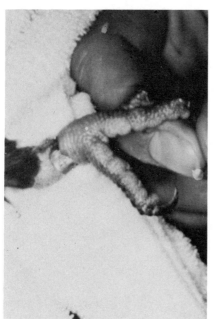

A leg band that has become too tight, causing swelling and injury to the leg.

The leg band should always be removed to avoid this problem.

Leg Bands

The leg bands found on some birds at the time of purchase are used to indicate, in code, where the bird was bred or that it has been through quarantine, or was simply put on for identification reasons by the breeder. Once pet birds have been in the home for about 30-60 days these bands should be removed. Too many birds have sustained serious leg injuries, or lost legs completely as a result of these bands becoming too tight or getting caught on something. If you haven't removed bands before, find knowledgeable assistance (preferably from a veterinarian) so as not to damage the leg. Be sure to save the band or copy down the number and store it for safekeeping.

Burns

A burn is an injury to tissue caused by exposure to heat, electricity or chemicals. Birds allowed to fly into the kitchen may land in a pot of boiling water or grease or on a hot burner. Chewing on the cord of a plugged-in electrical appliance can burn the area generally around the beak and mouth. A bird may also come in contact with some chemicals such as toilet bowl cleaners, drain cleaners or other similar substances.

Signs to Watch For:
Reddened, hot or swollen skin
Greasy feathers
Reluctance to move
Shock

First Aid For Burns:

Mild and Superficial Wounds ONLY

1. Spray the area with cold water, or if it can be done with minimal stress, immerse the burned area in cold water to relieve the pain. Gently towel dry.
2. Do NOT apply butter, grease or first-aid ointments. An anti-inflammatory powder or spray can be lightly applied.
   - For acid burns, apply a thin coat of baking soda paste (baking soda mixed half and half with water)
   - For alkali burns, apply a thin coat of vinegar to the affected area.
3. Keep the bird quiet and confined.
4. Watch the bird closely for the next several hours.
5. If there is listlessness or if you have any questions, consult your veterinarian.

Veterinary Care:

Burns can be very serious and shock is common following such an injury. Healing can be slow and require prolonged treatment. Bandaging may be necessary to prevent further damage by the bird picking at the area. Antibiotics may be necessary to prevent infection.

Convulsions (Seizures)

A convulsion is a temporary loss of control of the voluntary muscles resulting in spasms of these muscles. The episodes usually last from several seconds to one or two minutes and may be repeated frequently.

Signs to Watch For:

Sudden onset of apprehension and restlessness which usually immediately precede an attack

Violent muscle spasms (twitching leg, flapping wing, "wandering" head)

Loss of balance—often falling off perch

Loss of consciousness

Shock

Immediately after the attack, the bird may appear dazed and unresponsive to noise or people. It may even rest on the cage floor for a few hours before it climbs back up to its perch.

The causes are numerous and include: infections, low blood sugar or calcium, cancer, poisoning (i.e., lead or insecticides), electrolyte imbalance, head injuries, vitamin deficiencies, epilepsy, kidney, liver diseases, and other unknown causes.

First Aid For Convulsions:

1. Prevent injury to the bird.
   - Quickly clear the immediate area of any objects, such as toys and low perches which may injure the bird.
2. Provide a quiet and tranquil setting.
   - If the bird is in its cage, cover the cage with a towel.
   - Dim the lights and avoid loud noises.
3. Do not attempt to give any medications, place objects in its mouth or restrain the bird in any way.
4. Seek veterinary care immediately.

Veterinary Care:

A complete examination is vital. Anti-convulsants, dextrose, calcium, vitamins and other medications will be administered as needed. The bird should be kept for observation. Diagnostic testing may be recommended to aid in treatment.

Heatstroke

When the body's control mechanisms can no longer function normally due to prolonged high ambient temperature, the animal will collapse. The problem develops when a bird has been closed up in a car, aviary, or other enclosure without adequate shade, ventilation or water. Exercise and excitement produces extra heat making matters worse.

Signs to Watch For:
Excessive panting, slobbering
Profound weakness
Collapse and coma with hot, dry skin

First Aid For Heatstroke:

1. *Remove the bird from the hot environment.*
   - Body temperature must be lowered immediately to avoid permanent brain damage or death.
2. Reduce bird's body temperature.
   - Place bird in cage and in air-conditioned area or in front of a fan.
   - Use spray bottle with cold water to mist feathers.
3. If conscious, allow it to drink small amounts of water.
4. Seek veterinary attention promptly.

Veterinary Care:

Shock can be a common sequelae and requires immediate treatment. Oxygen therapy is often beneficial. Close observation for at least 24 hours is important.

Poisoning

Birds are curious creatures and commonly mouth or chew strange objects. If they find the taste appealing, they will swallow all sorts of dangerous materials. Especially if you have free flying birds, be aware that one of them may come in contact with a poison. Any product labeled poisonous for humans should be poisonous to birds.

Suspect Poisoning If You Observe:
1. Bird chewing or contacting any poisonous substance.
2. Opened, chewed or spilled containers of any poisonous substance.
3. A foreign substance noted on the feathers.

Signs to Watch For:
Sudden onset of regurgitation and diarrhea
Convulsions
Sudden onset of breathing difficulties, coughing
Depression
Shock

COMMON HOUSEHOLD POISONS

Alcoholic beverages
Ammonia
Antifreeze
Ant syrup or paste
Arsenic
Automotive products
Bathroom bowl cleaner
Bleach
Boric acid
Camphophenique
Charcoal lighter
Clinitest tablets
Copper and brass
  cleaners
Corn and wart remover
Detergents
Disinfectants
Drain cleaners
Epoxy glue kit
Furniture polish
Garden sprays
Gasoline
Gun cleaners
Hair dyes
Herbicides
Insecticides
Iodine
Kerosene
Lighter fluid

Model cement
Muriatic acid
Mushrooms
Nail polish
Nail polish remover
Oven cleaner
Paint
Paint remover
Paint thinner
Perfume
Permanent wave solutions
Pesticides
Photographic solutions
Pine oil
Plants
Prescription and non-
  prescription medicines
Rodenticides
Rubbing alcohol
Shaving lotion
Silver polish
Snail bait
Spot removers
Strychnine
Sulfuric acid
Super Glue®
Turpentine
Weed killers
Window wash solvent

Note: The nearest Poison Control Center can also be contacted. They have
been organized to help all poison victims. All available information on
virtually every toxic product is kept at these centers.

Common Poisonous Plants

Bird-proofing a home is much the same as child-proofing except there is
no such thing as out-of-reach.

Poisonous House Plants

Plant	*Toxic Part*
Rosary Pea	Seeds
(Jequirity Bean, Crab's Eye,	Note: Seeds are illegally
Precatory Bean)	imported to make necklaces
	or rosaries.
Dieffenbachia	Leaves
(Dumb Cane)	

Caladium	Leaves
Elephant's Ear	Leaves, stems
Philodendron	Leaves, stems
Daffodil	Bulbs

Common Ornamental Poisonous Plants

Plant	*Toxic Part*
Castor Bean	Beans, leaves
Daphne	Berries
Rhododendron	Leaves
Azalea	Leaves
English Ivy	Berries, leaves
Oleander	Leaves, branches, nectar of blossoms
Yellow Oleander (Yellow Be-Still Tree)	Leaves, branches, nectar of blossoms

Flower Garden Plants

Plant	*Toxic Part*
Lily-of-the-Valley	Leaves, flowers
Delphinium	All parts
Iris	Bulb
Monkshood	Leaves, roots
Purple Foxglove	Leaves

Plants in Wooded Areas

Plant	*Toxic Part*
Jack-in-the-pulpit	All parts
Marijuana	Leaves
Skunk cabbage	All parts
Tobacco	Leaves

Vegetable Garden Plants

Plant	*Toxic Part*
Rhubarb	Leaf blade

Trees and Shrubs

Plant	*Toxic Part*
Black Locust	Bark, sprouts, foliage
Yew	Needles, seeds

Plants in the Field

Plant	Toxic Part
Jimsonweed	Leaves, seeds
Nightshades	Unripe berries, leaves

Christmas Plants

Plant	Toxic Part
Holly	Berries
Jerusalem Cherry	Berries
Mistletoe	Berries
Poinsettia	Leaves, flowers

Note: Wild mushrooms can also be poisonous. It requires an expert to differentiate between poisonous and non-poisonous wild mushrooms. They grow in gardens, lawns, and wooded areas. Any wild mushroom should be considered poisonous until proven otherwise.

First Aid For Poisoning:

1. Remove the poison to prevent further ingestion.
2. Keep the bird quiet and warm.
3. Get immediate veterinary care.
   - Bring a sample of the suspected poison, any vomit, along with the most recent droppings.

If no veterinary care is immediately available, the bird is conscious, and you are sure that the poison was ingested and not just played with, the following medication can be given to coat the digestive tract and help prevent absorbtion of the poison.

Try one of the following—
- Raw egg white mixed with Kaopectate® or Pepto-Bismol®
- Activated charcoal mixed with a few drops of mineral oil and enough water to give a pasty consistency.

The dosage depends on the size of the bird—

Canary or budgerigar	0.15-0.3 cc	(3—6 drops)
Cockatiel or other		
small parrot	1-2 cc	(1/5—2/5 tsp.)
Large parrots	3-6 cc	(3/5—1-1/5 tsp.)

Note: These can be given slowly with a plastic eye dropper or may have to be force fed with a tube. If any problems are encountered with the administration, STOP immediately.

Veterinary Care:

Provide emergency care as indicated and treat for shock. This would include, flushing out the crop to remove any poison, tube feeding medication to help prevent absorption of the poison, oxygen therapy, fluids, corticosteroids, and administration of antidote if known. Hospitalization and observation are also very important.

Lead Poisoning

This is a common cause of poisoning in pet birds and deserves special mention. Lead is found in such things as leaded windows (stained glass, etc.), toys containing lead, curtain weights, some costume jewelry, lead pellets from pellet guns, lead fishing weights, and paint containing lead.

Signs to Watch For:
Depression/weakness
Regurgitation and wet droppings (frequently bloody).
Convulsions/uncoordinated behavior, head tilt

If lead poisoning is suspected, contact your veterinarian immediately. X-rays should be taken. If lead is present, it can be seen in the digestive tract in most cases.

Treatment For Lead Poisoning (Veterinary Care Only):

There is a specific antidote available. Calcium Disodium Versenate is given by injection and repeated for a few days. Significant improvement will often be noticed within a very short time after the first injection. However, even with this treatment not all birds can be saved. Other supportive care will be required and furnished as needed.

Teflon Poisoning

Teflon-coated pots and pans used for cooking have become commonplace in most contemporary kitchens. They are designed for moderate cooking temperatures. When these pans are accidentally left on the stove and the temperature becomes very high, the teflon will burn and in the process will give off strong fumes. These fumes can rapidly spread throughout the house and are often deadly to birds. Birds can die within 15-20 minutes and unfortunately there is no cure. However, some supportive care and oxygen therapy may be beneficial.

Insecticide Poisoning

The most common cause of insecticide poisoning in pet birds occurs when owners spray or "fog" the house for fleas. Since birds have such sensitive respiratory tracts, if they are brought back into the home too soon after spraying, poisoning can quickly occur. To avoid any problems, when spraying, take the bird out of the house. Do not bring it back in for at least 24 hours and not until the house has been well aerated by opening the doors and windows for a sufficient interval. Consult your veterinarian for the safest and most effective foggers to use. If signs of poisoning occur, contact your veterinarian.

How to Prevent Poisoning In Your Bird:

1. *Feed a nutritionally complete diet.*
   - Food and water should always be fresh.
   - All fruits and vegetables should be thoroughly washed before serving.
2. Before giving your bird any medications, consult your veterinarian.
3. Many household products are potentially poisonous, and should not be left open where a bird can reach them.
4. Do not use any products with strong fumes such as cleaning solutions around your bird.
5. Do not use any fungicides, herbicides, insecticides, or rodenticides around your bird. If you must, consult your veterinarian first as to which are the safest products and how to use them.
6. Do not let your bird near house plants. Both of you will be grateful!
7. Do not leave any cigarettes or other tobacco products around where your bird can get to them.
8. The kitchen area presents special problems, especially for free-flying birds. There can be cleaning solutions left open, strong fumes, open pots of boiling water, and excessive heat.
9. At the first sign of any abnormal behavior contact your veterinarian immediately.

11

Aches, Pains 'n' Problems

This chapter presents an overview of the most commonly-encountered diseases of pet birds. It is beyond the scope of this book to discuss these diseases in detail or to mention all the less-common illnesses. Hopefully, by reading this chapter you will be better able to understand the complexities of diagnosing and treating some of the multitude of diseases affecting birds.

We would all like an illness to be mild. To have a quick and uncomplicated recovery. Unfortunately, this cannot always be the case. If home treatment is elected and no improvement is observed within 24 to 48 hours, consult a veterinarian. The treatments discussed in this chapter are purposely kept simple and those drugs mentioned are usually readily available without prescription.

BEAK DISORDERS

Since the beak is the primary food-gathering organ, the entire body depends on its normal function for survival. When problems hamper its normal activities, the effects will be seen immediately. Most problems are quickly noticed and lead to difficulties with eating. Watch for difficulties with cracking seeds or repeatedly dropping food after it has been picked up.

Beak Deformities

The most common problem is simple overgrowth caused by a malocclusion or insufficient normal wear. The most common cause of malocclusion causing misalignment of the upper and lower beak is from an injury to the beak. In budgerigars, mites are the most common cause. Other less-frequently-seen causes are poor nutrition, infections and hereditary birth defects (although these birds frequently die shortly after birth). The cause should be determined and corrected when possible. Most deformities, however, are not correctable and the beak will just have to be trimmed periodically to maintain proper length.

Mite Infestation

This is a common problem in budgerigars and is discussed later in this chapter under PARASITES.

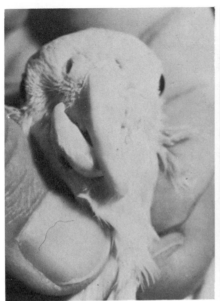

An overgrown beak.

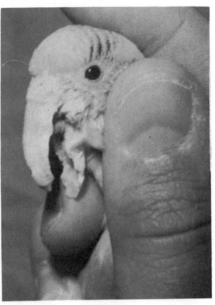

Budgerigar suffering from scaly face mite. Note the severe deformity of the beak and the white honeycomb-like crusting on the face. —*Dr. R. Woerpel*

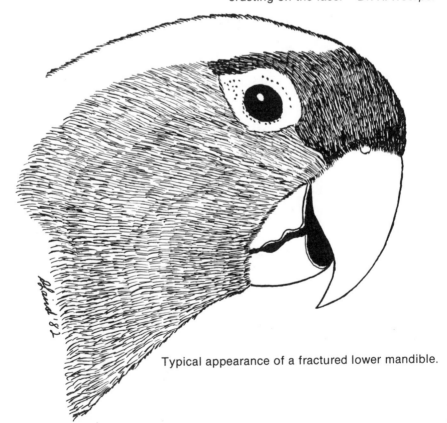

Typical appearance of a fractured lower mandible.

Trauma—Fractures

Birds allowed free flight in the house or contact with other animals are potential candidates for broken beaks. Simple fractures or splits may grow out normally as long as the base or root of the beak is not damaged. Veterinary care may be required to wire the fracture together for support as it grows out. Complete loss of a portion of the beak is far more serious. This often results in death since eating becomes difficult, if not impossible.

There are various methods of force feeding discussed in Chapter 14 that can be tried when necessary. Force feeding may have to be continued for a month or more, or until the beak grows out. Soft food is necessary. Daily weighing is helpful to know if enough food is being eaten.

Dr. Lafeber has noted that in budgerigars the beak grows about ¼" a month or about 3" per year. Overgrowth usually occurs at the tip of the upper beak. There are a variety of instruments suitable for trimming. For smaller birds, cuticle nippers or common nail clippers work very well. For larger parrots, common toenail clippers or dog nail clippers are excellent. Refer to Chapter 6 for the trimming procedure.

CERE DISORDERS

Brown Hypertrophy *(hyper = great, trophy = growth)*

In parrots, especially female budgerigars, the cere can become thickened, almost horn-like and brown in color. The condition is not serious unless it occludes the nostrils. The cause is unknown. A lanolin-base cream can be applied for a few days to soften the growth which can then sometimes be carefully lifted off. If bleeding should occur follow the directions given on page 116 and consult your veterinarian.

Inflammations

Sinus infections will commonly cause this area to become swollen and reddened. Often a nasal discharge or even bubbling from the nostrils will be seen. See the treatment for respiratory infections on page 136.

EYE DISORDERS

Signs to watch for:

Eyelids swollen and/or pasted closed
Frequent blinking
Any eye discharges, including excessive tearing
Cloudiness of eyeball
Rubbing eye or side of face

Any eye problem must be considered serious. Since a minor irritation can rapidly progress to irreversible damage and even blindness, never ignore an eye problem. If it does not improve within 24 hours see your veterinarian immediately. Never use any eye medication unless it specifically states for ophthalmic use or has been prescribed by your veterinarian. Do not use any medication that was prescribed for you or one of your other pets without first checking with your veterinarian. These medications have specific uses and if used improperly can lead to more problems.

Conjunctivitis

Conjunctivitis ("pink-eye") is an inflammation or infection of the membrane (conjunctiva) that lines the inside of the eyelids and outer area of the eyeball. It is the most commonly encountered eye problem. The causes are numerous and can include bacterial or viral infections, allergies, house dust, small seeds, many irritants such as aerosol sprays, and trauma.

Trauma

Traumatic wounds to the eyeball must always be considered serious and should receive prompt attention. They may be minor requiring only an examination and special ophthalmic medication. Deep wounds and lacerations are very serious and require immediate attention.

Corneal Ulcers

Corneal ulcers (wounds on the surface of the eyeball) are painful and serious. They can be caused by contact with objects such as a projecting wire, infections, irritating substances and quite often self-induced (excessive rubbing of the eye on the cage or from a foot). These ulcers are often invisible to the naked eye and can only be diagnosed with a special test using a florescein dye that stains the affected area green when viewed with an ultraviolet light.

Diseases in other parts of the body can also cause eye problems. Respiratory infections commonly cause both eyes to become inflamed and runny. Vitamin A deficiency can cause the eyes to become dry and inflamed. Eye tumors are occasionally detected.

First Aid for Eye Problems:

1. Remove the cause if readily apparent.
   • The eye can be examined by gently parting the eyelids. A bright light is useful. Look for any foreign objects. If they can be easily removed use a moistened cotton-tipped applicator (Q-Tip®) and very gently swab across the eye.
2. The surface of the eyeball and eyelids can be rinsed and cleaned with plain tap water. Apply water with plastic eye dropper or drip it off a wad of cotton or tissue paper. Alternately, artificial tears for people can also be used.
3. Over-the-counter eye drops containing boric acid or antibiotics

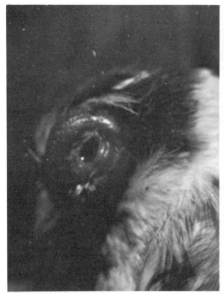

Photo by Author   *—Dr. R. Woerpel*

Eye problems can be detected early to properly treat and prevent problems from becoming as severe as these.

Birds normally breathe through their nostrils. Prolonged open-mouthed breathing such as this usually indicates a respiratory problem.   *—Dr. R. Woerpel*

without corticosteroids can be applied to the eyes three to four times daily.

4. Consult your veterinarian. It is important to prevent irreversible eye damage, such as blindness or loss of an eye.

Veterinary Care:

A correct diagnosis and specific treatment is vital for obtaining a rapid cure with the least chance of permanent damage. Foreign bodies must be removed correctly. Surgery is sometimes necessary to repair deep corneal ulcers or lacerations. Each type of eye problem requires specific medication which a veterinarian will be able to supply and give clear instructions for its use.

RESPIRATORY SYSTEM DISORDERS

Signs to Watch For:

Abnormal breathing sounds—wheezing, panting

Sneezing or coughing

Nasal discharge

Heavy breathing—shortness of breath, open-mouth breathing, tail-bobbing (pronounced up and down motions of tail)

Loss of voice

Loss of appetite

Respiratory infections, especially upper respiratory infections such as colds, are one of the more common diseases seen in pet birds.

Respiratory Infections

Colds and sinusitis (inflammation of sinuses) are seen the year 'round but are most common during the colder and wetter winter months. Nasal discharges, such as a watery bubbling of fluid out of the nostrils, runny eyes and sneezing usually accompany these infections. The causes vary and include various bacteria, viruses and fungi. Vitamin A deficiency is thought to be a major contributing cause or even one of the actual causes of the disease itself. Drafts and stress will also contribute to the infection.

Sinusitis of the area around the eye is often seen in large parrots, cockatiels and canaries. The most common appearance is that of a bird with a pebble-like and firm swelling above or below one or both of the eyes. Also, the affected eye tends to close, giving a droopy appearance. Surgery is usually necessary to lance and drain the swelling followed with infusion of antibiotics. Vitamin A injections will usually help cure the problem faster.

Inflammation of larynx, trachea (breathing tube), syrinx (bird's voicebox), and bronchi (air ducts leading into the lungs) do occur and are usually associated with upper respiratory infections or lower respiratory infections such as pneumonia.

Pneumonia (inflammation of the lungs) is a very serious condition and fortunately is rather uncommon in birds when compared to other respiratory infections. It also can be caused by a variety of bacteria, viruses and fungi. These organisms can gain entrance into the lungs, from a cold traveling down into the chest, an extension of an infection in other parts of the body via the blood stream, or a deep puncture wound around the chest area.

Air sacculitis, an inflammation of the air sacs, is often a chronic condition that can cause breathing difficulties for months or even years. Bacteria and fungi, especially one known as aspergillus, are the common organisms causing infection. Actually making this diagnosis in the live bird is very difficult. Although the bird may not appear sick in the early stages, it will show heavy breathing with tail bobbing especially after only very brief exertion. In the advanced stages, the respiratory distress worsens and can eventually lead to death. It is a difficult disease to treat.

SOME OTHER COMMON RESPIRATORY PROBLEMS

- Small seeds can lodge in the nostrils or in the roof of the mouth and can make breathing and eating troublesome.
- Tumors or abscesses can occur almost anywhere in the body. If they occur in the air passageways causing an obstruction breathing will become difficult.
- Air sac mites are seen most often in canaries and finches. These mites can cause severe breathing difficulties and are discussed later in this chapter under PARASITES.
- Psittacosis and Newcastle diseases can both show respiratory problems associated with them.
- Goiters are an enlargement of the thyroid glands that are located alongside the trachea at the base of the neck. These are uncommon but are still reported to occur occasionally in budgerigars that are eating nothing but seeds. Iodine is low in these diets and this deficiency can lead to goiter formation. Vitamin and mineral supplements should contain sufficient iodine to prevent this problem.
- Diseases of other organs can also cause breathing problems. Tumors in the abdomen, obesity and the presence of eggs are some of the things that will prevent the lungs and air sacs from fully expanding causing shortness of breath.
- Allergies probably affect birds but have yet to be fully explored and identified.

RESPIRATORY DISTRESS IS SERIOUS. YOU SHOULD ALWAYS SEEK OUT VETERINARY CARE AS SOON AS PROBLEMS ARE OBSERVED.

First Aid for Respiratory Infections:

1. Keep birds warm and rested. Minimize stress.
2. Wipe any discharges away from the nostrils if the bird can be easily handled.
3. Steam vaporization producing a fine, warmed mist of water is beneficial for soothing and moisturizing the inflammed linings of the respiratory tract. (Vaporizers are available at drug stores.)
4. Consult your veterinarian.

Veterinary Care:

All respiratory infections should be considered potentially life-threatening. For severe breathing difficulties oxygen therapy is vital. Diagnostic tests are useful to determine the exact nature of the disease and its most effective treatment. Antibiotics are usually essential to control infections. Hospitalization and observation may be necessary.

DIGESTIVE DISORDERS

Signs to Watch For:

> Diarrhea
> Regurgitation
> Straining to eliminate
> Crop distention
> Abdominal enlargement
> Poor appetite

The Mouth

Hypovitaminosis A is a Vitamin A deficiency affecting the epithelial cells lining the roof of the mouth. It causes white, "cheese-like" plaques to form. The larger parrots, especially Amazons and African greys appear to be most susceptible. Respiratory infections are often associated. Numerous bacteria and *Candida* species (a yeast) can also cause a similar problem or secondarily invade the mouth once the A deficiency weakens the epithelial barrier.

Signs to Watch For:

Affected birds exhibit appetite loss with corresponding weight loss, respiratory infections and a change of or loss of voice. It has also been shown to cause swellings or abscess beneath the tongue.

Veterinary Care:

A culture and sensitivity test is advisable to try to identify the organisms causing the infection along with the most effective drugs to control it. Vitamin A injections are important and will aid in a more rapid response. Antibiotics or anti-yeast drugs are necessary to treat the infections. Medications, such as an iodine solution may be used to swab the mouth and help remove the plaques. If the bird is not eating, then force feeding becomes essential until its appetite returns.

Seeds are deficient in Vitamin A. Therefore, as discussed in Chapter 3, it is important to supplement with other foods high in Vitamin A.

Pox Infection:

Mouth lesions can also be caused by a pox virus. It often causes tiny, dry and scab covered lesions in the mouth. They may also be distributed around the eyes, face and legs. Unfortunately there is no specific treatment. The bird will either die or recover after a period of time. However, antibiotics and Vitamin A therapy will help control any secondary bacterial infections.

REGURGITATION
A Sign of Affection? Or Disease?

Regurgitation is the expulsion of *undigested* food from the mouth or crop. It is usually composed of fluid, mucus and seeds. Vomiting is the expulsion of *digested* food from the stomach or bile from the intestines. It is largely composed of finely ground up food and fluid. It is generally considered that birds cannot vomit. Therefore what we see are birds regurgitating—NOT vomiting.

Regurgitation can indicate a crop infection or a blockage of of the upper digestive tract. It may also be due to a neurosis, an emotional disturbance. In male budgerigars regurgitation as a sign of affection can be directed onto a toy, mirror, another shiny object or even its owner. In larger parrots, they may attempt to feed their owners using dramatic head and neck bobbing. These love affairs are an imitation courtship behavior and not a disease. Removing the object of affection will usually cure the problem or be content to accept the attention.

Regurgitation can also be caused by a number of much more serious problems. Some of these disorders could include dietary change, indigestion, stomach or intestinal diseases (gastroenteritis), infectious diseases, gizzard foreign bodies, poisons, drugs, kidney disease and motion sickness. Most of these problems are discussed elsewhere in this book. Regurgitation can be very stressful and tiring for the bird. It also results in the loss of water, electrolytes, minerals and other essential nutrients.

NOTE: Be careful not to confuse the food and fluid associated with the act of regurgitation with that of the droppings. It's not always as clear cut as one might think, especially if the bird has diarrhea.

First Aid For Regurgitation
1. Remove or correct the cause when possible.

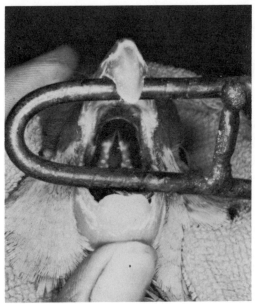

White plaques along the roof of the mouth are
suggestive of a Vitamin A deficiency.

Cockatiel with a large, abnormally distended
crop. Note the balloon-like swelling.

2. Remove the grit. Sick birds may overeat it and engorge themselves.
3. Confine the bird to its cage. Keep it warm and comfortable.
4. Kaopectate™ or Pepto-Bismol™ can be tried as an aid to soothing and coating the digestive tract. It should be given with a plastic medicine dropper. The dosage is as follows:

Finches/Canaries	1-2 drops every 4 hours
Budgerigars	2-3 drops every 4 hours
Cockatiels	5-7 drops every 4 hours
Amazon parrots	12-20 drops every 4 hours (0.6-1 cc)
Large Cockatoos and Macaws	20-40 drops every 4 hours (1-2 cc)

Veterinary Care:

If the bird looks in otherwise good condition the above treatment can be tried. However, if the bird looks weak and unstable on its feet and especially if the vomiting persists longer than 12-24 hours, a veterinarian should be consulted. Vomiting is often an indication of a very serious problem that requires more specific therapy.

CROP DISORDERS

Crop Impaction

Crop impaction is an obstruction of the normal passage of food through the digestive tract. The crop becomes large and will often be seen flopping over the breast at the base of the neck. Regurgitation is common. The swelling usually contains a mixture of seed, mucus, and fluid. The common causes include clumping of seeds, overeating of grit or an infection due to bacteria or a type of yeast known as *Candida.* Some of the less common causes include an abnormal functioning of the muscles or nerves to this area.

First Aid For Crop Impaction:

1. Place a few drops of mineral oil into the mouth using a plastic medicine dropper. Wait a few minutes and follow this with gentle massage of the crop in an attempt to break up the obstruction. This procedure may need to be repeated every couple of hours.

    There is always a risk associated with attempting to dislodge the obstruction. The bird could aspirate the crop contents into its lungs leading to very serious complications.
2. If the above procedure is successful, administer Maalox™ or DiGel™ to soothe the inflamed crop and neutralize the acid. Follow the dosages recommended for treatment of regurgitation.
3. Feed a soft, bland diet for a few days.

Veterinary Care:

Tube feeding of mineral oil or similar lubricant can be given in higher doses along with other supportive care. If this conservative approach is not successful, surgery would be required to remove the mass. Antibiotics will usually be administered directly into the crop.

Sour Crop

Sour crop is the common name given to a severe inflammation of the crop. The crop lining is usually irritated and the contents foul-smelling. Regurgitation of food or fluid frequently occurs. Some of the common causes include spoiled or moldy foods, bacterial or yeast infections and any obstruction that blocks or slows the passage of food through the digestive tract.

First Aid For Sour Crop:

1. Administer Maalox™ or Di-Gel™ to neutralize the acids, help eliminate the gas, and to soothe the inflamed crop lining. Follow the dosages recommended for treatment of vomiting.
2. Feed a soft, bland diet for a few days.

Veterinary Care:

The crop contents will be "milked out" two or three times daily followed by other supportive care. A tube can be passed directly into the crop and the material sucked out. Antibiotics are necessary for a few days following initial treatment.

PROVENTRICULUS AND GIZZARD DISORDERS

These organs do occasionally become inflamed causing something akin to an "upset stomach" or gastritis. However, these can be difficult diagnoses to confirm. Just as the gizzard retains grit, it also retains foreign bodies. Some of these objects have included wire, beads, string, chains, buttons, staples and rocks. Sharp objects can cause severe irritation to the linings, or worse, a perforation into the abdominal cavity. Regurgitation, appetite and weight loss, and abnormal droppings are common signs. Radiographs are needed to determine if foreign objects are present. Parasites do occur and these are discussed later in this chapter.

Most foreign objects must be surgically removed. The surgical procedure is difficult and should be attempted only when there are no other options available.

INTESTINAL DISORDERS

Intestinal infections, or enteritis, are also seen in pet birds. Poor appetite, weight loss, and diarrhea (with or without wet droppings) are usually found regardless of the cause. A great variety of factors can be the cause. These include bacterial (*E. coli* and *Salmonella* are the notorious ones), fungi, viruses, parasites, dietary changes or poor nutrition, poisons, tumors, diseases of other organs and almost any type of medication. Also, any change in the bird's environment or daily routine will be stressful and this alone can cause diarrhea.

An inflammation of the intestines is a very serious problem. When the gut linings become inflamed and irritated, bacterial and other poisons can more easily penetrate this normally effective barrier and get into the bloodstream. Once in the bloodstream other organs such as the liver, kidney and lungs can become affected. There is also excessive loss of water, electrolytes, enzymes and minerals which further lead to weakness and even shock.

First Aid For Simple Diarrhea:

1. Remove the grit. Sick birds may overeat it and engorge themselves.
2. Soft, bland and nourishing foods such as cooked eggs, bread, peanut butter, vegetable-type baby foods, cooked oatmeal and some seeds are beneficial. The food and water must always be fresh and clean.
3. Kaopectate™ or Pepto-Bismol™ can be given to soothe and coat the inflamed digestive tract. Follow the guidelines and dosages as listed for regurgitation.
4. Seek veterinary care if rapid improvement is not observed.

Veterinary Care:

Dehydration and loss of vital nutrients are a common complication associated with persistent diarrhea. Supportive care which includes broad-spectrum antibiotics, stronger-acting anti-diarrhea medications, vitamin injections and fluids can be very beneficial. As always, determining the cause of the problem aids in selecting the most appropriate treatment.

Constipation

Constipation is actually quite uncommon in birds. It would be suggested when there are either no feces noted in the droppings or only tiny amounts with excessive straining. Birds that are not eating will not produce feces and this can mimic constipation. The causes include abdominal tumor or an egg exerting pressure on the intestines, excessive fibrous material in the diet, grit impactions, hernia, poor muscle tone and obesity.

Treatment must first always be aimed at eliminating the basis for the problem. A thorough physical exam and often radiographs will reveal any tumors, grit impaction, eggs or hernias present. These problems are best left to a veterinarian since they are difficult to treat and can be very serious.

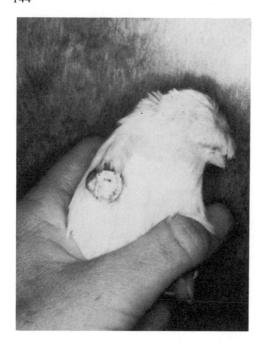

Wing abcess in a canary.
Note the white, crumbly
cheese-like material
causing the swelling.

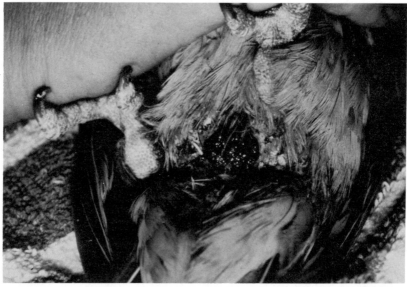

Cloaca prolapse in a parrot. This is an emergency often caused by straining
to lay an egg.   —Dr. R. Woerpel

CLOACA DISORDERS

Cloaca Prolapse

Cloaca prolapse is the expulsion or falling out of the cloaca tissue. It is caused by excessive straining as seen with persistent diarrhea, inflammation of the cloaca, and from efforts to pass a retained egg. A prolapse must be considered an emergency and your veterinarian should be consulted immediately.

Veterinary Care:

The treatment consists of first cleaning this tissue gently with warm soapy water. A little mineral oil can be applied to help soften and remove any debris. Granular sugar can be applied to help shrink the swollen tissue. Alternately, a combination of antibiotics and anti-inflammatory corticosteroids, added to medical grade DMSO then applied to the tissue can also be very effective. Then, with a blunt instrument, such as a glass thermometer, the tissue is pushed back in through the vent area from where it came. A suture may have to be placed around the vent and snugged down for 2-3 days to prevent further prolapsing. Antibiotics, fluids, and anti-shock drugs are usually needed along with warmth and rest.

LIVER DISORDERS

Liver diseases, namely inflammations and infections known as hepatitis, are commonly seen in pet birds. In general, this disease is not transmissible to man unless psittacosis is the underlying problem. The signs are not specific for liver disease and can include any of the following: poor appetite, weight loss, increased thirst, seizures, depression, diarrhea and often the urate portion of the droppings becoming yellow or green in color. It is impossible to diagnose liver disease without blood tests and sometimes radiographs are needed. The causes can be bacterial, viral and fungal infections, poisons, a disturbance in the fat and carbohydrate metabolism, and cancer. A severe intestinal infection can also lead to a liver problem.

Without proper treatment a bird can become seriously ill. Based on the cause the veterinarian will prescribe antibiotics, appetite stimulants, and even medication that may help to decrease the size of a fatty liver. Tube feedings for a few days are often needed to help strengthen the bird. When the blood tests indicate a liver disease, repeating them in about two weeks is valuable for evaluating the response to treatment.

PANCREATIC DISORDERS

Diabetes has been occasionally noted in birds. It has most commonly been reported in budgerigars. The pancreas fails to produce sufficient amounts of insulin and this deficiency keeps the blood sugar levels abnormally high. In other words, the energy normally derived from simple sugars is unavailable to the body. Signs to watch for include a dramatic increase in the food and water intake and very wet droppings. Daily insulin injections have occasionally proved successful in treating this condition in pet birds.

The pancreas also manufactures enzymes which are intimately involved in the digestion of food. If these are absent or present in insufficient amounts much of the food eaten will become unavailable to the body. This condition seems most prevalent in cockatiels where despite a ravenous appetite, weight loss becomes severe. The feces will also change and become large and clay-colored resembling "puffed rice." Supplemental enzymes can be added to the food but have not always proved effective.

LUMPS 'N' BUMPS

Strange swellings and growths do appear on the body from time to time. These are fairly easy to detect. Look for a group of feathers not lying smoothly or pointing in abnormal directions, or even excessive preening occurring over a particular area, as these could be indications of some type of problem. Listed here are some of the more common swellings or growths found on the surface of a bird's body. It will usually require a veterinarian to correctly diagnose the cause of the swelling and the best treatment.

Abscesses

An abscess is a localized collection of pus. In mammals, it is soft to the touch and filled with a foul-smelling, viscous liquid. However, in birds, an abscess is hard to the touch and filled with a white and crumbly, cheese-like material. The most commonly affected areas are just above an eye (look for a small pea-size mass), along the roof of the mouth and below the tongue (look for white spots), or on the underside of the feet where it is referred to as "bumblefoot." An abscess must be opened and all the debris removed. Then it is flushed with an antibiotic solution and occasionally sutured closed if necessary. Appropriate antibiotics should be given for a few days afterward.

Hematomas

A hematoma is a pooling of blood, similar to a blood clot, and is found just beneath the skin layer. It can be due to broken blood vessels and is usually caused by an injury to the affected area or a clotting defect. They are soft to the touch and easily compressed. The most common site is the breast area or on top of the head. The best treatment is usually to do nothing and let them go away by themselves. Since birds have only a small amount of blood, surgery will lead to more blood loss and this could prove very dangerous.

Large tumor on the leg of a budgerigar.

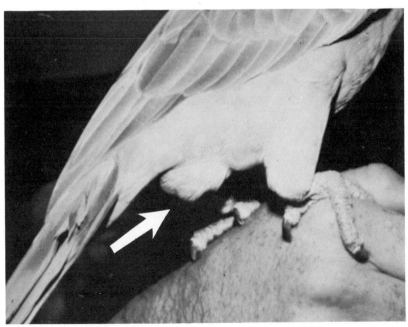

Hernia in a parrot. Note the ventral "bulge" behind the legs in the area of the vent.
—Dr. R. Woerpel

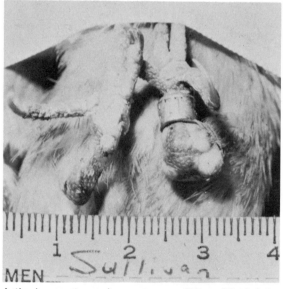

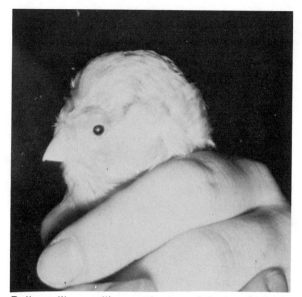

Balloon-like swelling on the top of the head of this canary is caused by a ruptured air sac resulting in subcutaneous emphysema.   —Dr. R. Woerpel

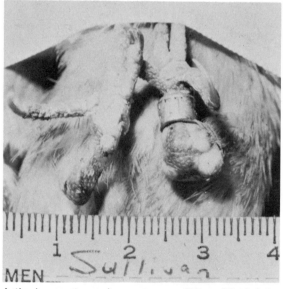

Articular gout causing severe swelling of the joints.

Tumors

A tumor is an abnormal enlargement or growth of tissue. Any part of the body can be affected. On the skin, one of the more common types is a lipoma. This is a fatty deposit that is soft to the touch and usually occurs over the chest or abdominal areas. Tumors are classified as either **benign** (non-cancerous) or **malignant** (cancerous) growths. Any tumor should be surgically removed and biopsied. Determining the type of tumor suggests the probability of it recurring and/or possibly spreading throughout the body. It also helps suggest the most effective treatment program.

Hernias

A hernia is an abnormal slippage of an organ into an area it does not normally enter. It can be caused by a tear in a tissue as a result of an injury or tissue weakness; it can also be present from birth. The most common site is the abdomen, right above the vent. The straining associated with egg laying is one of the more common causes. The swelling is usually soft to the touch and sometimes even the hole through the torn tissue can be felt. Hernias should be examined by a veterinarian and surgery may be required to close the defect.

Feather Cysts

A feather cyst is a swelling beneath the skin caused by the growth of an abnormal feather within its follicle. The follicle becomes inflamed and fills with a thick lumpy material. These are most commonly seen in canaries and finches on wing or tail areas. The cyst should be surgically opened and the young feather and debris removed. An antibiotic solution is then flushed into the area which may or may not be sutured closed.

Subcutaneous Emphysema

Subcutaneous emphysema is the abnormal accumulation of air beneath the skin. There is a striking balloon-like swelling over an area of the body. It is caused by a tear in an air sac which can occur from an injury or often just appear spontaneously. The signs can be mild to severe. Some of these swellings will clear right up without treatment, while others are very stubborn and require long-term therapy. The treatment requires bandaging of the affected area for varying periods of time. This exerts pressure over the affected area and helps compress the swelling. They may also recur after having appeared to heal.

Gout

Gout is a poorly-understood disease in birds caused by an abnormal increase in uric acid which becomes deposited in various tissues. There are two distinct forms. *Visceral gout* affects the internal organs and is very difficult to detect. *Articular gout* collects these deposits around the joints, ligaments and tendons of the lower legs and feet. It is most common in the budgerigar and appears as multiple cream-colored shiny swellings bulging up through the skin. It is painful and the bird becomes noticeably lame.

There is no effective treatment for gout. Changing the protein level in the diet may help and there are certain drugs that affect uric acid levels that can be tried. Occasionally lancing the swellings to lessen the pain may be helpful but should be done only if absolutely necessary since the healing is poor. Pain medication, padding the perches and using different perch sizes and shapes are also helpful. Food and water should always be within easy reach.

Obesity

Too much food from over-indulgent owners and a lack of exercise can lead to obesity in caged birds. Fat deposits may develop over the breast and abdominal areas. The bird should be examined to be sure it is indeed fat and not a tumor and that it is otherwise healthy. Limiting food intake, when acceptable to the bird, selecting low-fat seeds, and increasing fruits and vegetables in the diet are also beneficial. Exercise will also help.

KIDNEY DISORDERS

Kidney diseases are seen in birds. It is not possible to diagnose these without using laboratory tests.

Determining the exact cause of the disease is difficult to do in live birds since kidney biopsies are not safe at this time. Some kidney diseases are treatable and some are not. The signs are generally vague and may not be suggestive of kidney problems. They include appetite loss, increased thirst, generalized weakness, depression, and wet droppings. The protein in the diet should be kept low, fruits and vegetables should be increased. Antibiotics and other drugs may be helpful and vitamins are essential.

FEATHER DISORDERS

Feather problems are caused by a number of factors including nutrition, parasites, hereditary disorders, metabolic disorders, injuries, infections, and commonly, self-induced feather damage. The cause should be determined and treated whenever possible. The broken or split feathers need to be removed or trimmed back. If this is not done the bird will often begin picking at the area even more. Regardless of the cause, any broken or split feather should always be removed.

Abnormal Molt

It can be difficult to differentiate a normal heavy molt and an abnormal one. You should become familiar with the normal molting pattern for your bird. An abnormal molt should be suspected when a bird is losing feathers and not showing signs of replacing them or replacing the molted normal feathers with others that appear abnormal.

Heavy molts can be due to abrupt temperature changes, temperature extremes, changes in light periods, shock or severe fright. However, in these instances new feathers should grow back in within the normal six- to eight-week time period required for feather regrowth. A hormone imbalance and other unknown factors can also cause a heavy molt. In these imbalances feather regrowth would be slower.

Slow feather growth can result from poor nutrition or an abnormally functioning thyroid gland. Diets high in protein, calcium and other minerals are especially important during the feather growth period. Thyroid hormone supplementation can be helpful to stimulate the feathers to grow. Other hormones may also be helpful. Remember that when feathers are missing birds must be kept warm. Their insulation and normal temperature control afforded by the feathers has been lessened.

French Molt

This is a non-fatal condition that primarily affects young budgies at about six weeks of age. The flight and tail feathers either drop out or break off at about the time the birds are ready to leave the nest. These birds are called "creepers" or "runners" since they are unable to fly. The exact cause is unknown but suspected to involve the feathers' blood supply and/or a virus. There is no cure and many of these birds will never grow normal feathers again.

Feather Picking

Birds are social animals and when forced to live in a cage, as opposed to their natural wild state, neuroses may develop. Remember imported birds are used to having the freedom associated with flight, plenty of space to escape dangers, and places to hide. Also, searching for food and socialization eliminates boredom and inactivity.

Feather picking or plucking is the major cause of feather loss in parrots. Picking may start as a vice associated with boredom and end up becoming a pastime. The causes, as with all emotional problems, can be numerous. They include boredom, insecurity, too-small cage, heavy molt, lack of sleep, infrequent bathing, poor nutrition, a new owner or the owner spending less time with bird, incompatibility with cagemate, and all other causes of stress. It is important to also realize that some birds will begin plucking out their feathers during the breeding and nesting season. The hallmark of this disease is a normal feathering of the head and neck. The degree of plucking or self-mutilation is variable. It may only involve certain areas such as the chest or inner wing areas and from here spread to include the entire body except for the head and neck.

Before attempting treatment a veterinarian should examine the bird to rule out any health problems that may be contributing to the picking. Just as there are no two personalities alike, there are no two birds alike. What may work as a cure in one bird is not necessarily going to work in another. With this in mind, Dr. Chuck Galvin has made an excellent list of suggestions that have helped control feather picking in many birds. In some cases owners have tried all of the following and never cured the problem. In others, just trying one of the following has helped. Ideally, the cause of the picking should be eliminated but this is not always possible. Frequently, the cause is not even known.

1. Make sure nutrition is adequate. Protein, calcium and other minerals are necessary for feather growth. Nutritional supplements are recommended.
2. Give your bird lots of direct attention.
3. Some birds respond favorably to radio or television. You may want to leave the radio on while you are away from home.
4. Toys, mirrors, swings, bells, chains, colored yarn, chicken bones and other novelties can be placed in the cage so long as they do not frighten the bird. Also, don't overcrowd the cage. Make sure all toys are kept clean and avoid any toys that can injure birds. Playpens are another excellent idea. Toys and playpens are discussed in more detail in Chapters 4 and 5.
5. Try moving the cage to another area of the house. Perhaps near a window or in a room with more family activity. Most birds do not like to be left alone and want to feel that they are part of the family. Avoid drafts.
    Note: Is your bird picking only when you are gone?
6. Provide a cage of adequate size to allow ample room for physical activity.
7. Allow eight to 12 hours of sleep in a darkened area.
8. Be sure to remove the feathers that fall to the bottom of the cage. Some people feel that if a bird has the opportunity to play with the plucked feathers that it can aggravate the problem.
9. Frequent baths or spraying with water has helped. See the section on BATHING in Chapter 6.
10. Try using a tree branch with the bark left on. It should be clean and free of insecticides. The bird can occupy its time by picking at the bark.
11. When possible, increase the bird's exercise time by allowing it to fly around the house.
12. Avoid stressful situations, i.e., other pets that threaten or people who tease.
13. Try feeding the bird so that it has to work harder to reach its food.
14. Sometimes changing the photoperiod helps. That is, alternating between hours of light and darkness every couple of weeks.
15. Try playing a tape recording of bird sounds. These can also be left on while you are away.

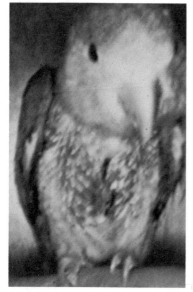

Feather picking is the major cause of feather loss in pet birds.

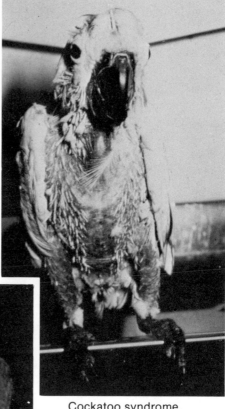

Cockatoo syndrome.

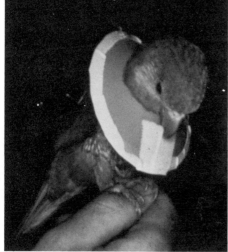

Collars can be one of the most effective methods to control feather picking.

16. If other attempts fail, relief *may* be obtained by acquiring a companion bird. If there is already a companion bird try separating them.
17. Tranquilizers, steroids, and hormones as prescribed by a veterinarian can be tried.
18. Teaching the bird new tricks may help to distract its attention from its feathers.
19. Often nothing less than physically preventing the bird from picking and chewing at its feathers will work. An Elizabethan collar that fits around the neck can be a very effective restraint. Most birds will become accustomed to a collar within a couple of days. However, some birds may never accept one and it will have to be removed. Also, if the bird really wants to destroy the collar with its beak it can do so rather easily. There are many different shapes and materials that can be used. In our experience, radiograph or other lightweight flexible transparent plastic works best. The inner hole that fits around the neck is padded with tape and the edges are held together with superglue. Transparent materials seem to work best and this may be because the bird can still view its lower body through the collar. The stress factor with a collar can be great and many birds will go off their food initially. They must be watched very closely. It is best to let a veterinarian apply a collar since they are more experienced and know how to handle problems that can arise. The collar is left on for about six to eight weeks, until the new feathers have grown back in. When removed, the bird may go back to picking. In these cases, the collar may need to be left on indefinitely along with attempting to modify the bird's behavior with other methods.

- Feather mites have been purposely not discussed in this section. They are frequently suspected as a cause of feather problems, but are uncommonly at fault. See the next section for the PARASITE discussion.
- There is a feather problem that affects a small percentage of cockatoos. It is called the **Cockatoo Syndrome** and its cause is still not known. It is not caused by feather picking. The feathers begin to fall out or the bird picks at them and they never grow back in normally. Unfortunately, there is no treatment, but in spite of the problem many birds can still live reasonably normal lives.

PARASITES

Parasites are defined as organisms nourishing themselves at the expense of another, often causing adverse effects to the host. Fortunately, parasites in pet birds are not a common problem. If your bird has been purchased from a reputable dealer, and especially if it has been born in the United States, the chance of its having parasites becomes even smaller. If your bird has been imported or lives in an outdoor aviary, especially one with dirt floors and where it can be exposed to wild birds and rodents, then the potential for parasite problems is going to be greater.

This section deals with the most commonly encountered parasites of pet birds.

SKIN PARASITES

Scaly-Face or Scaly-Leg Mite (Knemidokoptes)

Host:	All birds, but most commonly budgerigars
Appearance:	Tiny, insect-like creatures almost invisible to the naked eye.
Spread:	Possibly from parents to offspring while nesting but still not known for sure. Some birds will harbor the mite their entire life but never get any apparent disease.
Mite Life Cycle:	Spends entire life on bird. They burrow into the top layers of the skin and lay eggs in the tunnels formed by the burrowing.
Signs to Watch For:	White honeycomb-like crusts found primarily around the beak, cere, eyelids, and also the legs and vent area. If untreated these mites can cause severe deformities of the beak.
Diagnosis:	The crusts on the birds have a very characteristic appearance upon physical examination. If necessary to confirm a diagnosis, the crusts can be viewed under a microscope and the mite can usually be found.
Treatment:	At home, a light coating of mineral oil applied with a cotton-tipped applicator can be used daily to soften the crusts and smother the mites. Use a circular motion and gently lift the crusts off as they begin to soften. Keep the oil off the feathers. A veterinarian will often use Eurax Cream™ to kill the mites. This medication is safe, non-greasy and very effective. A new injectable medication, *Ivermectin* (Equalan™) is now available and is also very effective against this mite. Be sure to clean the cage, perches and toys as the mite could be living in the crusts that have fallen off.
Prevention:	Have your new bird examined by a veterinarian before it comes in contact with any other birds.

Feather Mites (Red Mite)

Host:	All birds, but the mites are uncommon in all birds.
Appearance:	Rapidly moving tiny greyish-white or red specks.
Spread:	Brought in by an infested bird or by wild birds in an outdoor aviary.
Life Cycle:	These mites hide under perches, food and water cups, droppings, and around the cage. They feed on the bird's blood only at night. The female mite lays eggs in the cracks and crevices of the cage. The eggs hatch in 48-72 hours in a warm, moist environment. The baby mite grows into an adult mite in only a few days.
Signs to Watch For:	Scratching, skin irritation and restlessness primarily at night.
Diagnosis:	Cover the cage with a white sheet at night and examine the underside of it first thing in the morning. Alternatively, try using a flashlight and shine it into the cage at night. Look for the moving red specks. A magnifying glass may help.
Treatment:	You must clean and disinfect the cage and furnishings. Flea and tick powders for dogs containing pyrethrin or cabaryl are effective against mites. Use them sparingly on the bird.
Prevention:	All new birds should be isolated for 30 days. The feathers and cage can be examined. Purchase new birds from a reputable dealer.

Lice

Host:	All birds, especially chickens and birds of prey, but uncommon in pet birds unless exposed to wild birds.
Appearance:	Small, swiftly-moving, wingless insects with flattened bodies.
Spread:	If your pet bird comes in contact with infested wild birds transmission can occur. Heaviest infestations usually occur on those birds that are sick or injured. Most lice are very host-specific, and as a result, do not commonly move from one bird to another.
Life Cycle:	Lice spend their entire life on the bird. Clusters of eggs called *nits* are attached to the feathers and appear as tiny white clusters. Within each egg a tiny nymph will develop into an adult in about three weeks.

Signs to Watch For:	Constant scratching and skin irritation. The feathers may develop a "moth-eaten" appearance.
Diagnosis:	Finding the tiny white eggs, nymphs or adults attached to the feathers.
Treatment:	Flea and tick powders for dogs containing pyrethrin or cabaryl are effective against lice. Use them sparingly. Must clean and disinfect cage and furnishings.
Prevention:	Avoid contact with birds that have an unknown history. Purchase new birds from a reputable dealer.

Fleas and Ticks

Fleas are wingless, brown, blood-sucking insects. Ticks are fat, brown and bean-shaped parasites that attach themselves to the skin. Fortunately, these parasites are uncommon on birds. For fleas, a pyrethrin or cabaryl insecticide applied sparingly to the bird and the cage can be used. Ticks are removed by grasping the head parts with forceps at the surface of the skin and pulling them out.

RESPIRATORY SYSTEM PARASITES

Gapeworms (Syngamus)

Host:	All birds, but uncommon.
Appearance:	Red, Y-shaped elongated worms found in the breathing tubes.
Spread:	Birds eat the worm larvae directly or their transport hosts, such as earthworms or snails. Adult birds can also infest their young.
Life Cycle:	The worms lay eggs in the bird's trachea. They are then coughed up and either are expelled onto the ground or swallowed and passed out in the feces. The eggs develop into larvae which are then eaten directly by the bird, or by a transport host such as earthworms, slugs and snails. In birds, the larvae migrate from the intestines to the respiratory tract.
Signs to Watch For:	Severe breathing difficulties with coughing and "gaping," stretching the neck in order to make breathing easier.
Diagnosis:	Microscopic exam of the droppings for eggs. In larger birds it may be possible to swab the trachea and draw out a sample containing the worms.

Treatment:	Thiabendazole prescribed by a veterinarian.
Prevention:	All birds should have their stools checked for parasite eggs. Birds quartered in outdoor aviaries with dirt floors are at an increased risk.

Air Sac Mites

Host:	Primarily canaries and finches; occasionally other birds.
Appearance:	Moving minute black specks in the trachea and air sacs.
Life Cycle:	Unknown. Young birds may become infested from their parents.
Signs to Watch For:	Severe breathing difficulties, coughing and gasping. Poor overall physical condition.
Diagnosis:	Difficult in live birds. In an aviary situation, a sick bird may have to be sacrificed to get an accurate diagnosis.
Treatment:	Cabaryl or malathion insecticides. These can be administered in different forms so consult a veterinarian.
Prevention:	In aviaries with the problem, pest strips may help. The birds should not be able to get to them and the enclosure should be large and well ventilated.

DIGESTIVE SYSTEM PARASITES

Roundworms (Ascarids)

Host:	All birds.
Appearance:	Long, thin, white worms.
Spread:	Eating the larvae from the soil.
Life Cycle:	Larvae are swallowed and grow into adults in the intestines. The adults then lay eggs and these are passed out with the stool.
Signs to Watch For:	Diarrhea or constipation and weight loss.
Diagnosis:	Stool examination. On occasion may even see the live worms passed out in the stool.
Treatment:	Piperzine or levamisole as prescribed by a veterinarian.

Prevention:	Good hygiene and sanitation. Clean the floors in aviaries often. Have stool samples examined when a problem is suspected.

Capillaria ("Threadworms")

Host:	All birds.
Appearance:	Round thread-like worm.
Spread:	Eating the larvae from the soil.
Life Cycle:	Larvae are swallowed and grow into adults in the crop or small intestines. The adults then lay eggs and these are passed out in the stool.
Signs to Watch For:	Diarrhea and weight loss. May see difficulty in swallowing.
Diagnosis:	Stool examinations.
Treatment:	Levamisole or piperazine as prescribed by a veterinarian.
Prevention:	Good hygiene and sanitation. Clean the floors in the aviaries often. Have the stools examined when a problem is suspected.

Tapeworms (Cestodes)

Host:	All birds, but African greys seem especially susceptible.
Appearance:	Flattened and segmented white worms. May pass individual segments called *proglottids* that look like cooked white rice grains when dried out.
Spread:	Birds must eat transport host such as infested insects or mollusks.
Life Cycle:	Worms attach to small intestines and adults pass eggs in stool which are eaten by insect or mollusk where they develop into larvae. Transport host with larvae inside is eaten by the bird and then develops into adult in the small intestines.
Signs to Watch For:	General weakness and sometimes diarrhea. The bird may harbor worms without showing any signs of disease.
Diagnosis:	Stool examination. May observe segments passing in stool.
Treatment:	Yomesan™ as prescribed by veterinarian.

Prevention:	Obviously, birds should not be eating insects and mollusks. However, they are a good nutritional source and they will usually not cause a problem. Have stool samples checked if a problem is suspected.

Giardia

Host:	All birds, primarily budgerigars.
Appearance:	Microscopic, invisible to unaided eye.
Spread:	Cysts in feces from infested bird are eaten by another bird.
Life Cycle:	After cysts are eaten, they grow to maturity in the small intestine.
Signs to Watch For:	Long-standing diarrhea, usually foul-smelling. Poor appetite and weight loss, even death.
Diagnosis:	Stool examination—must be a very fresh sample. In aviary may have to sacrifice one of the sick birds to get an accurate diagnosis.
Treatment:	Dimetridazole (Emtryl®) or Metronidazole (Flagyl®) as prescribed by a veterinarian.
Prevention:	Good hygiene and sanitation. Have stool samples examined when a problem is suspected.

Trichomonas

Host:	All birds, but primarily pigeons where the disease is called canker, birds of prey, where the disease is called frounce, and also canaries and finches.
Appearance:	Microscopic, invisible to the unaided eye.
Spread:	Unknown.
Life Cycle:	Unknown. They are found mostly in the throat, esophagus, crop and intestines.
Signs to Watch For:	White cheese-like material along the roof of the mouth, poor appetite, diarrhea, weakness, and shortness of breath.
Diagnosis:	Microscopic exam of cheese-like material.
Treatment:	Dimetridazole (Emtryl®) or Metronidazole (Flagyl®) as prescribed by veterinarian.

Prevention: Prevent contact with wild birds. Keep water fresh
                            and clean.

WARNING: It is ill-advised to worm any bird unless there is good evidence
that parasites are present. Worming medications also pose a potential health
risk. Their method of administration and dosage level must be correctly
selected. Also, as is evident from this disucssion, there are many types of
parasites and each requires a certain type of medication.

12

Diseases—"The Biggies"

There are a few diseases affecting birds with which all bird fanciers should become familiar. These are mentioned frequently and have far-reaching implications, not only for your bird's health, but also for yours.

Psittacosis

Psittacosis is a widespread and serious disease that can be transmitted to man by infected birds. The name comes from the word *psittacidae,* the name of the family of birds which includes parakeets, cockatiels, parrots, macaws and all other parrot-like birds. In turkeys, chickens and other non-psittacine birds, the same disease is called *ornithosis.*

It is most common in young, newly-acquired birds that have been particularly stressed due to crowding, chilling, shipping or intensive breeding. In birds that have been smuggled illegally into this country, the incidence of psittacosis is much higher. Fortunately, it is less common in birds that have been in the home environment for a long time. Recently purchased birds are at the highest risk.

The disease is spread by close contact with sick birds shedding the organism in their feces and in the air via respiratory secretions. Young birds are more susceptible to a severe debilitating infection than are adult birds. The disease can take from a few days to many months to become apparent. The bird may also become a carrier of the disease without showing any signs.

THERE IS NO GROUP OF SIGNS THAT ARE DISTINCTIVELY CHARACTERISTIC OF PSITTACOSIS. However, the following signs in a bird *may* suggest the possibility:

- Lack of appetite or weight loss
- Depression and listlessness
- Watery green droppings
- Sneezing or nasal discharges
- Sudden death

Positive diagnosis in live birds is difficult. Your veterinarian relying on the history, physical exam, and sometimes blood tests and radiographs can make a tentative diagnosis of psittacosis. Isolation of the causitive organism is required for a positive diagnosis in a live bird.

The only approved drug for treatment of psittacosis is chlortetracycline. The use of correct dosages and length of treatment, which is 45 days, is critical. Methods of administration are also variable and your veterinarian can decide on the best course. Often other forms of supportive care will also be necessary. Even with proper treatment some birds will not survive.

Birds legally entering this country are quarantined and treated with chlortetracycline for only 30 days. Though this will not completely eliminate the disease, it will greatly reduce its incidence.

In addition to properly treating the bird or birds affected, other important steps include:

1. ISOLATE ALL SICK BIRDS.
2. Thoroughly clean and disinfect the cage and its surroundings.
3. Keep circulation of feathers and dust to a minimum.
4. Bird droppings and all other contaminated equipment should be incinerated or saturated with disinfectant and placed in plastic bags before disposing, so as not to pollute the environment.
5. Keep human contact to an absolute minimum.

In man, the infection occurs through contact with a sick bird or a bird shedding the psittacosis organisms. The symptoms are similar to an influenza-like illness characterized by fever, headache, respiratory distress, and lethargy. If any of these symptoms appear, consult your physician and let him know you have had contact with birds.

Newcastle Disease

Newcastle disease is a serious viral disease found in all domestic birds and many wild birds all over the world. It was first seen in Newcastle-on-Tyne, England in 1926. From there it spread worldwide and was discovered in the United States in 1944. It is the most feared bird disease. Not only does it have a near 100% death rate in affected birds but also it can spread quickly to poultry causing enormous losses of entire flocks.

The are several forms of the disease. The abbreviation VVND (VELOGENIC VISCEROTROPIC NEWCASTLE DISEASE) is the most frequently encountered form. It is highly contagious to poultry and can literally wipe out an entire flock within a few days.

Infected exotic birds may spread the disease to poultry. Bird droppings, respiratory discharges and contaminated equipment can also transmit the disease. Newly-acquired young birds, especially smuggled ones are at the highest risk.

Signs to Watch For:

• Nervous disorders are common and include paralysis of wings or legs

- Muscle twitching
- Head and eye twitching
- Severe respiratory infection
- Diarrhea, often bloody.

THERE IS NO GROUP OF CLINICAL SIGNS THAT ARE DISTINCTIVELY CHARACTERISTIC OF NEWCASTLE DISEASE. Many other far less serious diseases will appear similar.

Most all birds with Newcastle disease will die within a week. A definitive diagnosis is dependent on sophisticated laboratory tests which are usually run at government veterinary laboratories. All birds found to have the disease must be destroyed. There is NO treatment available.

In any outbreak the government will become involved and will advise the owners as to the best course of action. This disease is actually uncommon in caged birds, but because of its great importance to the poultry industry we must always be on the lookout for it.

The strict importation and quarantine laws presently in existence have originated largely as a result of efforts to limit the spread of both psittacosis and Newcastle disease.

Pacheco's Disease

This viral disease is usually associated with areas where multiple birds are kept. This would include quarantine stations, aviaries, pet shops, or individual birds that have been recently obtained from one of these places. Only psittacine birds are affected. Finches, canaries and mynahs have not been found to be susceptible.

About the only consistent sign is rapid death in one or many of the birds that are kept in nearby quarters. It usually takes only a few hours and sometimes up to a day or two after the first hint of illness is detected for them to die. The only signs may be diarrhea first, followed in the later stages with appetite loss and depression.

Stress is implicated as being an important factor in the onset of disease. Once again, stress lowers the birds' resistance to infection. The disease is probably transmitted by infected droppings contaminating the food and water supply. Diagnosis requires sophisticated laboratory tests and is done on the dead bird. In multiple-bird households accurate diagnosis is important to help control outbreaks.

Patagonian and Nanday conures are suspected of being carriers transmitting Pacheco's to other birds. No treatment is available. It is not transmitted to poultry or man and therefore does not get the notoriety that surrounds outbreaks of psittacosis and Newcastle diseases.

Important Points to Remember:

1. Vaccines are not available for use in pet birds. They are available for the protection of poultry. Never use poultry vaccines on pet birds as

they may cause serious side effects. In the years to come, we hope that vaccines will be available for pet birds against some of these dreaded diseases.

2. Isolating all new birds for at least 30 days before introducing them to other birds will help minimize any disease outbreaks.

3. Buying new birds from reputable breeders or pet shops will greatly minimize the risks of disease. These infamous diseases are uncommonly seen in birds that have been well-cared-for prior to sale.

4. Remember that newly-purchased birds are at the highest risk. Avoid birds that may have been smuggled into the country and *NEVER* bring birds of uncertain background into immediate contact with your other birds.

13

Veterinarians: When to Seek Professional Help

If your bird is sick, it's always best to consult a veterinarian knowledgeable in avian medicine. ONLY a veterinarian is capable of diagnosing the problem and administering the treatment that is most likely to succeed. Remember that diseases of birds, and all animals for that matter, are every bit as complicated and varied as diseases of humans.

More and more veterinarians are now developing the skills needed to work with birds. The newly-formed Association of Avian Veterinarians is a nationwide group of practitioners dedicated to advancing the knowledge of avian medicine. Many serious avian veterinarians are now members.

To find a good avian veterinarian talk with local pet shops, bird clubs, veterinarians and the local veterinary association for the names of the doctors that treat birds. Do this before an emergency arises. Keep the doctor's name handy for quick reference. It is also a good idea for both you and your bird to become acquainted with the doctor you have selected. Be sure to find out about his weeknight/weekend emergency care coverage—*before* an emergency occurs.

Veterinarians: When you need their help—

- Emergencies
- Whenever your bird isn't acting right and you want the best possible care.
- When home treatment fails.
- For any problems requiring radiographs, laboratory tests or surgery.
- For any problems requiring prescription drugs, including antibiotics.
- For well-bird examinations, including newly purchased birds and yearly check-ups.
- Whenever you have questions about your bird, in both health and disease.

Important: If your bird is ill, don't let it go for days before seeking veterinary

167

care. The sooner the disease is under proper treatment, the better the chances are for an early and uneventful recovery.

Evaluating the Doctor

It is easy to know if you like the doctor and feel comfortable in personal communication. But, it's another thing to evaluate the doctor's medical skills.

Choosing your veterinarian is as important as selecting your family doctor. Here are some suggestions that should help.

- You must feel comfortable with him/her. Confidence and trust in the doctor's ability is first and foremost.
- Time should be spent explaining the nature of the problem to you and its treatment in simple and understandable terms.
- All your questions should be answered.
- Your bird should be handled gently and carefully.
- The doctor's age is not important. Knowledge of and experience with birds are what matter.
- A good veterinarian will recognize his or her own limitations and will refer the patient to a specialist when these limitations are exceeded.
- Knowledge in avian medicine is growing rapidly. Ask if your veterinarian keeps current and attends continuing education meetings.
- A diagnosis cannot, unfortunately, be made over the phone. However, your veterinarian should be available for questions on cases currently under his/her treatment.
- Emergency coverage should be available.

Evaluating the Hospital and Staff

- The hospital should be clean.
- The staff should be knowledgeable, well-groomed and friendly.
- Many veterinarians will be happy to offer a tour of their hospital at a convenient time.
- The hospital should be well-equipped to handle birds. Some of the more important "tools-of-the-trade" include: an oxygen cage and heat source, radiograph machine, laboratory facilities, anesthesia and surgery equipment. There should also be an assortment of small, hand instruments and a wide variety of medications.

The Complete Exam

The cornerstones of any examination are a thorough history and physical examination. When visiting your veterinarian you should be prepared to answer these questions about your bird.

- Approximate age and sex, when known.
- Length of ownership and where purchased (private breeder, pet shop, etc.)

Waiting room

—Tony Costanza

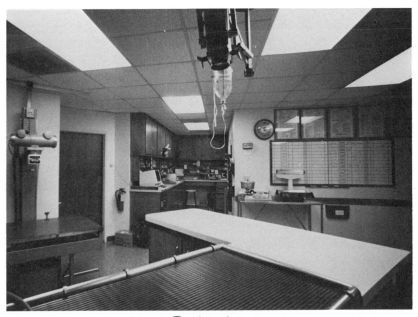

Treatment room

—Tony Costanza

- The main complaint. What are the signs and when did they begin?
- Has the bird been exposed to other birds? Are any other birds sick? Are there any newly-acquired birds in the house? Are any family members ill?
- Are there any previous medical problems? (If your bird has been treated by another doctor have the records forwarded to your new veterinarian.)
- Breeding history, if applicable.
- Appetite—bird's diet including types of seeds and any vitamin and mineral supplements it is receiving.
- Questions concerning the behavior and activity level of your bird. For example, the amount of playing or talking that your bird is doing. Is it exhibiting any abnormal behaviors?
- Have there been any changes noticed in the feathers? Molting? Picking or pulling at the feathers?
- Have there been any recent changes in the bird's home environment? Has the cage been moved? Is the bird in a new cage? New roommate or loss of an old roommate (yours or the bird's)?
- Type of housing.
- Free flight or confined to the cage?
- Any chewing on objects in cage or around the house?
- Has any home treatment been attempted? If so, what and for how long?

In Chapter 8 the basics of the visual examination of a bird were discussed. It is easy to teach someone the steps involved in conducting a complete examination. It is another thing to have acquired the knowledge and practical experience of determining what is normal and what is abnormal, and how to differentiate one problem from another similar-appearing problem. This is where the avian veterinarian plays such a critical role.

A complete examination should include:

1. Examination of the bird's environment, when possible, i.e. cage and furnishings.
2. Observation of the bird from a short distance (See Chapter 8).
3. Physical examination of the restrained bird. This must include a systematic evaluation of all areas of the body.

Note: In cases of a severe respiratory infection or shock, your veterinarian might choose to avoid the physical exam all together. It could prove to be too stressful and life-threatening.

Veterinarians and Their Fees

Veterinary fees are variable. They are based on the cost of at least eight years of college education and the costs of maintaining a full-service, fully-equipped hospital, along with a reasonable profit.

Hospital cages with oxygen and temperature control are a valuable aid in treating sick birds. These were designed and built by Paul Ridgway. *—Tony Costanza*

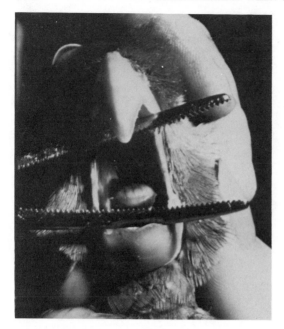

The mouth is examined to determine signs of infection or nutritional deficiencies.

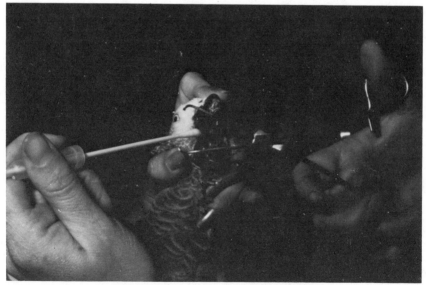

Collecting a sample of bacteria from the mouth for a culture and sensitivity test.

Your veterinarian should discuss the fees before any testing or treatment is undertaken. An estimate of the charges should be available. However, at times it can be difficult to give an exact figure.

Going to the Veterinarian—What to Bring

1. Bring your bird in its own cage. (Do not clean it so that the actual environment, including the droppings, can be examined.) If the cage is too large to move, use a cardboard box or other similar container. Be sure there are holes for ventilation. Fold up the cage paper and bring it along.
2. Empty the water cup just before leaving so it doesn't spill in transit.
3. If there is grit, remove it. Sick birds can overeat it and get an impaction of the gizzard.
4. Lower or remove the perches if your bird is showing any instability or excessive weakness.
5. Bring any medications or other supplements that the bird has been given.

DIAGNOSTIC TESTING

The most worthless and expensive therapy given a patient is when an improper diagnosis leads to the administration of incorrect treatment. Veterinarians perform laboratory tests to help them arrive at an accurate diagnosis and this is often the key to effective treatment and rapid recovery. The tests have become very sophisticated and ultimately have led to the better health and longevity of our fine feathered friends.

There are numerous diagnostic tests available. No one test will consistently yield an answer. Sometimes it becomes necessary to run a few different tests so that the puzzle can be correctly pieced together for the correct diagnosis and most effective treatment.

Below is a brief explanation of the most commonly performed diagnostic tests. Some of these tests may not be available in all parts of the country at this writing.

Blood Tests

Since blood flows to every organ in the body, an abnormality in one of the organs will frequently cause changes in the blood picture indicating an abnormality.

Blood tests are especially valuable for early detection of diseases before any outward signs become apparent and before reaching crisis proportions. It is an excellent test to perform on newly-purchased birds and for yearly check-ups. The blood is usually collected from clipping a toenail short or occasionally from a blood feather or from one of the veins in the neck, wing or leg. New techniques have been developed that now allow a variety of blood tests to be done on very small amounts of blood.

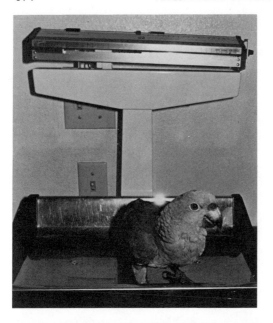

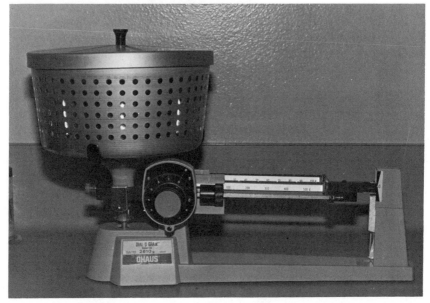

Daily weighings of hospitalized birds gives important information. It can quickly be determined if birds are eating sufficient amounts to maintain their weight or if supplemental feeding will be required.

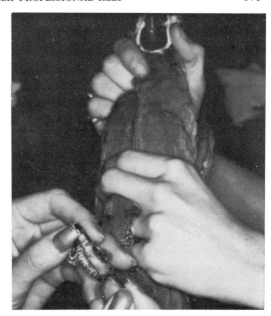

Collecting blood from a macaw. —*Tony Costanza*

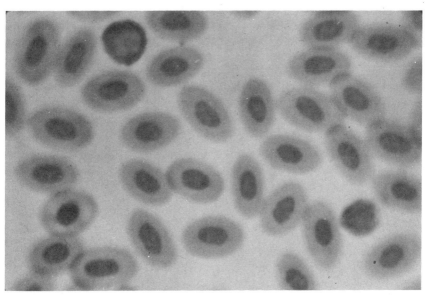

A microscopic look at blood cells from a bird.

Urinalysis

This test is not commonly performed on birds. It is helpful when diabetes is suspected. In this instance the urine will contain large amounts of sugar.

Radiology

Birds are ideally suited for radiographs because of their anatomy. Their system of air sacs surrounding the internal organs, allow for excellent contrast and visibility of the other organs. The ability to "see" inside the body often proves invaluable for diagnosing a variety of problems. These include abnormal changes in the shape and size of the organs, visualizing foreign bodies and fractures.

Radiographic equipment is expensive, but should be available in most veterinary hospitals. As one would imagine, it is almost impossible to have birds hold still to take the pictures. There are many "tricks-of-the-trade" which include sedation and specially developed bird restraint devices that are safe, painless and lessen the stress of handling.

Tissue Biopsies

A piece of tissue can be surgically removed and submitted to a laboratory where a veterinary pathologist can examine the tissue microscopically and interpret the findings. This is an excellent way to arrive at a diagnosis, as well as determining the potential for healing of the organ. Virtually any tissue can be submitted. Tumors or any abnormal growths should be biopsied.

Bacteriology (Culture and Sensitivity)

Samples of the bacteria causing an infection are commonly taken from the mouth, nostrils, eyes, skin and droppings. The bacteria are grown (cultured) on special media, then tested with a variety of antibiotics. The effectiveness of the tested antibiotics (sensitivity) for killing the bacteria can be measured in this way. This information is important because it eliminates the guesswork in selecting the most effective antibiotic. This will help lead to a rapid recovery and minimize the risk of it spreading to other parts of the body and to other birds.

Fecal Exam

All birds should have their feces checked periodically for parasites. When present, they can cause weakness, weight loss and diarrhea. A fresh sample should be submitted to your veterinarian for examination.

Endoscopy

An *endoscope* is a small diameter precision optical instrument that can be inserted into the abdomen through a small incision. Many of the internal

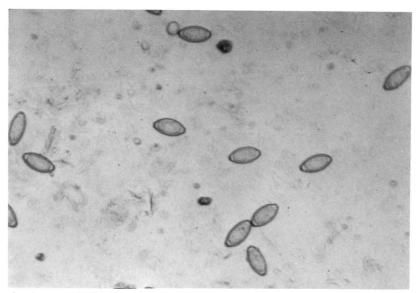

A microscopic look at parasite eggs from the droppings of an infested bird.
—*K. Mahoney*

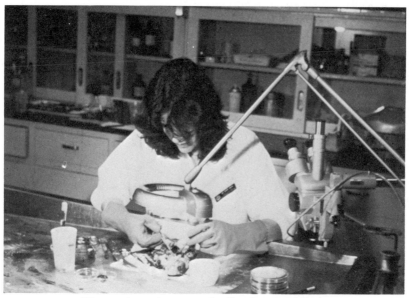

The post-mortem examination is valuable
to determine the exact cause of death.

Surgical Removal of Foreign Bodies

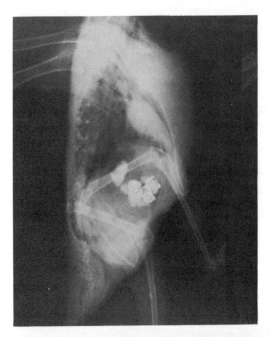

The radiograph at the left clearly shows a quantity of foreign bodies in the gizzard of the affected bird. In the photograph below, the anesthetized bird receives medication just prior to surgery. The plastic tube leading into the mouth is the *endotracheal tube* that administers the anesthetic agent.

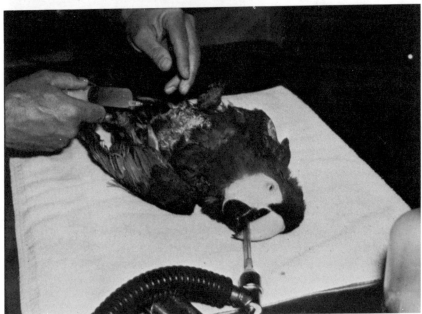

he Gizzard of a Scarlet Macaw

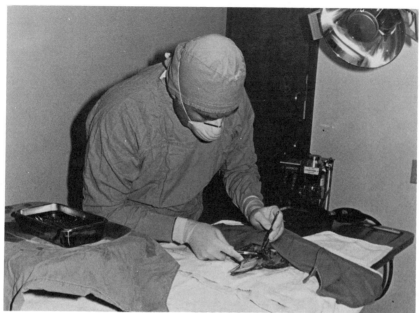

Surgery to remove the foreign bodies is being performed by Dr. Ron Ridgway (above) while the inset shows the various items this bird ingested. No wonder it got sick! A week following surgery the patient continues to do nicely.

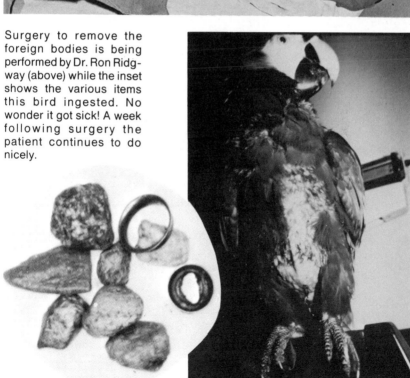

organs can be seen and some abnormalities can be detected. This is also the instrument commonly used to surgically sex birds. This is a wonderful tool and in the years to come will, no doubt, find many more uses.

Post-Mortem Examination

Unfortunately not all birds can be saved. When a bird dies, a post-mortem examination to determine the exact cause of death can be very informative. It is especially valuable when other exposed birds have been showing similar signs. Disease outbreaks can then be more effectively controlled or prevented altogether.

The dead bird should be wrapped in newspaper or placed in a plastic bag and refrigerated. Do *not* freeze. Submit the body to the veterinarian as soon as possible.

Therapy

Some of these diagnostic tests take a day or more to obtain the results. In these instances, your veterinarian will still begin treatment immediately. Then, when the test results are in, the therapy can be changed or altered to achieve the best response.

Over the past few years, the medical and surgical care of birds has been improved dramatically. More birds are now being saved than ever before. This trend is continuing as our knowledge of birds continues to grow. Specific treatment of bird diseases is discussed elsewhere in this book.

Surgery

Surgery is often necessary to achieve a cure. Such problems may include fractures, foreign bodies, tumors, abscesses, crop impactions, hernias and occasionally egg binding. Your veterinarian should take the time and explain the benefits and the risks of performing the surgery.

The actual procedure is very similar to surgery on other animals:

- Prior to anesthesia, blood tests and radiographs may be necessary. This is not only to diagnose the problem correctly, but also to rule out any other diseases that might complicate the anesthesia or surgery and increase the risks.
- The bird must be very relaxed prior to surgery and is, therefore, usually hospitalized at least a few hours, if not, the night before.
- Medication will usually be administered prior to anesthesia to make the bird more relaxed.
- Once anesthetized, the feathers around the surgical area are plucked and the skin thoroughly cleansed.
- The heart rate and respiratory rate are closely monitored to determine the depth of anesthesia and to help minimize any potential problems.
- Surgical instruments designed for human eye surgery are most often used because of their small size.

- Blood loss is always kept to a minimum.
- Speed is important, but close attention to details is critical for proper healing to take place.
- Suture material of small diameter is used to close the wounds both internally and on the skin.
- Birds may flop around while awakening from anesthesia and must be watched closely so as not to injure themselves.

GENERAL INSTRUCTIONS FOR BRINGING YOUR BIRD HOME FROM THE HOSPITAL

1. Remove all grit from the cage for at least a week, then begin to mix only small amounts into the food gradually over the next few weeks as has been previously mentioned.
2. Provide a relaxing, quiet environment. It's usually best to separate the bird from other pets until recovery is complete.
3. The environmental temperature should be kept at 80°-85° F.
4. Avoid drafts and frequent changes in temperature.
5. Follow the instructions of your veterinarian. Any medications sent home must be given the correct number of times each day spread out over a 24 hour period. Be sure to also give it for as many days as instructed.
6. Watch for adequate food and water intake.
7. Watch the droppings. If they were abnormal, as your bird starts to recover, the droppings should begin to return to normal.

14

Home Medical Care

BIRDS ARE GOING TO GET SICK. Regardless of your best efforts, it's inevitable that your bird is going to become sick at some time or another during its life. By following the suggestions in the book and practicing good preventive medicine you will minimize disease but never eliminate it.

When your bird does become ill, follow these simple guidelines. Put them into effect immediately.

BASIC REQUIREMENTS FOR ALL SICK BIRDS:

1. Warmth
2. Food and water within easy reach
3. Rest and relaxation
4. Medication, if needed

Warmth

All sick birds need an environment that is 80°-85° F (27°-30° C). If the cage is small, a heating pad can be used. Cover it with a towel and place the cage on top of it. A heating pad can also be attached to the cage wall, but be careful that bigger birds do not chew on it. Start off with a low setting. Try a space heater placed eight to ten feet from the cage. (The days of turning up the central heat are over!) Overall, an infra-red heat lamp is usually the best source of heat. Placed two to four feet away from the cage, it gives ample warmth and soft lighting. A standard light bulb is not recommended. The bright light can be stressful and can also change the bird's photoperiods.

It may also be a good idea with any of these heating sources to cover two-thirds of the cage with a blanket or towel. This helps keep the heat in and the drafts out. A thermometer, especially the thin plastic aquarium-type, is an excellent way to monitor the temperature. Attach it to the inside or outside of the cage, but in a place where it will be inaccessible to the bird.

If the bird becomes too warm it will keep its body feathers in close, its wings outstretched and panting will be excessive. If this happens, immediately lower the temperature and refer to the section on overheating.

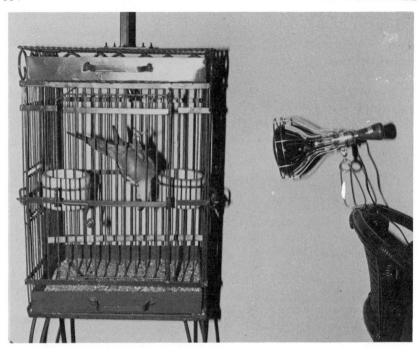

Heat is a necessity for sick birds. A heat lamp placed a few feet from the cage is a very effective and safe way of supplying the needed warmth.

—Tony Costanza

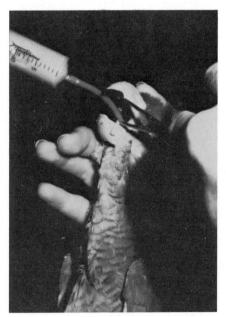

Tube-feeding showing correct placement of feeding tube in esophagus and crop.

Rest and Relaxation

Minimize stress and increase the sleeping time to twelve to sixteen hours a day. Keep the noise level down. Dimmed lighting when possible is also a good idea.

Water

Dehydration can be a very serious problem and must be corrected rapidly. Sick birds often do not drink adequate amounts. If the droppings are excessively wet, dehydration can become a real problem. Try feeding more fruits.

For rehydration as well as providing quick energy, try the following:

1. Honey or Karo Syrup™ added to water (4 tbsp/qt)
2. Gatorade™
3. Orange Juice

Amounts of Fluids to Give

Finches/canaries	2-3 drops
Budgerigars	5-8 drops
Cockatiels	10-15 drops
Amazon parrots	1-2 cc
	(1/5-2/5 tsp)
Large cockatoos and macaws	2-5 cc
	(2/5 tsp)

These fluids are given slowly by plastic dropper. They can, if necessary, be given every 20-30 minutes and repeated a few times.

Food

Every effort must be made to see that your bird keeps eating. Many sick birds lose their appetite. This serves only to make them weaker and less able to fight off the disease. Whether your bird is perching or on the cage floor, keep the food nearby. If the bird is on the floor, scatter the food around it. (This is not hygienic, but in the circumstances, hygiene is not important.) Feed the most highly-favored foods. It may become necessary to force feed a sick bird.

VARIOUS FEEDING METHODS FOR SICK BIRDS

1. Hand Feeding or Dropper Feeding

This is a good safe method, but it is not practical for giving large amounts of food. For dropper feeding, try using a plastic medicine dropper, small spoon, syringe, rounded end of a chopstick or a small piece of cardboard. The food should be the consistency of thick paste and the recipe is the same as discussed under tube feeding.

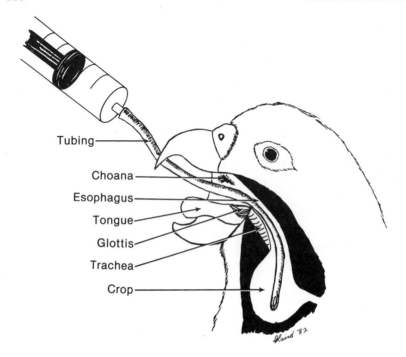

Fig. A

Tube feeding a bird.

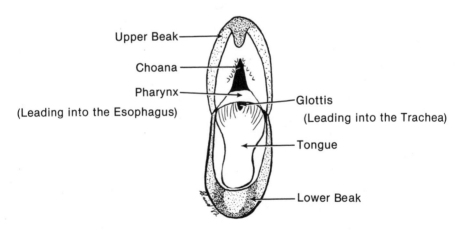

Fig. B

Simplified internal view of major structures seen when looking into a bird's mouth.

2. Tube Feeding

This is often one of the most important treatments for critically ill birds. Most diseases cause a marked decrease in appetite at the very time that nutritional needs are highest. Good nutrition is essential to help fight disease and repair damaged tissues. Rapid weight loss will usually occur due to the bird's high metabolic rates. Force feeding can be life-saving because it will provide the needed nutrients to help the body fight off the disease. It will keep the bird alive while the medication is working and the body begins to mend. The description of the technique is included but SHOULD NEVER be attempted without first having the technique demonstrated by a veterinarian. In inexperienced hands, severe injury to the bird can result. If the tube is accidentally passed down into the trachea, pneumonia and even death can result.

TUBE FEEDING TECHNIQUE

1. The food should be prepared and warmed prior to handling the bird.
2. Use a flexible rubber or plastic tube attached to a syringe. The end should be rounded or smooth so as to avoid traumatizing the tissues. A veterinarian can best advise as to the correct type and size of tubing and syringe based on the type of bird.
3. Measure the distance from the tip of the beak to the base of the neck and mark the tube accordingly.
4. Proper restraint is essential. Wrap the bird in a towel. Keep the body upright and hold the head firmly.
5. Stretch the neck to straighten the esophagus and provide a straight shot into the crop. The mouth may have to be forcibly opened using a speculum, gauze strips or other techniques as needed. The use of these can be explained by a veterinarian.
6. Moisten the tip of the tube with water, then, from the side of the beak pass it into the mouth. Slide it along the roof and with gentle pressure the tube should slip into the esophagus. Pass it down into the crop to the level of the mark on the tube. Note: If the tube does not go down gently, stop. Remove it and try again. Be sure the neck is stretched. DO NOT FORCE THE TUBE! The tube can be felt in the esophagus by gently feeling the neck on the right side. This is a good idea to do to be sure that the tube is not mistakenly in the trachea.
7. Administer a small amount of food at first and if it goes down smoothly, continue. Be careful not to put any pressure on the crop as it is filling.
8. Immediately after administering the formula, put the bird back into its cage. If regurgitation should occur, do not continue to restrain it. Allow it to shake its head. Regurgitation usually indicates the crop filled up and too much food was given at one time.

Frequency of Tube Feeding

This is variable and depends on the condition of the bird. For the first few days it may be necessary to feed every eight hours. After this, decrease the frequency and amount of feedings to encourage self-feeding. If the crop is still full from the previous feeding, do not give any more food.

Tube Feeding Recipes

There have been many recipes devised, and no one formula is magical. The formula must be balanced; be high in energy and protein; contain extra vitamins and minerals; and have sufficient bulk or fiber to stimulate gut motility. Here are a few suggestions:

Formula #1

1 part quality dry dog or cat food
1 part grain cereal: Cream of Wheat™, Wheat Hearts™, oatmeal
1 hardboiled egg
Avian vitamins
To this a small amount of fruit such as apple, banana or orange can be added. Peanut butter can also be added. Place these ingredients together in a blender and mix well. Warm water can be added if needed to make a creamy consistency.

Formula #2

1 part Gevral™ Protein—Therapeutic Nutritional Supplement
1 part Gerber™ Mixed Cereal
2 parts Gerber™ Strained Mixed Vegetables
Add water to make a creamy consistency

Note: Gevral™ Protein Powder
        Lederle Laboratories Div., American Cyanamid Co.,
        Pearl River, NY 10965

Formula #3

Lafeber's Emeraid II™—"Therapeutic Nutrition for Sick Birds"
Manufactured by Dorothy Products
7278 Milwaukee Avenue
Niles, IL 60648

Amounts to Feed:

Canaries/finches	dropper feed (1/4-1/2 ml)
Budgies/lovebirds	1-3 mls
Cockatiels	3-6 mls
Amazon parrots	12-20 mls
Large cockatoos and macaws	30-40 mls

Medications

When used correctly, drugs are an aid to the ultimate healer—Mother Nature. Drugs will help relieve pain, control disease and promote healing. When used incorrectly, they can harm the patient, causing even more serious problems. Selecting the best drugs and their correct dosage is essential and only a veterinarian is qualified to do this. Birds present even more challenges than other animals, because drug knowledge in pet birds is still in its infancy. New drug information is being learned all the time, and these insights are helping us to save more birds than ever before.

Before giving any medication to your feathered friend, check with your veterinarian first. Your bird's life is at stake, so don't reach for the first drug a friend or salesperson says to try. If in doubt, don't give any medications. Accurate drug dosages are based on the correct weight of the animal and this must be known before administering any drugs.

There are many diseases that display the same general signs yet are very different and each requires specialized therapy. The "cure-all" medications that can be purchased over-the-counter are usually of minimal benefit. They are very general forms of treatment that rarely do much good. Never use human medicines unless directed by your veterinarian.

Antibiotics

Antibiotics have saved many lives that otherwise would have been lost. These chemical compounds are produced by microorganisms or synthesized by man. They inhibit the growth of other microorganisms, namely bacteria. Antibiotics are not effective against viruses, but are often used in viral infections. In these instances, they are given to prevent bacterial overgrowth in the animal's weakened condition. Many times antibiotics are combined with other drugs or treatments such as surgery, to achieve their greatest benefits.

There are numerous antibiotics in use because not all antibiotics are effective against all the various types of bacteria. A veterinarian will select the most effective antibiotic based on the probable bacteria causing the disease. A culture and sensitivity test may be recommended to determine the most effective antibiotic.

If these drugs are used incorrectly, then no benefits are gained. In fact, the bacteria can develop a resistance to the antibiotics or the infection may recur. In addition to selecting the right antibiotics, it is essential to use the correct dosage at the proper frequency and for the necessary length of time.

With any drug, there is a potential for unwanted side-effects. If you suspect a problem, discontinue the medication and contact your veterinarian immediately.

In addition to antibiotics, there are many other drugs that are used to control disease. Some of these more common drugs have been mentioned in the disease chapters of this book.

There are several ways of administering drugs. The same medication may be available in different forms, i.e., injectable, liquid, spray, powder, ointment or pill. The form in which it will be used depends upon the nature of the disease under treatment and the condition of the bird.

Some of the more common routes of administration include:

- *Medicating the water:* Remember a sick bird's water consumption usually decreases. This makes accurate dosing of medication very difficult. Some drugs may also change the color or taste of the water making it even less appealing. Some drugs, however, are best added to the water. Also, for flocks or an individual bird when an owner is unable to properly handle them, this is the preferred method.
- *Medicating the food:* Once again, accurate dosing becomes almost impossible. Sick birds usually eat less and the medication may collect at the bottom of the feeding dish. However, there are tetracycline-impregnated pellets or seeds which are effective for treating certain diseases such as psittacosis.
- *Medication given by mouth:* This is an ideal method for birds that can be handled easily, since near exact dosing of medication is possible. Occasionally the bird may shake some of the medication from its mouth. Try giving the liquid medication slowly, drop by drop, and allow the bird to swallow after every few drops. This will help eliminate this problem and also should minimize the risk of the medication entering the trachea and lungs which can cause serious problems. Use a plastic medicine dropper or plastic syringe. Most birds will, of course, have to be properly restrained while administering the medication.
- *Medication given by injection:* Many drugs are only available in injectable form. The exact dosing of medication also is possible. Learning to give injections and acquiring the knowledge of how often to give them and where on the body to give them requires considerable expertise. It is best left to a veterinarian unless under their supervision they demonstrate the technique and give explicit instructions on how often to give the drug. Intravenous injections are used by veterinarians to gain rapid effects of drugs in life-saving situations. Intramuscular (into the muscle) and subcutaneous (immediately beneath the skin) injections are most often given into the pectoral area.
- *Eye medications (Ophthalmics):* Use only medications that specifically state on the label that they are for use in the eye. Before home medicating any eye problems, check with your veterinarian.
- *Skin medications:* Powders or sprays are best. GREASY MEDICATIONS SHOULD BE AVOIDED SINCE THEY CAN DAMAGE THE FEATHERS.
- *Nose medications:* Antibiotics or decongestants are often used in the nose for birds with colds.
- *Medicating the air (Vaporization):* The use of a vaporizer or nebulizer to produce a warmed fine liquid mist is very helpful for treating most

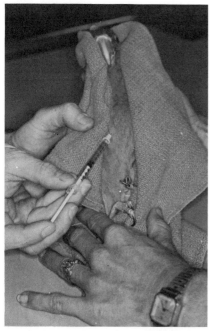

Giving an injection into the pectoral muscles of a bird. This procedure is best left to a veterinarian unless your doctor recommends it and properly demonstrates the technique. —*Tony Costanza*

Method for administering oral medication using a small syringe. Note: In most instances the bird will have to be restrained in a towel.

respiratory infections. It helps to soothe and moisturize the inflamed linings of the airway. Veterinarians will often add medications to the solution for greater benefit for some infections, especially those in the lungs and air sacs.

HOME EMERGENCY KIT

Scissors
Tweezers
Needle-nose pliers

Cotton-tipped swabs (Q-Tips®)
   Feeding tube and syringe
    (if provided and demonstrated
     by veterinarian)
Masking tape (1/2″ width)
Plastic medicine dropper

Sterile gauze pads
Towels

Heat source:
   Heat lamp or space heater
Environmental thermometer

Styptic powder
Hydrogen peroxide or
betadine solution
Telephone number of veterinarian:

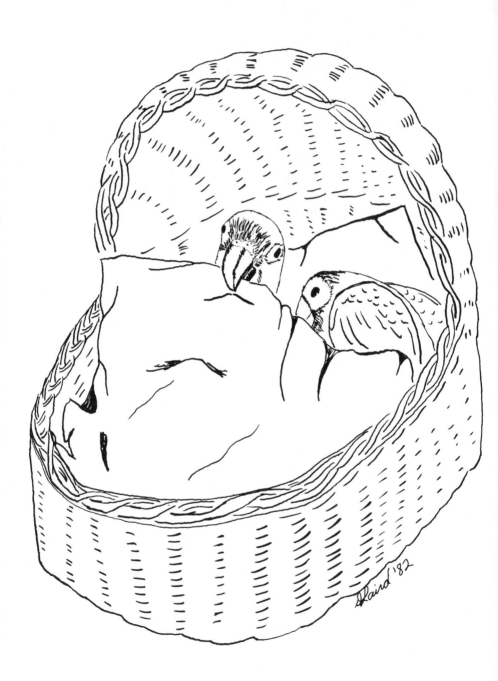

15

Bird Breeding

Co-author Betty Byers

Quick profits—minimal time. These are common misconceptions many people have about breeding birds. If breeding birds was easy, birds would be inexpensive and many more people would be in the business. Successful breeding usually requires many years of experience, a great deal of time and numerous frustrations before it begins to pay off. Think of it as a labor of love.

Before investing large sums of money, spend a little time first learning about birds and how to breed them. Pairs will produce young in a few months, years, or never. Visit with some breeders, bird clubs, and talk with as many knowledgeable people as possible. An excellent book to include in your library for those interested in bird breeding is Rosemary Low's *Parrots, Their Care and Breeding* (Poole and Dorset: Blandford Press, 1980.)

Captive-bred and/or hand-raised birds usually make the best pets. Wild-caught birds are generally more nervous and frightful. They are rarely as good pets as are domestically-raised birds. In the years to come, it will become increasingly difficult to export birds from their native countries. It is for these reasons that we must all work together towards perfecting our skills and enhancing our knowledge for improved bird breeding.

The following discussion is an overview of the factors necessary to begin your breeding program. It is not meant to provide all the answers. For some of the specific breeding requirements for each species refer to Appendix A, "Everything You Always Wanted To Know About . . ."

MATCHMAKER, MATCHMAKER

Factors Influencing The Choice of Species For Breeding

- Eye appeal and personality
- Breeding tendencies
- Neighbors and noise
- Feeding and housing requirements
- Time and attention required

For the beginning breeder, birds such as finches, budgerigars, and cockatiels are the ideal choices. It makes good common sense to start out with these for the following reasons:

- They breed readily in captivity.
- The sexes are usually distinguishable by coloration.
- They have minimal housing and feeding requirements.
- They provide good insights into bird management and behavior.
- Most importantly, they let you find out if you enjoy bird breeding without investing large sums of money.

The larger birds, such as cockatoos and macaws, though possibly more beautiful and a greater status symbol, are not necessarily as desirable. They are also far more difficult to breed and require much more experience in order to achieve success.

Note: Birds that are born with any abnormality should not be used for breeding. The deformity could be passed on to future generations. However, birds that have acquired a deformity during their life can still make good breeders.

SEXING YOUR BIRD

or

"Gee, it laid an egg. I thought it was a boy!"

Although uncommon for most species, cycling females can spontaneously lay eggs which are infertile and with no male nearby. For most birds, since there are rarely any sexually distinct physical or behavioral characteristics observable, other methods of determining sex have had to be evolved.

The first requirement necessary for a successful breeding program is a true pair, and therefore, it is essential to know your birds' true sexes. If you are not going to breed your bird, then remember he or she knows what sex it is and will be just as happy whether or not you know its sex.

The correct determination of sex has been a long standing problem. Over the years many methods have been tried, some very scientific and others quite the opposite. A few of these are very reliable and many of them are consistently unreliable.

The ideal method to match pairs is to place a large number of the same species in an enclosure and let them pair off themselves. With the larger birds this is not practical and is very costly. Therefore, other methods have had to be developed. These include:

1. *Surgical sexing:* This is currently the MOST reliable method. A knowledgeable veterinarian must perform the procedure. The bird is restrained with or without sedative drugs and a small incision is made

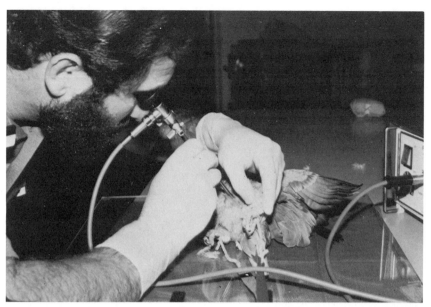

The author surgically sexing a bird using an *endoscope.* *—Tony Costanza*

Galvanized wire cages are a good way of housing a breeding group of small birds.
                                                                    —Tony Costanza

into the left flank. Using an otoscope (also used for ear exams) or an endoscope (a precision optical instrument used for visual examination of body cavities), it is inserted into the abdomen and the ovary or testicle is viewed directly. An experienced veterinarian will have a very high success rate with minimal risk to the bird.

2. *Fecal steroid analysis:* The San Diego Zoo first began this research measuring the ratio of estrogen and testosterone in the feces. There are still testing problems associated with this method. At this time it is not reliable enough to make it a practical sexing procedure.

3. *Genetic sexing:* This involves examining the chromosomes in blood cells or the pulp in a growing feather. This method is still in its infancy, not widely available, and expensive. It may become more practical in the future.

4. *Observation:* There are still many other methods that are suggested for determining sex. Unfortunately, with one exception, physical observations are unreliable. An experienced breeder who becomes very familiar with one species may be able to sex chicks within the first few months of their life. This is based on their physical and behavioral characteristics.

MANAGEMENT

Regardless of the size of your operation, it is important to develop a regular routine so as not to forget to perform all the varied and necessary tasks. Caring for birds is time-consuming; the temptation to buy more birds is tremendous, but do not own more than you have time to adequately care for or too many problems will arise.

Good management of your birds today will pay off with large dividends in the future. Your routine should include the following:

Daily Routine

1. *Feeding and watering:* Do this in the early morning hours at about the same time each day. Remove any uneaten fruits and vegetables at the end of the day.

2. *Inspection/Observation:* All birds should be looked at and observed for any problems. Watch for abnormal droppings, decreased food intake or ruffled appearance.

3. *Social contact:* It is important that your birds get to know you. It will have a calming effect on them, make them feel more secure and less likely to injure themselves from fright.

4. *Environmental temperature:* Watch for temperature extremes and avoid abrupt temperature changes. Note: Healthy birds adapt well to cold. However, dampness and cold together can cause sickness.

5. *Treatment of sick birds as needed:* These birds must be kept isolated from the others.
6. *Cleaning cages and flights:* Cages should be cleaned daily. Flights should be cleaned every few days. Concrete floors should be hosed down daily and dirt floors should be raked daily. The entire enclosure should be disinfected periodically.

Additional Routines

1. *Rodent control:* This can be a major problem. Rodents can carry disease, contaminate and eat the food, and disturb nesting birds.
2. *Nest box inspection:* During the breeding season, quietly examine the boxes twice daily looking for eggs and any problems that might arise. During the rest of the year check the boxes weekly for rodents.
3. *Seasonal management:* This is mainly for outdoor aviaries. In cold climates, enclosed shelters are a good idea. Check for water freezing and consider installing some kind of warming system. Be sure the food is of the highest quality. During severe cold weather, the inexpensive polyethylene plastic sheeting can be used to cover the outer walls. In hot weather, be sure good ventilation is present. A sprinkler or misting system can be installed to cool the enclosures and shower the birds.
4. *Record keeping:* Like any business, good financial records are important. Also, each bird should have its own record consisting of breeding history, number and size of clutches and health history. Each chick should have its growth rate charted. Include space for general observations on each bird. This information can be shared and is helpful for other breeders as well.

HOUSING

Proper housing is necessary to keep your birds happy and healthy. They must be comfortable and protected from weather extremes and unwanted visitors such as wild animals, dogs, cats, and mischievous people.

Major considerations:
Cages vs. Flights
Indoors vs. Outdoors

Factors to be considered before construction:

Space available	Species breeding
Neighbors and noise	Number of birds kept
Zoning laws	Future expansion plans
Climate	Hobby vs. Occupation
Expense	

SITE SELECTION

Careful thought and planning is necessary to achieve the most ideal end result. In addition to the factors listed above, select the area that is best protected from foul weather. Consider the direction from which most storms come and build on the opposite side of the house. In warm areas avoid sites that are in the direct sun.

Indoor housing is ideally suited for the smaller birds. Basements, attics, garages and spare rooms provide good locations.

HOUSING CONSTRUCTION

Welded wire cages are ideally suited for indoor use, and can be easily made by the do-it-yourselfer to the desired size. These are not strong enough for the large parrots with powerful beaks, such as macaws. Any wire used for these birds should be chain link.

There are many companies now offering an excellent assortment of prefabricated flights in a variety of shapes and sizes. For the do-it-yourselfer the possibilities are endless.

Design Considerations

The best of both worlds would be an indoor shelter connected to an outdoor flight cage.

The conventional shape is rectangular. The dimensions depend on the species to be kept and the space available. The length is most important for birds such as cockatiels, grass parakeets, and rosellas that like to fly. These can be as long as 20 feet. The width should be at least 2½ feet for the small birds and six feet for the larger parrots. The height is normally six feet, making it suitable for the owner to stand upright inside the aviary.

Be sure to design your aviary for easy cleaning. A "safety area" using a set of double doors spaced a few feet apart or an enclosed walkway will minimize problems with escaped birds. Feeding and watering stations and nest boxes should be easily accessible for both you and your birds.

The doors should open to the inside, be at least four feet high and not reach the full height of the enclosure. Use a heavy safety latch that can be padlocked.

Construction Materials

Wood has long been the conventional building material. Its two major disadvantages are that it cannot be disinfected and it is easily gnawed on and damaged by the larger birds. With steel or plastics, such as PVC plumbing pipe, these problems can be avoided. The wire gauge depends on the types of birds. For the larger macaws and cockatoos be sure to use heavy chain link. Galvanized wire will help prevent rust. Pull the wire very tightly so beaks and

Nest boxes come in all sizes and shapes.
—*Tony Costanza*

Flight cages are ideal for housing larger parrots. —*Dale R. Thompson*

feet do not get caught in the corners. Painting wire black not only has added eye appeal, but the birds are more easily viewed. Always use two layers of wire between adjoining cages, or better yet, keep them separated by a few inches to prevent birds from hurting their neighbors.

Flooring Materials

Concrete laid over wire mesh for reinforcement is best and also the most hygienic. Lay it on a slight slope and place a drainage hole at the lower end so it is easier to hose down. Dirt or grass flooring is impossible to adequately clean and disinfect.

Roofing Materials

A variety of materials such as wood, tile, and asphalt shingles work well. In very cold or warm climates, consider using a double roof with a six-inch space between the two layers. This will help avoid temperature extremes, especially if insulation material is added.

Nest Boxes

These are important for stimulating birds to start breeding. They also offer a quiet, secluded retreat. They are usually made of wood, but metal, such as trash cans, are often used for the larger birds. The wood should be at least 3/4 inch thick for insulation and for minimizing the effects of gnawing. The side dimensions should be approximately equal to the bird's body length, which will make it cozy for the two birds. The height should be two to three times the width. The entrance hole should be barely large enough for the birds to squeeze through. Wooden dowels or small pieces of wood forming steps are a good idea to place on the inside wall leading up to the entrance hole. An inspection door located at the top or side of the box is essential. The box must be kept dry and dark as possible. Attach it high up in a sheltered area of the aviary wall or on the outside of the cage.

Egg Laying

Depending on species, the hen will lay from one to eight eggs, usually a day apart. Just before laying begins, she will spend increasingly longer periods of time in the nest box, the lower abdomen will become swollen and the droppings looser.

Egg Incubation

Incubation or "egg sitting" usually begins shortly after the first egg is laid. Usually the female has this responsibility, but in some species this is shared.

Occasionally it may be necessary to artificially incubate the eggs in an incubator. The reasons will include: parents failing to incubate, parents

Egg incubator

—Tony Costanza

breaking the eggs, or as a means to increase egg laying leading to greater productivity. The correct temperature and humidity are vitally important to achieve the best results.

Determining Egg Fertility

After five to seven days the eggs can be "candled." At this stage, holding the egg over a flashlight will determine if it is fertile or not. A circular red spot with blood vessels coming out from it indicates a fertile egg. An infertile or "clear egg" lacks this spot.

Egg Hatching

Eggs will usually hatch in two to five weeks, depending on species. The chick will "pip" using its egg tooth to puncture the shell and then in up to 72 hours will break out. The parents rarely assist in this ritual.

Newly-Hatched Chicks

The first two to three weeks are always the most critical. When the parents are feeding their young, it is best to feed them increased amounts of

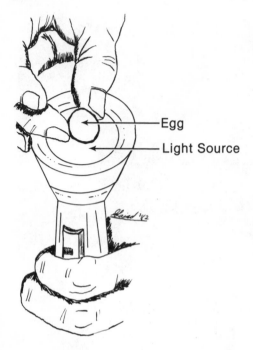

Fig. A

Candling egg to determine
fertility.

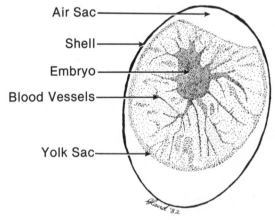

Fig. B

General appearance of
candled fertile egg at about
the 7th day of development.

food high in protein as discussed in Chapter 3. Be sure to inspect the nest box daily to be certain the parents are feeding their young.

The young birds will leave the nest box fully feathered from a few weeks of age to a few months, again, depending on species. These birds should begin feeding themselves shortly after leaving the nest while the parent feeding will be slowly eliminated.

Chicks raised entirely by their parents are technically wild birds. If the parents will permit it, play with the chicks daily while they are in the nest to get them used to human contact. Hand-feeding, beginning at a few weeks of age, is strongly encouraged for birds that are meant to be pets since they will become very trusting of people.

COMMON MISCONCEPTIONS ABOUT BREEDING

1. *Hand-fed birds do not make good breeders.*
   In most instances they will make fine breeders. Occasionally, especially with older birds, they may become so attached to their owner that they just won't accept another bird for a mate.
2. *A particular variety of bird is difficult to breed.*
   This can be true. However, some breeders seem to have better success than others when breeding certain varieties. When possible, develop a special expertise with a certain variety or species of bird and you are likely to achieve more fruitful results through your crop of specialized knowledge.
3. *Other frequently heard comments:*
   Nest box too large or too small, cage too small or too large, indoor breeding best, outdoor breeding best, etc. Rarely does an absolutely right way or wrong way exist. Use common sense and closely observe your birds. Develop a feeling for their needs and wants. Follow your instincts and keep an open mind when talking with other successful breeders.

Hand-feeding

Reasons for Hand-Feeding Young:
- Eggs that were artificially incubated
- Parents fail to feed the chicks
- One or both parents become sick or injured
- Parents mistreat the chicks
- For pets, hand-fed chicks make the most affectionate and trusting of all birds.

HAND-FEEDING REQUIRES A CONSIDERABLE AMOUNT OF TIME. Do you have it to give? Working full-time makes hand-feeding impossible. There are experienced people who can be hired to hand-feed when desired.

The chicks should be taken from their nest when they are only two to three weeks old to begin hand-feeding.

CARING FOR YOUNG CHICKS

Housing

To begin with, the chick must be completely separated from its parents. A nest box can be used temporarily. A small aquarium is preferred since it can be cleaned and sterilized easily and allows the chick and people the added benefit of viewing each other. A cardboard box cannot be easily cleaned and does not have windows.

A bed of paper toweling that is changed frequently or wood shavings is preferred since they will better absorb the droppings and help keep the chick clean. Occasionally birds have been reported to have ingested the shavings. If this occurs, switch to paper toweling.

As the birds continue to grow, after a few weeks they can be moved to a cage with a low perch.

Chicks from the same clutch can be housed together. To avoid the possibility of transmitting disease, it is best to keep birds from different clutches separated.

Heat

For their first few weeks of life chicks must be kept between 88°-94° F. After this period the temperature can be gradually decreased to 85°. A heating pad placed half under the box or aquarium works well. Additionally, a 40-60 watt red or blue light bulb placed near the top or a commercially available cage-top heater with thermostat makes a good heat source. Use a thermometer to monitor the temperature. Also place a small cup of water in these temporary quarters to increase the humidity.

If the birds become too warm they will begin to pant, and if too cold, they will shiver slightly.

Feeding

Spoons, plastic syringes or plastic eyedroppers are all good feeding utensils. An eyedropper is preferred by these authors since the outlet hole can be made variable in size with a pair of scissors. This method seems to be less messy.

THE CHICK MUST BE KEPT CLEAN AT ALL TIMES. If not, it will develop sores on the skin. Dried food becomes very difficult to remove, especially from the young bird's soft beak. A cotton ball moistened with warm water should be readily available and used as soon as droppings or food are noticed on the bird.

Conure with eggs and newborns in the nestbox.   *—Tony Costanza*

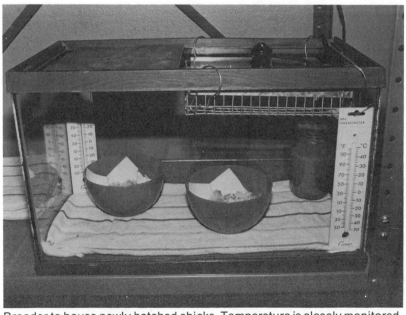

Brooder to house newly hatched chicks. Temperature is closely monitored.
                                                        —Tony Costanza

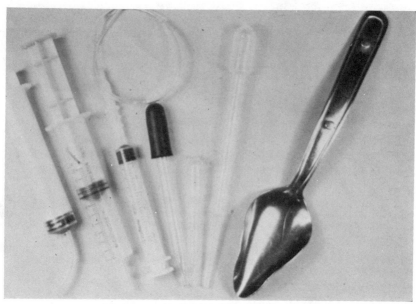

Various utensils used for handfeeding.

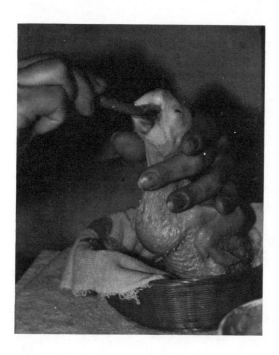

Handfeeding young
macaw. Notice the bal-
looning crop filling with
food. —*Tony Costanza*

Feeding Frequency

These young birds need a constant food supply to provide for their rapid growth. Their parents would be feeding them almost continuously. After removing them from their nest, wait for their crops to empty (indicating passage of the parent-fed food) before beginning hand-feeding.

For the first week, a newly-hatched chick must be fed every two hours around the clock. During the second week, the night feeding can be eliminated and the day feeding can be every 3-4 hours. When the pin feathers start to show, the birds can then be fed 3-4 times daily.

With a little experience, observing the crop-emptying time will give a good indication when to begin the next feeding. It is not necessary to wait until the crop is completely empty to feed again.

Weighing

The chicks should be weighed first thing every morning before feeding on a gram scale and their weight charted. With this information, normal patterns of weight gains will be known and any problems in the early stages can be quickly noted.

Hand Feeding Recipes

A readily available, quick, and easy formulation:

Gerbers™ Strained Mixed Vegetables	1 jar
Gerbers™ High Protein Cereal	1/4 cup
A quality dry dog food	1/4 cup
Avian vitamins	

To this can be added peanut butter and part of a hard boiled egg. The ingredients can be mixed in a blender. Add enough water to make a pasty consistency. It should be made up fresh daily, kept in your refrigerator and warmed before feeding.

San Diego Zoo's Hand-Feeding Formula

1½ cups water
½ cup Masa Harina™
1 raw egg yolk
½ cup hulled
  sunflower seeds
½ cup Wheat Hearts™
  cereal

1 tsp. trout chow
2 tsp. dark Karo™ syrup
½ ripe papaya
1 leaf greens (spinach,
  chard, etc.)
3½ tsp. Premix*

Bring water to a boil, add Wheat Hearts™ and trout chow and cook for three to five minutes. Let the mixture cool and add contents to a blender. Add the remaining ingredients and additional water as needed for a pasty consistency. This formula can be frozen. Try using ice cube trays. Thaw and serve warm as needed.

*Premix is a nutritional supplement and is available from:

> Zeigler Brothers, Inc.
> P.O. Box 95
> Gardners, PA 17324

Baby Bird Food:

*Lafeber's Nutri-Start is available from:

> Dorothy Products
> 7278 Milwaukee Avenue
> Niles, IL 60648

Weaning

When the chick becomes more difficult to feed and begins eating less, it is ready to be weaned. The age is, of course, variable depending on species, but can range from five weeks of age up to twelve weeks. It is normal for some weight loss to be noticed, particularly if weighing daily, as the growing chick prepares for flight.

This is their curious stage so begin to add seeds, both whole and shelled varieties, to their feeding cup and spread some out on the cage floor. Some fruits and vegetables can also be tried. The hand-feedings should be decreased to about two feedings daily, and over the next couple of weeks, slowly eliminated.

Before completely eliminating hand-feeding, be sure the bird is eating ample amounts of its new food. Watch it closely over the first few days after hand-feeding is stopped. By now the bird will be a few months old.

REPRODUCTIVE PROBLEMS

Mother Nature isn't perfect. A breeder, regardless of experience and care given his or her birds, will have breeding failures and other problems—it's inevitable.

Here are some of the more commonly encountered breeding-related disappointments:

Causes of Breeding Failures
- Both birds are the same sex
- Incompatibility of pair
- Birds are too young or too old
- Inadequate housing
- Disease

Common Causes of Chick Deaths
- Failure of parents to care for the young
- Disease
- Birth defects

EGG LAYING PROBLEMS

Egg Binding

Egg binding occurs when the egg gets stuck inside the hen and is not passing out when it should. During the egg-laying period some signs to watch for include "fluffing-up," straining, depression, exhaustion, and the hen is usually not on the perch but on the cage floor.

A spasm of the oviduct often prevents normal passage of the egg. The causes of this are:

- Stress, such as chilling
- Poor muscle tone, as in old age and being out of condition
- Calcium deficiency
- Soft-shelled eggs
- Large or misshapen eggs
- Overbreeding
- Diseases

First Aid for Egg Binding:

This is an emergency and treatment must begin immediately. Place the hen in a small, darkened cage or cardboard box. Increase the temperature to 85°-90° and be sure to provide water. Often these steps alone will be sufficient and help the egg to pass out.

Veterinary Care:

If within a few hours nothing happens, consult a veterinarian. Radiographs are helpful to confirm the diagnosis and help in selecting the best course of treatment. A few drops of lubricating jelly (K-Y®) or mineral oil placed carefully into the vent, combined with gentle manipulation may help to release the egg. Caution, this is very dangerous for an inexperienced person to attempt since the oil can get all over the feathers and the egg can easily break inside creating a life-threatening situation. Sedation may be given to relax the hen and aid in this obstetrical procedure. Calcium injections along with other medications are often given and help stimulate normal contractions of the oviduct. If these measures are not successful, surgery may be recommended to remove the egg.

There are numerous other reproductive problems that are seen in birds. It is beyond the scope of this book to discuss them here. The reader is referred to the bird disease books listed in the BIBLIOGRAPHY.

16

Rules for Transporting Birds

***Bringing Pet Birds Into The United States
(Quarantine Regulations)***

For those of you who will be traveling outside the U.S. and are planning on bringing a pet bird or two back with you, there are some special regulations with which you must become familiar.

The following is a pamphlet that is reprinted with permission from the United States Department of Agriculture—Animal and Plant Health Inspection Service (USDA-APHIS).

SPECIAL RULES FOR BRINGING PET BIRDS INTO THE UNITED STATES

What is a Pet Bird?

A pet bird is defined as any bird—except for poultry—intended for the personal pleasure of its individual owner and not for resale. Poultry, even if kept as pets, are imported under separate rules and quarantined at USDA animal import centers. Birds classified as poultry include chickens, turkeys, pheasants, partridge, ducks, geese, swans, doves, peafowl, and similar avian species.

Importing a Pet Bird

Special rules for bringing a pet bird into the United States (from all countries but Canada):

- USDA quarantine
- Quarantine space reservation
- Fee in advance
- Foreign health certificate
- Final shipping arrangements
- Two-bird limit

211

If you're bringing your pet bird into the country, you must . . .

Quarantine your bird (or birds) for at least 30 days in a USDA-operated import facility at one of nine ports of entry. The bird, which must be caged when you bring it in, will be transferred to a special isolation cage at the import facility. Privately owned cages cannot be stored by USDA. Birds will be cared for by veterinarians and other personnel of USDA's Animal and Plant Health Inspection Service (APHIS).

Reserve quarantine space for the bird. A bird without a reservation will be accepted only if space is available. If none exists, this bird either will be refused entry or be transported—at your expense—to another entry port where there is space. In any case, the fee described below must be paid before the bird is placed in quarantine.

Pay USDA an advance fee of $40 to be applied to the cost of quarantine services and necessary tests and examinations. Currently, quarantine costs are expected to average $80 for one bird or $100 per isolation cage if more than one bird is put in a cage. These charges may change without notice. You may also have to pay private companies for brokerage and transportation services to move the bird from the port of entry to the USDA import facility.

Obtain a health certificate in the nation of the bird's origin. This is a certificate signed by a *national government* veterinarian stating that the bird has been examined, shows no evidence of communicable disease, and is being exported in accordance with the laws of that country. The certificate must be signed within 30 days of the time the birds arrive in the United States. If not in English, it must be translated at your cost. Please note that Form 17-23, referred to later, includes an acceptable health certificate form in English.

Arrange for shipping the bird to its final destination when it is released from quarantine. A list of brokers for each of the nine ports of entry may be requested from USDA port veterinarians at the time quarantine space is reserved. (See addresses to follow.) Most brokers offer transportation services from entry port to final destination.

Bring no more than two psittacine birds (parrots, parakeets and other hookbills) per family into the United States during any one year. Larger groups of these birds are imported under separate rules for commercial shipments of birds.

Rules Effective January 15, 1980.

Why All the Rules?

Serious diseases of birds and poultry can be carried by pet birds entering this country. Parrots from South America are believed to have caused an outbreak of exotic Newcastle disease in southern California in 1971-74. Eradication cost $56 million and the destruction of 12 million birds, mostly laying hens. Import rules for personally owned pet birds were put into effect in 1972 and strengthened in 1980. These new rules, effective January 15, 1980, provide a better defense against the introduction of this highly contagious disease.

Ports of Entry for Personally Owned Pet Birds

Listed below are the nine ports of entry for personally owned pet birds. To reserve quarantine space for your bird, write to the port veterinarian at the city where you'll be arriving and request Form 17-23. Return the completed form, together with a check or money order for $40* made payable to USDA, to the same address. The balance of the fee will be due before the bird is released from quarantine.

PORT VETERINARIAN
ANIMAL AND PLANT HEALTH INSPECTION SERVICE
U.S. DEPARTMENT OF AGRICULTURE
(CITY, STATE, ZIP CODE)

New York, New York 11430
Miami, Florida 33152
Laredo, Texas 78040
El Paso, Texas 79902
Nogales, Arizona 85621
San Ysidro, California 92073
Los Angeles, California (Mailing address Lawndale, CA 90261)
Honolulu, Hawaii 96850

*Persons planning to import pet birds should first contact the veterinarian in charge of the import facility for current costs.

The Quarantine Period

During quarantine, pet birds will be kept in individually controlled isolation cages to prevent any infection from spreading. Psittacine or hookbilled birds will be identified with a leg band. They will be fed a medicated feed as required by the U.S. Public Health Service to prevent psittacosis, a flu-like disease transmissible to humans. Food and water will be readily available to the birds. Young, immature birds needing daily hand-feeding cannot be accepted because removing them from the isolation cage for feeding would interrupt the 30-day quarantine. During the quarantine, APHIS veterinarians will test the birds to make certain they are free of any communicable disease of poultry. Infected birds will be refused entry; at the owner's option they will either be returned to the country of origin (at the owner's expense) or humanely destroyed.

Special Exceptions

No government quarantine (and therefore no advance reservations or fees) and no foreign health certificate are required for:

• *U.S. birds taken out of the country if special arrangements are made in advance.* Before leaving the United States, you must get a health certificate for the bird from a veterinarian accredited by USDA and make certain it is identified with a tattoo or numbered leg band. The health certificate, with this identification on it, must be presented at the time of re-entry. While out of the country, you must keep your pet bird separate from other birds. Remember that only two psittacine or hookbilled birds per family per year may enter the United States. Birds returning to the United States may come in through any one of the nine ports of entry listed earlier. There are also certain other specified ports of entry for these birds depending upon the time of arrival and other factors. Contact APHIS officials for information on this prior to leaving the country.

• *Birds from Canada.* Pet birds may enter the United States from Canada on your signed statement that they have been in your possession for at least 90 days, were kept separate from other birds during the period, and are healthy. As with other countries, only two psittacine birds per family per year may enter the United States from Canada. Birds must be inspected by an APHIS veterinarian at designated ports of entry for land, air, and ocean shipments. These ports are subject to change, so for current information, contact APHIS/USDA officials at the address listed in the section on U.S. agencies.

Pet birds from Canada are not quarantined because Canada's animal disease control and eradication programs and import rules are similar to those of the United States.

Other U.S. Agencies Involved With Bird Imports

In addition to the U.S. Public Health Service requirement mentioned earlier, U.S. Department of the Interior rules require an inspection by one of its officials to assure that an imported bird is not in the rare or endangered species category, is not an illegally imported migratory bird, and is not an agricultural pest or injurious to humans. Also, of course, the U.S. Customs Service maintains a constant alert for smuggled birds. For details from these agencies, contact:

Division of Law Enforcement
Fish and Wildlife Service
U.S. Department of the Interior
Washington, DC 20240

Bureau of Epidemiology
Quarantine Division
Center for Disease Control
U.S. Public Health Service
Atlanta, Georgia 30333

U.S. Customs Service
Department of the Treasury
Washington, DC 20229

For additional information on USDA/APHIS regulations, contact:

Import-Export Staff
Veterinary Services, APHIS
U.S. Department of Agriculture
Hyattsville, Maryland 20782

Two Serious Threats to Birds

Exotic Newcastle Disease

As a bird owner, you should know the symptoms of exotic Newcastle disease, the devastating disease of poultry and other birds mentioned elsewhere in this pamphlet. If your birds show signs of incoordination and breathing difficulties—or if there should be any unusual die-off among them—contact your local veterinarian or animal health official immediately. Place dead birds in plastic bags and refrigerate them for submittal to a diagnostic laboratory. Keep in mind that this disease is highly contagious and you should isolate any newly purchased birds for at least 30 days. Although exotic Newcastle disease is not a general health hazard, it can cause minor eye infection in humans directly exposed to infected birds.

Smuggling

If you're tempted to buy a bird you suspect may have been smuggled into the United States . . . don't! Smuggled birds are a persistent threat to the health of pet birds and poultry flocks in this country. Indications are that many recent outbreaks of exotic Newcastle disease were caused by birds entering the United States illegally. If you have information about the possibility of smuggled birds, report it to any U.S. Customs office or call APHIS at Hyattsville, Maryland (301) 436-8061.

Issued January 1980
Slightly revised November 1980

Author's Recommendation

(The following is not part of the USDA/APHIS rules and explanations you have just read, but rather a prudent measure the author suggests you follow for the protection of your own bird(s). Please note that what follows is *not* required by law.)

Psittacosis requires 45 days of continuous treatment to effectively combat. Unfortunately, these birds are quarantined for only 30 days. Therefore, under the care of your veterinarian, have the bird examined and, if necessary, treated for an additional period of time with chlortetracycline. Be sure to isolate your bird from any other birds during this time also.

17

Taming and Training Birds

by Steve Martin

Introduction

The well-trained parrot can be one of the most affectionate, enjoyable, and entertaining pets a person can have. However, not all birds are at this stage when first acquired. Untrained, or improperly trained, parrots are often a source of confusion and frustration to the new owner. The following sections are designed to give guidance to the novice bird owner, as well as to lend new ideas to the experienced bird trainer.

I have described the procedures I use to bring a bird from the wild state to the point of having that bird perform behaviors in a show. I also deal with the problems one might encounter along the way.

This section should also help many people realize that bird training is not for everyone. Training demands a time commitment that not everyone can afford. More important is the person's emotional attitude toward the bird. Patience, compassion, and a sincere love and respect for the bird are just a few things that a good bird trainer should have.

There are many different methods used to train birds. Since no two birds are exactly alike, some methods work better with certain birds than with others. Yet, with all birds, there is one common denominator that promotes successful training: *communication*. The basis of this communication is understanding the bird and being aware of its emotions. Too many people either do not give their bird credit for its emotions, or simply are not sensitive to those emotions. These are usually the people that have the most difficulty communicating with, or training, their bird.

Keep in mind that birds cannot be treated like dogs. They are emotionally more independent, and yet more sensitive. At the same time, they are intelligent and capable of learning behaviors even more quickly than dogs.

Finally, not all birds will make good pets. Some birds don't adjust to captivity as well as others. If this is the case with your bird, you might consider captive breeding instead of training. Some parrots are now being bred successfully in captivity. Hand-fed baby parrots are easier and better birds to work with. There is nothing like starting your relationship with a parrot when it is only a few weeks old.

Training and taming may seem a bit difficult at first to the beginner, but have patience. The experience of each successful step will bring encouragement to you and your bird. Soon you will realize that your bird is actually starting to make progress. What this really means is that you are starting to communicate with your bird!

HAVE PATIENCE. Do your best to be sensitive to your bird's feelings and you will be communicating with your bird before you know it. Remember that experience is the best teacher.

Professional Parrot Trainers

If at all possible, train your bird yourself and avoid professional parrot trainers. If you take the time to do it yourself, you will develop a better understanding of your bird, and thus, a better relationship with it.

If you do decide to seek the aid of a professional trainer, consider the following points:

- Is the cost reasonable? (Prices vary greatly.)
- Does the person's training method meet with your approval? The trainer should discuss the method with you *before* you use his or her services.
- Does the trainer have references? If the person is successful, he or she should be able to provide you with a list of references you could contact before proceeding.
- Will the trainer be available to help with future problems? There will probably be questions or problems that arise after the training course is completed.
- Will the trainer be willing to spend time with you once you get your bird back to instruct you on how to handle and work with the bird? THIS IS A MUST if you are to continue what the professional trainer has started.

Biting

Biting is one of the most common problems associated with having a parrot. It is also one of the most difficult problems to interpret, understand, and deal with. Parrots don't just bite for something to do, THEY BITE FOR A REASON. They bite when they are afraid, nervous, upset, angry, and sometimes even when they are happy and playful.

A bite from a parrot that is angry is often vicious and can cause considerable injury. A bite from a bird that is playing rarely breaks the skin, but still can hurt. Young birds have a teething stage during which they investigate objects by biting or chewing. Usually a sharp "NO!" will startle the young bird enough that it will soon learn how hard to pinch, or not to pinch, a finger. Keep in mind that birds use their beaks as a third foot, often grasping things in their mouths. It is important to teach your bird to discriminate between grasping and biting, as well as know it yourself.

The bird that bites when it is angry and bites to hurt you is another problem altogether. The best way to remedy this problem is to figure out why the bird is biting and deal with that first. Chances are you will realize that the bird bites you when you are trying to make the bird do something it doesn't want to do.

People commonly get bitten when they are trying to get their bird on their hand or off their shoulder. These birds haven't been *trained* properly to get on the hand or off the shoulder. If you teach your bird to do these for a treat, the biting will usually stop.

Some birds will bite when they are nervous or frustrated. For instance, if a bird is particularly nervous outside of its cage and you take it outside the cage, it may bite you. The key to stopping this biting problem is to notice when your bird is upset and correct the situation by putting the bird back in its cage before it bites you.

Some birds learn to bite to get a desired response. If you try to get your bird on your hand and it bites you, causing you to leave it alone, the bird will soon learn to bite you when it wants to be left alone. The best way to correct this problem is to train the bird to get on your hand for a treat so the bird will *want* to get on your hand. Then, if the bird still bites you, you can leave the bird alone as a disciplinary action by denying it the opportunity to earn a treat.

TAMING

Definition: Taming is the act of bringing a bird from its native wild state to a state of domestication. It is based on building a positive relationship with your bird and establishing trust, confidence, and communication between you and your bird. Taming should be more emotional than it is physical. You have to give the bird a reason to like you rather than try to make it like you.

The best approach to taming a bird is to understand and work with the bird's emotions. Understanding your bird's emotions leads ultimately to a better communication. This communication is the groundwork for a very positive and rewarding relationship.

Allow your bird to first adjust to its environment by placing it in a cage in the room where it will live, and leave the bird alone. Make sure that your bird has everything it needs—food, water and all other creature comforts, but don't try to force your presence upon the bird. After a week or two, you can start to build a relationship with your bird. There are several ways to "win" your bird over, the easiest and most reliable being to give it something it wants. Instinctively what the bird desires most is food.

Taming is best achieved on a positive reward system. To establish an effective reward it is necessary to find your bird's favorite treat. When you offer it a full variety of seeds and fruits, notice which ones it eats first and most. Usually this will be sunflower seeds since chances are that is what it has eaten most of since it left the jungle. If your bird is of a smaller species, you might try millet spray (millet seeds on a stem). It is also important to figure out how many seeds per day is the proper amount for your bird according to its dietary needs. A general rule is that roughly one third of a bird's seed intake consists of sunflower seeds, while seeds overall account for, again roughly, 75% of the total diet.

Once you have determined your bird's favorite treat (for our example we will use sunflower seeds), remove all the sunflower seeds from the seed cup.

This action will accomplish two things: first, it will prompt your bird to eat a better-balanced diet. Often a bird will eat more sunflower seeds (or whatever its preferred treat) than it actually needs, causing the bird to neglect the other seeds and fruits that are essential for a proper diet. By restricting the sunflower seeds, it will usually begin to eat more of the other foods it has previously neglected. Secondly, by taking away its favorite food, you enhance its desire for that particular food, making it a special treat to the bird much as a favorite snack is to a child. This will also strengthen its representation as a strong and positive reward. (Remember that food usually makes more of an impression to a parrot than companionship, discipline, or affection, particularly if the food in question is its favorite treat.) However, never deprive your bird of its full ration of food daily, including its treats.

Now that you have confirmed your bird's favorite treat, you need to establish it as a reward eventually getting the bird to take it out of your hand. Some birds may accept you and do this already, however, most birds will not naturally eat out of your hand. Most likely, as you approach your bird's cage, it will move to the far side to get away from you, or perhaps even jump to the bottom of the cage, lie on its back and hiss. Again, don't force your presence upon your bird. Instead, as you walk by its cage, drop two or three sunflower seeds (treat) in its cup, then leave the room. When it realizes that you're a safe distance away your bird will get back up on its perch. After some time your bird whould see the seeds and eat them. Then, do it again. Consistency is important here so that the bird can learn to expect the seeds each time you come by the cage. Now, instead of thinking "Oh, no! Here he comes", it will be thinking "Oh, boy! Here he comes." Soon your bird will look forward to you coming by its cage. Although your bird may still run, it will be developing a more positive attitude toward you. If you don't have time to work with your bird should see the seeds and eat them. Then, do it again. Consistency is its regular food.

You'll find that a day or two later it will be waiting on its perch for you to come by with the goodies. By now your bird should realize that nothing negative happens when you are near, and that you will give it its favorite treat. At this stage it shouldn't be necessary for you to leave the room after dropping the seeds, just walk to the other side of it. Wait for it to eat the seeds out of the cup, then go back and drop a few more seeds, this time walking only halfway across the room. When the bird will eat the seeds with you in the room, you have achieved a major step—your bird is starting to accept you.

It's important not to stand next to your bird's cage too soon; be aware of feelings and watch for signs of nervousness. For instance; when your bird stops looking for another seed, or if it takes a seed then drops it, you may be progressing too fast. Always end a session on a positive note (even if it means going back a step to regain its confidence) because that is what your bird will remember at the start of the next session. Be sure your bird is comfortable with the rate of progress by noticing its behavior and respecting its feelings. Remember that you are not trying to get your bird to obey, you are trying to win a friend.

Once you have encouraged your bird to walk up to its seed cup with you in the room, gradually progress to the point where it will take the seeds right after you drop them in the cup. When your bird will do this comfortably, it is ready to learn to take a seed from your hand.

Getting Your Bird to Eat Out of Your Hand

Hold the seed between your thumb and forefinger about 1/2 inch outside the bars of the cage. If your bird is ready for this step, it will take the seed from your fingers. It may take sometime for your bird to be comfortable with this, so do not progress too fast.

Once your bird is accepting seeds through the bars, begin to work your hand around to the door of the cage. Holding the seed at the very tip of your thumb and forefinger so it can be picked out easily, open the door and offer the seed to your bird at the cage door. If your bird looks angry or nervous, go back to the previous step (between the bars) to build up its confidence again. *This is a delicate step,* so be aware of your bird's feelings. If your bird looks eagerly for another seed, this is usually a good time to progress.

At this point, being careful not to make any fast motions, move your hand just inside the cage door. Hold 20 to 30 seeds in your palm and let your bird pick one out. When your bird is comfortable with this you have achieved a major step. You have won the trust of your bird and can now begin training.

Eventually you will want to introduce your parrot to other people. Although your bird may seem quite comfortable with you, do not subject it to strangers or other animals too soon. While you may represent a positive figure, others may not. Gradually introduce your bird to strangers by having them offer the bird a seed through the bars and then have them follow the same "get acquainted" procedure that you followed.

Taming Summary

Remember that taming is best accomplished through the positive approach of building mutual trust for each other.

- Be aware of your bird's feelings and emotions.
- Do not use physicial discipline.
- Use treats as positive reinforcement.

- Progress only at a rate that is comfortable to your bird.
- Remember that quick actions frighten birds.
- Realize signs of nervousness: not eating or eating only part of the seeds, paying attention to others rather than you.

Discipline

I discourage physical discipline when working with birds for the simple reason that they do not understand it. Some people try to dominate or be the master of their bird; treating their bird very much like they treat their dog. Few birds will understand and accept this sort of taming approach. Physical discipline may work with a dog because they instinctively understand it. Their instincts are similar to wild dogs that travel in packs. In these packs there is usually a dominant animal that uses physical aggression to control the others.

Most birds show aggression only when an intruder comes too close to their territory or nest. These confrontations are rarely more than a vocal display. There is almost never any physical contact, and the intruder usually retreats without an argument.

Therefore, emotional disciplines work best with birds.

Emotional Discipline

Covering the Cage: This is a good method to stop your bird from screaming or making other annoying noises while in its cage. If the bird continues to scream with the cage covered, try bumping the cage lightly. Don't let your bird know that it is you bumping the cage; let the bird think that its screaming causes the cage to shake.

Putting the Bird Back in Its Cage: This only works if your bird prefers to be outside its cage with you instead of inside its cage alone. When your bird does something wrong outside the cage, place it back in the cage denying your bird the opportunity to be with you outside the cage.

Placing the Bird on the Floor: With the possible exception of hand-fed babies, most birds don't like to be on the floor. They feel insecure and vulnerable in this position. When your bird does something wrong, you can place it on the floor for a few seconds and the discipline will be felt. The bird will probably look to you for security when you pick it up off the floor.

These emotional disciplines should be used immediately after a bird does something wrong, such as bite or scream. The emotional discipline should also be preceded by a verbal reprimand ("No!") to make it most effective. The bird will associate the sound of the word "No" with the emotional discipline which follows. Soon you will only need to use the word as a threat of a possible upcoming emotional discipline.

Squirt Bottles

The use of squirt bottles can be an effective way of discipline for certain wrongdoing, such as screaming. The bird is simply squirted each time it does something wrong. The water doesn't hurt the bird, merely startles it.

Some birds will learn to accept the squirt, and some even grow to like it. Some parrots learn that when you don't have the squirt bottle in your hand, you can't squirt them and they will continue to misbehave while the bottle is not in sight.

If you decide to try the squirt bottle method, here are some guidelines:

- Be consistent. It will make more of an impression on the bird if it is squirted *each* time it misbehaves.
- Try to be out of the bird's sight when you squirt it. Remember that you just want to startle the bird. If the bird does not see the squirt, it will be even more surprised.
- Don't soak the bird. One or two squirts are plenty.
- Hide the bottle between squirts. If your bird sees you pick up the bottle each time before you use it, the bird will learn to stop misbehaving when you go for the bottle. You want to catch the bird "in the act" to make the best impression.
- Try not to hit the bird in the face with the water. A squirt to the body will be just as effective and less likely to cause injury or problems such as foreign particles in the eyes or the bird inhaling some of the water.

TRAINING

Definition: Training is teaching your bird to perform a desired behavior or action when you want it to. This action is performed for some type of reward.

The reward can be an edible treat, a scratch on the head, verbal praise, or anything that will provide the bird with emotional or physical enjoyment. Training is best accomplished by using the bird's favorite food as a treat.

Although styles may vary, there are certain guidelines that are universal to all trainers:

- Use food that doesn't take long for the bird to eat. If a bird spends a lot of time consuming the reward (such as a peanut), the time factor just might make your bird forget why it got the reward in the first place.
- Always have the food ready. The quicker you are with the food, the faster your bird will learn.
- Conduct your training sessions daily. If possible, once in the morning, once after work, and a third time before going to bed. Fifteen minutes per session is a good average, if a time needs to be set. However, if things are going poorly, feel free to end the session early, always on a positive note. Likewise, if everything is going great, extend the session a few minutes to finish a behavior that's close to completion. Keep in mind that some behaviors can be trained in a single session, while others may take more than a week. The amount that can be accomplished is dependent only upon the particular trainer and bird.

- A bird's cage is similar to a baby's security blanket. Place your bird back in its cage if it is frightened or nervous. However, a word of caution: a common mistake to make is placing your bird back in its cage if it has done something wrong. Being back in the security of its cage is possibly what your bird wants, so you actually end up rewarding your bird for doing something wrong by placing it back in its cage.
- There are effective forms of discipline other than physical ones. A verbal reprimand works just as well; a sharp "NO!" being the most common. Emotional disciplines, mentioned earlier, are another good way of getting your point across: placing your bird on the floor and denying it the security of its cage, or placing your bird back in its cage when it wants to remain out with you, thus denying it your companionship. A verbal reprimand coupled with an emotional discipline is most effective. *Be consistent* with your use of these so your bird can easily discern right from wrong.

Behaviors

A trained, desired action by your bird is referred to as a trick or behavior. These two terms are interchangeable, however, most professional trainers prefer the word behavior.

Behaviors fall into two categories: the first is a *learned behavior, when you* create the situation by showing your bird what to do. The second is the *innovative* situation in which you either wait for your bird to offer a new behavior on its own, or simply catch it doing the behavior on its own. An example of innovative behavior is if your bird bobs its head up and down to amuse itself, and you reward it for bobbing its head. Soon it will realize that by bobbing its head, it will get a reward, and continues to do it, forming a trained behavior.

Bridging Stimulus

The bridging stimulus plays an important part in training. A bridging stimulus is a sound that signals an upcoming reward. There are several different types of bridging stimuli, or bridges. The two most common are a clicker and a verbal bridge. The clicker is a child's toy that can be obtained at most variety stores. The clicker can be inconvenient, particularly when the behavior calls for the use of both hands. Or there may be times when your bird will catch you unaware and offer a spectacular behavior, but your clicker is not around. I prefer not to be caught without a bridge, therefore I use the verbal bridge "Good!" Any word will do, tone inflection is also important. Stress the word in a pleasant tone as you say it and always use the same word as your bridge.

The bridge is used in conjunction with food, the food reward is given always immediately following the bridge.

Training Summary

- Break down the behavior into small steps *before* you begin training.
- Have your food ready, immediately bridge then reward your bird when it does something right.
- Work at your bird's pace. Do not rush it.
- Be consistent with your cues, your bridges and rewards, and your disciplines.

As you continue to gain experience in training, you also gain knowledge of your bird, and training becomes easier.

Training Sessions

Training sessions should be held in a quiet atmosphere, free of distractions.

- It is best to have two or three sessions per day.
- The average session should be 15 minutes, although the length will vary according to how well your bird is responding.
- Learn to recognize your bird's attention span and try not to work past that point.
  The warning signs of your bird losing its attention span are:
  - Not wanting the treats or rewards
  - Taking the treats, but dropping them without eating them
  - Reluctance to perform a behavior it already knows
  - Not paying attention
  - Unusual nervousness
  - Unusual aggression
- Figure out how many treats you want to give your bird in any given day. Divide these treats into equal portions according to the number of sessions you plan to work with your bird. Be careful not to feed your bird too many treats per day or it may neglect its other food.
- It is best to end the training session on a positive note, or before the bird has exceeded its attention span.
- If you begin a session and find that you don't have your bird's attention, stop the session and wait a few hours or until your next planned session.

Getting Your Bird to Stay On Your Hand

Before you start to teach your bird behaviors, it is important that you teach the bird to stay on your hand. A bird that is constantly walking up your arm, instead of sitting on your hand, is out of control.

- Encourage your bird towards your hand with some seeds. When the bird reaches your hand, bridge and reward it. If your bird starts to go up your arm, tell it "No!" and encourage it down toward your hand again.

Before a bird is taught any behaviors, it must learn to sit calmly on the hand.

The "Kiss", in which the bird touches the trainer's lips with the curve of its upper beak, is one of the more familiar behaviors taught to pet birds.

- Be consistent about only rewarding your bird on your hand and not on your arm. Soon the bird will learn to stay on your hand.

BEHAVIORS TO TEACH YOUR BIRD

Waving:

Definition: The bird stands on one foot, with the other it reaches out and moves that foot up and down in a waving motion.

This is usually a simple behavior which can be trained in one or two sessions. Timing is critical: you should be very quick with your bridge.

- With your bird on its T-stand, hold your hand out for it to step onto. As soon as your bird picks up its foot to step onto your hand, bridge it. Catch your bird in the act of picking up its foot.
- Repeat the above step, this time using a cue. For instance, the verbal cue "wave", and the hand cue, a waving action with your left hand. The hand cue can gradually be made into a subtle wiggle of a finger on the left hand.
- Gradually move your hand further away from your bird. Soon your bird will figure out that it can't reach your hand, and that you are bridging it just for picking up its foot.
- Now move your hand up and down. Your bird should try to follow your hand with its foot. Bridge and reward your bird when it moves its foot up. Next time delay your bridge until the bird has moved its foot up *and* down.
- Gradually move your hand even further away (10-12 inches), using your cues to coax the bird. As soon as your bird takes the initiative and starts moving its foot up and down as you deliver the cue remove the hand cue altogether.

Kiss:

Definition: The bird touches the trainer's lips with the curve of its upper beak.

If you are right-handed, start with the bird on your left hand.

- Place one seed between your lips and another between your right thumb and forefinger. Using the seed in your hand, direct your bird to the seed between your lips. When your bird takes the seed from your lips, bridge it and give it the seed in your hand. You may have to wait for your bird to finish eating the first seed before giving it the one in your hand.
- Repeat this process a few times. Usually after four or five times the bird will not wait to be directed to the seed in your lips and will proceed on its own. At this point put the seed between your teeth. As your bird

attempts to take that seed, cover it with your lips. When your bird makes contact with your lips, bridge and reward it with the seed in your hand. *Do not give it the seed in your teeth.*

- Repeat this process a few times. Soon your bird will go directly to your lips without even seeing the seed in your teeth. At this point there is no need to keep the seed between your teeth any longer. Presently you are still directing the bird with the seed in your hand. This action will be one of the cues you will use to stimulate the behavior. The other cue will be the word "kiss." Start making your hand cue less obvious by *not* directing the bird all the way to your lips. You should gradually phase out the hand cue and use the verbal cue "kiss."

- *Do not* reward your bird if it pinches your lip. Teach your bird to touch you only with the top of its beak. You can do this by tipping your head slightly forward as you make contact with the bird's beak. Contact should be made with your upper lip against the curve of the bird's upper beak.

Nod Head "Yes":

Definition: The bird bobs its head up and down as if responding "yes" to a question.

- With your bird sitting on the perch, place a seed between your thumb and forefinger and hold it three to four inches in front of the bird, just out of its reach.

- Start to move the seed up and down. Your bird should follow the action with its head. When this happens, bridge it (say "Good!"), and reward the bird with the seed.

- Gradually start moving your hand away; six inches, twelve inches, etc. At first your bird will follow your hand thinking it can grab the seed from your fingers. As you move your hand further away, your bird will start to realize that it is being rewarded for a particular action.

- Try to get your bird to take the initiative of moving its head on its own instead of merely following the seed and your hand. You want your bird to realize that it is being bridged and rewarded for moving its head up and down.

- As soon as your bird does one action, either moving its head *up* or *down,* bridge and reward it.

- Wait a little bit longer next time to bridge your bird. Maybe its own frustration will cause the bird to move its head in both directions. This will usually happen in a short period of time.

- Sometimes parrots will move their heads up and down in play. If this is the case with your bird, catch it doing the action. By catching your bird doing the behavior and rewarding it a few times, the bird will soon do the action on its own.

Shake Head "No":

Definition: The bird shakes its head back and forth as if responding "no" to a question.

- This behavior is trained basically the same way as the "yes" behavior.
- With your bird on its perch, hold a seed between your thumb and forefinger and move it back and forth a few inches in front of your bird.
- Bridge and reward your bird every step of the way (when the bird turns its head in either direction). Eventually hold your bridge until your bird moves its head in both directions several times.
- Gradually move your hand away. Watch carefully for your bird to take the initiative; promptly bridge and reward it.
- Another way to train this behavior is to place a small piece of scotch tape on the back of your bird's head. Your bird may shake its head to get the tape off. Bridge and reward the action.
- The easiest way to teach this behavior may be to simply catch your bird doing it on its own. Many birds will shake their heads when they rouse (shake their feathers). If you can catch your bird doing this a few times soon the bird should start to realize the behavior results in praise and reward.

Eagle:

Definition: The bird spreads both its wings out and holds them extended for a few seconds.

There are a few different ways to teach this behavior. If your bird likes to be scratched under the wings, try the following method first.

- With your bird on its perch facing you, place your right index finger under its left wing and your left index finger under its right wing. Your bird should spread its wings at this point; bridge and reward it.
- After repeating this a few times, start to phase out the hand cue. Make the same motions as before but don't actually touch the bird. Your bird should spread its wings in anticipation of you touching it. At the same time you should be using a verbal cue, "eagle" or whatever word you want to use.
- Say the verbal cue as you give the hand signal. After a few repetitions, you will able to eliminate the hand cue and your bird should perform the behavior on a verbal cue alone.

Birds that don't like to be scratched under their wings can be taught this behavior using another method.

- Place your bird on your hand and hold it away from your body. Roll your hand slightly to offset the bird's balance. As your bird spreads its wings to catch its balance; bridge and reward it.
- Repeat this a few times, saying the verbal cue as you roll your hand.

- Gradually phase out the hand cue (rolling your hand). Your bird should soon open its wings on the verbal cue alone.

Some birds flap their wings during play or out of excitement. You can sometimes catch your bird doing this and train the behavior that way. Teach your bird to hold its wings open by delaying your bridge a little each time.

Potty Training:

Definition: The bird is taught to defecate in a certain spot on a verbal cue.

Most people don't realize that a bird can be taught to pass its droppings on cue. Like any behavior, not all birds will do this one. It takes a tame bird that likes to be with you and the luxury of time on your part. Once you decide to teach your bird this behavior, work on it for a few days in a row, at least.

- Sit down on the couch with your bird on your hand or next to you and wait for it to have to defecate. Most parrots will have to defecate about every fifteen minutes depending upon their diet and the amount eaten.
- Birds usually display certain symptoms just before they have to defecate. Some will get nervous and start walking around, others will stop and get a fixed stare in their eyes. Most will squat down and drop their flank feathers, sometimes wagging their tail back and forth. Look for these signs as you are sitting with your bird.
- When you see your bird start to display any of these signs, interrupt its train of thought—distract your bird from what it is about to do. Place the bird on its T-stand or wherever you want it to defecate, and wait for it to happen. This may only take a few seconds, or up to ten or fifteen minutes, depending on how much you interrupted its train of thought. As soon as your bird defecates bridge and reward it. Sit back down on the couch with the bird again and wait for the next time.
- The key to training this behavior is to notice the signs before your bird defecates. Always have your bird defecate in the same place.
- You can put this behavior on a cue if you like. For instance, in anticipation of your bird defecating, say the word "Go" repeatedly. When it does, bridge and reward it.

Even a parrot that has been trained this behavior will sometimes defecate where and when it has to. However, the bird *will* first make an effort to get to where it is supposed to defecate—how good an effort depends on the bird.

This behavior is more difficult to train than the others, but the rewards are worth the extra effort.

TALKING: WHY DO BIRDS TALK?

The most commonly-asked question in pet shops is, "Does this type talk?" Most types of parrots can talk, no matter what their age, and most will if they meet the following requirements.

Parrots talk when they are healthy, happy, and at ease in their environment. They talk to amuse themselves.

Parrots mimic sounds they hear often and sounds they like to reproduce. You can't *make* any parrot mimic a sound that it doesn't want to mimic.

A positive relationship with your bird is the first step to encouraging your bird to talk. Once your bird has accepted you and its new environment, it will start doing things to amuse itself, this leads to talking. Some birds are stimulated to talk by a person's presence simply because they are happy when that person is near.

Records and tapes will sometimes help to teach your bird to talk. Some birds learn very well from them while others don't learn a thing. I usually recommend giving them a try.

One very good way to teach your bird to talk is by bringing in another bird (in a separate cage) that already talks. Birds learn to talk better from one another than they do from people. On the other hand, two birds in the same household that don't talk will usually take longer to learn to talk because they are interested in each other and not as likely to mimic human sounds.

A bird that is not tame can still meet the requirements to talk. If the bird is not handled, harassed, or made nervous, it will adjust to its environment with time. Once your bird has adjusted to its environment, it may learn to mimic sounds around it to amuse itself. However, it will only mimic sounds that it hears in a comfortable atmosphere. For instance, if your bird is not comfortable with people, it may mimic sounds that it hears when people are not present (dogs barking, phones ringing, etc.).

Some parrots learn to talk when they are only a couple of months old, others don't start until they are twenty years or more. The key factor here is the list of requirements outlined earlier: healthy, happy, at ease in their environment. Not all birds talk, but most that meet the requirements will.

Talking On Cue

Once your bird begins talking, you'll probably want to show off its vocal talents to your friends. You may find that when company comes over, your normally talkative bird suddenly becomes mute. Before you trade your parrot in for a canary, ask yourself why it won't talk. It is possibly nervous about the people huddled around the cage or maybe even your incessant prompting to talk. What can you do? Train your bird. Teach it to talk on cue.

- Many birds that talk will talk at a predictable time. Some birds talk in the morning; others talk in the evening. Some birds are stimulated to talk by household sounds such as the vacuum cleaner, telephone, television, etc. Others are stimulated by certain actions: when you leave the room, they might say "goodbye", or "hello" when you enter their room.
- Once you can predict that your bird will talk at a given time or in a given situation, you have half the battle won. Now you simply have to

create the situation and be ready with your bridge and reward. After you reward your bird a few times for saying a word, your bird should start getting the idea. When it starts saying the word right after eating the treat, you'll know that everything is starting to make sense to your bird.

- By this time you should be using a cue, either verbal or a hand cue, or both. For example, let's suppose your bird says "Hello" when you wave your hand *and* when you say "Hi." After rewarding your bird for saying "Hello", and as you anticipate the bird saying it again, repeat your cue word and wave your hand. After a few times your bird will start associating the wave of your hand as well as the word "Hi" with the word it is saying. Always be sure to bridge your bird immediately after each correct response.

- To test whether or not your bird understands your cues, leave the room for a couple of minutes. When you return, give your bird both verbal and hand cues. If it responds correctly, the word is trained. If your bird has learned some other behaviors, it's a good idea at this time to test its ability to discriminate one behavior from another. Your bird should be able to respond correctly to any cue in any given order. These new behaviors should be run through at least a couple of times a day until your bird performs them without error.

- You'll probably find that after you get one or two words or phrases on cue, the others will come easier. Your bird will probably learn new words at a quicker pace, too.

- *Be careful not to reward your bird for saying a word you trained on cue if you haven't given the cue to say it.* Your bird will still say words on its own to amuse itself and that's okay. But, if you reward your bird for saying a word you haven't cued you'll soon have a bird that says one word repeatedly every time it sees you.

MOST-COMMONLY-ASKED QUESTIONS
ON TAMING AND TRAINING

Q. How many members of a family should train the bird?

A. All the members of the family can work with the bird. This discourages the bird from taking preference for one person over another. However, it is best to have only one person train the bird, or have different people train different behaviors. No more than one person should train a particular behavior. The different training techniques of the people may confuse the bird when two or more people attempt to train the same behavior.

Q. Is it better to have two birds in the same household?

A. 1) If one bird is tame it will usually give the other confidence and speed up the taming process.

A combination of beauty, personality and the ability to learn many behaviors has made several of the cockatoos natural candidates for training. In this photo, a Sulphur-crested "scene-stealer" displays his crest, and his considerable charm for the widely-known aviculturist and writer, Betty Byers.

2) If neither bird is tame it will usually slow down the taming process for both birds.

3) A bird that doesn't talk will learn to talk quicker from one that does than it will from people. However, a bird that talks will often stop talking when put with another bird.

Q. Do all parrots talk?

A. No. Most parrots have the ability to mimic sounds but not all have the desire. Parrots raised in captivity make the best talkers.

Q. How do I make my bird talk?

A. You don't make your bird talk, you *let* your bird learn to talk. A good relationship and comfortable surroundings will help to encourage your bird to talk.

Q. After the bird is trained in a few behaviors, do I have to work the bird daily on these behaviors so it won't forget them.

A. No. Most birds will remember behaviors for weeks if not months. Some of my birds which work in the show for three months and take six months off will only need about a week's refresher course to regain the quality of their behaviors. (To make sure your bird doesn't forget its behaviors, it is best to put the bird through its paces a couple times per month if possible.)

Q. How many behaviors can a bird learn?

A. Each bird has its own capacity for learning just like people do. The number of behaviors a bird can learn is limited only by this capacity, and the limit of its trainer's imagination.

Q. How long does it take to teach a bird its first behavior?

A. A new trainer should be able to teach a tame bird with a good attention span a simple behavior, such as the kiss or wave, in three or four sessions.

Q. Should I clip my bird's wings before training?

A. It is usually best to have the bird's wings clipped before you bring it home. A bird with clipped wings will be easier to tame and train and less likely to injure itself flying around the room.

Q. How often should I trim my bird's toenails?

A. Parrots' nails grow constantly and should be trimmed when they become uncomfortable on your hand or arm. Be sure to have your bird's nails trimmed before you start taming so you won't have to upset your bird during this delicate time. It is best to have someone else do the trimming of the toenails and clipping of the wings so that your bird doesn't blame this uncomfortable process on you. Some veterinarians, as well as pet shops, offer this service.

Q. *What is the best type of talking parrot?*

A. For their ability to mimic sounds, African greys and yellow-naped Amazons are my choice for talking parrots. Which of the two is the best depends on the individual bird.

18

Wild Birds:
Attracting Them to Your Yard

Co-author Ron Ridgway, DVM

Wild birds are welcome visitors in most of our backyards. Their beautiful array of colors, their sounds and movements all make for a warm and peaceful setting. If you are going to attract a regular crowd of birds it will require a little time and planning. You must first provide for their basic needs and that means supplying food, water and shelter in a comfortable and protected environment. If these things are available, the birds will be flocking to your yard within a short time.

Food Preferences

It is important to know the types of birds in your area, as well as their food preferences. An attempt should always be made to duplicate their diet as closely as possible. A well-thought-out garden that supplies ample food, shelter and nesting materials will attract many birds. It is important to remember that a garden designed with birds in mind may not be the cleanest and best groomed yard in the neighborhood. Dense vegetation and compost piles are important additions. A neatly arranged and "spotless" yard works to the disadvantage of attracting birds.

An assortment of plants, including trees, shrubs, vines and flowers, perform several functions. These include a source of food such as seeds, fruits, flowers and they also attract insects. In addition to the plants, supplementary foods should be supplied year round. They help provide the extra nutrients birds need to fuel their high metabolic rates and keep warm.

Supplementary Foods

- All birds eat some seeds, even insect-eating birds. Almost any seeds are acceptable as long as they are fresh and not moldy. Your local pet shop or feed store should stock a supply that you can mix yourself or offer the prepackaged wild bird seed mixes. Make sure a variety of seeds is always available to appeal to the widest range of birds.

237

- Suet, the fat trimmings from meat, is especially relished by insect-eaters and provides a quick energy source. Serve it just as it comes from the butcher; it can be set out in chunk form and nailed to a feeding tray. To prevent the larger birds from carrying the pieces away, the suet can be placed beneath ½" wire mesh screen. Suet can also be combined with a variety of seeds or peanut butter and formed into small cakes. (These cakes stay fresher longer.) The recipes are available in the books listed in the BIBLIOGRAPHY.
- Kitchen foods such as peanut butter, baked goods (stale or fresh), hard-boiled eggs, raisins, nuts, crackers, cheese, dry dog food, fresh fruits and "veggies" can all be good sources of nutrition. The size of the pieces should be large enough to prevent the larger birds from flying away with them. They can also be placed under the wire mesh. In this way, the birds will stay in your yard to eat.
- Minerals, vitamins, and grit, as discussed in Chapter 3, can also be fed to wild birds.

Some Additional Recommendations

- Don't stop feeding once you start, especially during the winter months. Many birds will become dependent on your food and could die if it disappears. Remember to locate the feeders in easily accessible areas to make it more convenient for you to keep them filled.
- Keep seeds fresh, dry and clearly visible for the birds.
- As far into the winter as possible, continue to spade and turn over the compost pile to uncover worms, bugs, seeds and natural grit.
- Birds do most of their feeding in the morning hours, so try feeding them at this time.

THE FOOD PREFERENCES OF WILD BIRDS

These birds eat invertebrates (insects, spiders, worms, etc.):

Blackbirds	Hummingbirds	Swallows
Bluebirds	Jays	Tanagers
Bushtits	Kinglets	Thrashers
Catbirds	Martins	Thrushes
Chickadees	Mockingbirds	Titmice
Creepers	Nuthatches	Vireos
Cuckoos	Phoebes	Warblers
Flickers	Roadrunners	Woodpeckers
Flycatchers	Robins	Wrens
Grackles	Starlings	

These birds eat fruit when it is available:

Bluebirds	Orioles
Catbirds	Robins
Flickers	Starlings
Grackles	Tanagers
Jays	Thrushes
Mockingbirds	Waxwings

These birds eat seeds:

Bobwhites	Juncos
Cardinals	Nuthatches
Chickadees	Quail
Doves	Sparrows
Finches	Starlings
Grackles	Titmice
Grosbeaks	Towhees
Jays	

These birds eat nectar:

Hummingbirds	Orioles

Feeders

There are many ways of feeding birds. Before placing the feeders, watch the birds as they fly into your yard. Where do they land first? Where do they spend most of their time? Where do they fly for protection? Be sure to locate feeders in areas that are not only convenient and protected for the birds, but also convenient for you to keep them filled.

Feeding Stations

Scattering food on the ground, windowsills or garden wall is the simplest feeding method of all. However, this can also attract unwanted animals like mice, rats or predators such as cats. During the winter months ground feeding is impractical due to the weather conditions in many parts of the country.

Feeding Tables

These are easy to make and consist of a "table" usually made of wood and attached to a post five to six feet off the ground. The table top should measure approximately 18″ - 24″ square. The table edges should be raised to prevent food from spilling or blowing off. Leave a small opening in one corner and tilt the table slightly to allow for water runoff, or leave a small opening in each corner to provide drainage.

A well-stocked pet shop, feed dealer or garden supply outlet should have a good variety of bird feeders for the species found in your area. Select the feeders designed for the birds you want to attract.

Feeders

Feeders are the most practical way to furnish sustenance to wild birds. Feeders provide a roof that keeps the food dry and protects the birds from many of their natural enemies.

Most feeders can be easily designed and built at home with a minimum amount of time and materials. They can be very simple or elaborate. Imagination is the only limitation. There are many books offering plans on the building of feeders. For the person who is not a "do-it-yourselfer," feeders are commercially available at hardware or outdoor supply stores.

In addition to wooden feeders, many other objects can also be used:

- Buckets or cans: Can be placed on their sides and suspended from a branch or nailed to a post.
- Coconut shells: Drill a two-inch hole in the side, then hollow it out. Place a small hole in the bottom for drainage and at the top for attachment of a chain and suspend it from a branch.
- Cinder blocks: Use the openings to hold the seed and they can be placed most anywhere.
- Plastic bottles: Cut a hole in the side and suspend it from a branch. A small perch made of wood doweling makes it easier for birds to land and feed.
- Logs: Drill a few holes in the log, add a perch below each of the holes and hang it upright from a tree or place it on a post.
- String: Small bits of fruit and nuts and even popcorn can be strung and hung from a branch.

Guidelines for Placement of Feeders

- All feeders should be at least five feet off the ground. Metal cones placed above the feeders when they are suspended by a branch or placed around the pole below the feeder will keep unwanted animals away.
- Place the feeders eight to 10 feet from a fence, house or plantings. This is far enough away so that cats can't jump on it.
- Select an area protected from adverse weather. Pay particular attention to the direction from which most storms come and locate feeders on the opposite side of trees or the house.
- Rather than one large feeder, try a few small ones. This will help create less competition between the birds.
- At first, you may want to locate the feeders far from the house, and as birds become more accustomed to them, gradually begin to move them in closer.

Bird Baths

Regardless of the weather, birds need daily access to clean, fresh water. It's especially important during hot weather when they can be seen drinking, bathing and splashing around in their newly found "watering hole."

In wilderness areas, birds depend on streams, ponds, rain puddles, dew and snow for their water. In urban areas these natural sources of water rarely exist and the bird baths are certainly a welcomed addition.

The material used for the bath is not as important as its shape. Many commercial bird baths are too deep and the sides too steep. There should be a gradual transition from a very shallow depth of ½″ to a maximum of 3″ deep. The surface and edges of the bowl should have a slightly rough texture to avoid slipping. Baths made of terra cotta or concrete are commercially available, but be sure they are designed correctly.

Additional Considerations

- Birds will come to depend on this water source so be sure it is always available.
- The water should be changed every two days. The bath should be cleaned and scrubbed out periodically.
- Running water is excellent for attracting birds. It can be something as simple as a faucet dripping into the bath or an elaborate fountain.
- Birds still need water for drinking during the winter months. Boiling water can be added fresh each morning. More elaborate set-ups can include heating elements built right into the bottom of the baths.
- The basic guidelines for placement of baths are similar to the placement of feeders. Locate them eight to 10 feet from shrubs or from a fence. Remember, wet birds are slower moving and need extra protection.
- There are also many other types of small receptacles around the house that work well. These include: earthenware pie plates, flower pot saucers, and shallow dishes.
- Some birds even like dust baths. A sand box filled with dry dust (Fuller's earth), sifted dirt, or fine sand acts like talcum powder to condition the feathers and help control parasites.

Nesting

Breeding season begins in the early spring and it is during this time that nests are built. Depending on the type of bird, nests will be built almost anywhere in the trees or around the house. An ample supply of materials can be furnished to assist in the construction of these nests.

Good nest building materials include:

Cotton	Cloth strips
String	Bark
Wool	Feathers
Yarn	Straw
Thread	Down
Moss	Lint from a dryer
Animal hair (i.e., dog or horse)	

Mud should always be available for those birds, such as robins, that use it to line their nests.

- These materials can be placed in an easily accessible container or loosely attached to a bush or branch.
- The pieces should be no longer than 4" - 6" in length.
- Some birds will even use a hand-made nesting box. These must be carefully built with a particular type of bird in mind.

INJURED AND ORPHANED WILD BIRDS: HOW TO CARE FOR THEM

Whether you live in the city or the country, sooner or later, you may come across an injured or orphaned bird. For those of you who ask, "What do I do now?" Here's the answer.

First determine if the bird is actually injured or just resting. Stand back and observe the bird for a short time. Is it active? Is it hopping around? Can it flap its wings? If the answer to these questions is yes, then it is probably not injured and it should be either left alone or gently placed on a nearby branch.

It must also be determined if the young, unfeathered or partially feathered bird found away from the nest is orphaned or not. The young bird may be away from its nest practicing flying or it may have fallen out of the nest. An orphaned bird is usually weak and quiet. It should be returned to the nest whenever possible. Observe the nestling for a few hours to see if the parents return to care for it. Contrary to popular belief, the parents will continue to care for their offspring even if it has been handled. You can also try placing the nestling in another nest with other young birds of a similar type and age. The parents will usually raise the new addition as if it were their own. After one to two hours if the parents do not return, then it is safe to assume the bird has been abandoned.

How to Handle an Injured Bird

Approach the bird from behind whenever possible. If it is alert, anticipate that it will struggle when first caught.

1. For small birds, pick them up with your bare hands or use a lightweight cloth.
2. For birds of prey, use a heavy towel, blanket or jacket and cover them completely. These birds use their feet with their sharp talons as their primary means of defense. If you are grabbed by these it can be very painful and cause serious injury, so be careful.
3. As the bird calms down, gather the covering together with the wings lying smoothly against the body.
4. For transporting, the covering can be made into a sack using a shoelace. Extreme care must be used on warm days since overheating can occur rapidly.

5. Another excellent method for transporting birds is to use a cardboard box filled to the top with shredded newspapers. Place the bird in the box and then cover. In this way, the bird remains more quiet and if any broken bones are present, the shredded newspaper helps give some external support.

How to Care For an Injured Bird

Basic rules to follow:

- Provide warmth.
- Handle only when necessary.
- Provide good nutrition. The shape of a bird's beak can be a useful guide to the type of food it eats. You can consult a bird manual to compare the beak shapes and help identify your unknown bird.

  Note: Always isolate these wild birds from any other birds to prevent the possibility of spreading any disease.

Most of the guidelines discussed in Chapter 14, HOME MEDICAL CARE, will also apply to wild birds. However, wild birds should be left alone and not handled except when absolutely necessary such as feeding and administering medication.

An injured bird requires immediate care. Don't wait! It is always best to contact organizations or individuals that are experienced and have a working knowledge of caring for wild birds. In this way, many more can be saved and returned to their natural environment. These organizations or individuals include:

Audubon Society
Department of Fish and Game
Humane organizations
Local veterinarians
Natural history museums
Wildlife rehabilitation groups
Zoos

You should be aware that there are many federal and state laws designed to protect most wild animals. All birds of prey are protected and it is illegal for any person to possess one without a license. The above listed groups will either have the necessary licensing to care for these birds or will be able to direct you to someone that does. It should be everyone's goal to return these animals to the wild as soon as they are fully recovered.

How to Care For an Orphaned Bird

It is very important that the bird be correctly identified so that it will be fed the correct types of food. Don't hesitate to contact local bird organizations for positive identification. A wildlife rehabilitation group or a natural history museum should be helpful with this.

Basic Rules to Follow:

1. Check for injuries.
2. Keep the bird warm. A room temperature of 85°-90° F is essential.
3. Handle the bird only when necessary.
4. Provide company whenever possible. When two birds are raised together they will help stimulate each other, provide additional warmth and will not become too tame.
5. Provide good nutrition. To best evaluate an adequate feeding program:
   - Weigh the bird daily and expect a steady weight gain.
   - Feel the pectoral area—the bird should be plump and there should be no sharpness to the keel (breast bone).
   - Count the daily droppings—there should be at least 20 to 25 per day.

Immediate Care

An orphaned bird will probably be weak, thin and cold. Treatment should begin immediately to help strengthen the bird. For rehydration, try the following:

- 1 quart of water mixed with 3 teaspoons of Karo syrup or honey, and ½ teaspoon salt.
- Gatorade
- Orange juice

Depending on the size of the bird, give five to 20 drops every 15 minutes. Give it slowly and allow the bird time to swallow. Keep the bird warm—about 85° F.

Housing and Feeding of Orphaned Birds

- Keep them in a cardboard box with narrow slits cut out for "windows" and a wire mesh formed for a roof. Line the floor with wax paper and place several layers of newspaper on top of it.
- A heating pad set to "low" and wrapped in a towel can be placed half under the box so that the birds can move to the most comfortable temperature area. A heat lamp will also work well. A thermometer can be used in the box to monitor the temperature.
- Provide a quiet and draft-free environment.
- Diet:
   —Canned or dry dog food
   —Baby bird food
   —Lafeber's Nutri-Start available from:
      Dorothy Products
      7278 Milwaukee Avenue
      Niles, IL 60648

Feeding Technique

- Place food in the back of the mouth using a whittled-down ice cream stick, rounded end of a flat toothpick, watercolor brush or plastic eyedropper. Normally the young bird should gape (stretching the neck and opening the mouth) for the food. If the bird does not do this, open the beak with gentle pressure then feed. The bird will stop gaping when it has had enough or when its crop is full.
- These birds must be fed every 30 minutes during the day and about every one to two hours during the night. As the bird grows the times between feedings can be increased.
- If the crop is full, skip the feeding.
- The bird will usually have a dropping immediately after feeding.
- After every feeding the bird should always be cleaned with a cloth and warm water. Do not allow food to cake and dry on the feathers because it will be very difficult to remove.

At about four to six weeks of age, the birds should gradually be changed over to foods they would naturally eat in the wild.

- It is also at this age that the preparation for release should begin. Begin short flying practice sessions in the house. However, you may need to use a net to catch them afterward. Begin to take them outside in their cage to get them accustomed to the outdoors. Begin to reduce human contact.
- You may have to teach the bird to eat and drink on its own.
- At maturity, which is six to eight weeks of age in good health, the bird should be released. Good weather should be forecast for the next three days, at least. Continue to keep food and water near the release site for the following week in case the bird stays in the area.

BIRDS OF PREY (eagles, hawks, falcons and related species)

Raptors, as these magnificent creatures are known, are a very special and unique group of birds. It is illegal to possess any raptor without a license issued by the government. Unfortunately, these birds are often victims of target practice and injured or killed by gunshot wounds, as well as, electrocution from electrical wires and other environmental pressures that are transforming their natural paradise into a cultivated landscape.

The sport of falconry has been practiced for over 2000 years and involves the art of training raptors to take wild quarry. This ancient form of hunting was extremely popular with all classes of people during the Middle Ages. Now, falconers, as they are called, are a very select group of people that spend hours every day caring for and training their birds. To become a licensed falconer means passing a rigorous written exam covering all areas of bird care such as: the care and management of raptors, their life history, diseases and

The peregrine falcon has been a popular hunting bird for centuries. It is also one of the most widely distributed of all raptors.

Birds of prey have intrigued and inspired man before the pyramids cast their shadows across the Egyptian desert. Even today, a devoted group of enthusiasts keeps falconry from becoming a lost art.

Oil-damaged birds are a major concern to the modern conservationist and environmentalist. Those living in coastal areas who are involved with the well-being of bird populations must be familiar with the various procedures used in rescuing such unfortunate victims.

sanitation problems, identification, and of course, the art of falconry. Once the exam is passed and adequate housing facilities are available, an apprentice license is given and this person must be sponsored by someone holding a general or master falconer's license. The sport does not jeopardize the populations of native birds, since only certain raptors are allowed to be kept and, in fact, captive breeding of these birds is also on the increase.

Anybody seen harming these creatures should be reported to the authorities immediately. Follow the guidelines in the previous section on injured birds if you find an injured raptor.

OIL-DAMAGED BIRDS: THEIR CARE AND TREATMENT

This problem usually affects only sea birds. However, even pet birds have been known to accidentally get into household grease or oil. Death will often result in untreated birds due to chilling, exhaustion, starvation, drowning due to loss of buoyancy, or toxic effects of ingested oil. If you observe an oil spill or oiled wildlife, immediately contact the U.S. Coast Guard and the U.S. Fish and Wildlife Service.

Oiled feathers lose their insulation properties and, hence, their ability to control body temperature and these birds can easily become cold. They are unable to swim and unable to fly in many of the more severe cases. The humane death of a bird should be considered in cases where treatment has little chance of being successful and pain and suffering is apparent.

Immediate Care

1. If the bird is aggressive, loosely tape the beak closed with masking tape or secure it with a rubber band. Do not cover the nostrils.
2. Wipe any oil from the eyes, nostrils and beak.
3. For the eyes, a mild ophthalmic medication should be applied.
4. Increase the room temperature to 85°-90° F and provide a draft-free environment.
5. Dehydration can be corrected with 5% dextrose or three ounces of Karo syrup mixed into one quart of water. These solutions should be tube fed at one ounce per pound of body weight every four to six hours initially.
6. Feeding is important and should always be similar to the bird's natural diet. Force feeding should only be started if the bird repeatedly turns down food for one or two days.
7. Rest and relaxation to minimize stress is always important.
8. Delay the de-oiling treatment until the bird is warm, dry and well hydrated.

Removal of Oil or Grease

Note: The Department of Fish and Game, Wildlife Rehabilitation

Organization, or other organizations familiar with this process should be contacted first. Their experience should greatly help achieve a more successful outcome. The general guidelines are as follows:

1. Prepare a few bowls of cleaning solution using a 15% solution of an industrial detergent called *Amber Lux* manufactured by Lever Brothers. The water temperature should be 105°-110° F.
   Note: A mild dishwashing soap can be used for light oiling problems.
2. If the bird is oiled with grease or crude oil, dissolve it with mineral oil and wipe off as much as possible.
3. Protect the bird's eyes with eye ointment and wear rubber gloves.
4. Immerse the bird in warm detergent. Handle the feathers gently and follow their natural contour. Wet all the feathers. Dip the bird slowly in and out of the detergent solution for one or two minutes.
5. If the bird is still oily, transfer to the second and third bowls of detergent and repeat above step. All the oil must be removed as it will retard the normal water-proofing process.
6. Immediately after the washing, rinse the bird well with a warm water spray. Thorough rinsing and removal of all detergent is essential.
7. Immediately after rinsing, blot dry with towels. Do not rub.
8. Thorough drying should be done with a hair dryer. Do not hold it too close and do not use it on the highest heat setting.
9. Wrap the bird loosely in a towel and place it in a warm cage or cardboard box. Once it is rested and relaxed, provide the bird with food and water.

Severely oiled birds may need to have this process repeated in a couple of days after they are rested. The bird should not be released until it can maintain buoyancy and can easily swim for at least one hour several times daily. The down feathers should remain dry indicating normal waterproofing. Hopefully, these birds will not have to be kept for more than one week.

Appendix A

Everything You Always Wanted to Know About . . .

by Betty Byers

CANARIES

Common Name:	Canary
Scientific Name:	*Serinus canarius*
Country of Origin:	Canary Islands, Madeira and the Azores
Color:	Originally they were all green with some yellow-brown. Today they are various shades or combinations of brown, orange, yellow, white, blue and red.
Length:	They are four and a half to seven inches long from the head to the tip of the tail.
Life Span:	Five to fifteen years
Maturity:	One year
Sex Determination:	Males have a definite "song", and during the breeding season the vent area in a male becomes enlarged and prominent while the hen's vent area becomes only slightly prominent.
Cage Requirements:	12"L x 12"H x 10"W (minimum)
Diet:	See Chapter 3.

Breeding Requirements

Cage:	36"L x 16"H x 12"W
Flight:	6'L x 6'H x 3'W (minimum)
Nest Box:	A concave bowl or pan about four to five inches in diameter is used. Provide fine grasses, hay or string for nesting material.
Breeding Season:	Predominantly in the spring

Clutch Size:	Four or five blue spotted or creamy-colored eggs are laid every 24 hours. Eggs usually hatch in 13 to 14 days. The young are independent at three to four weeks.

Clutch Size: Four or five blue spotted or creamy-colored eggs are laid every 24 hours. Eggs usually hatch in 13 to 14 days. The young are independent at three to four weeks.

Additional Information: Indoor cage breeding is recommended since canaries are very susceptible to the cold. After the first two eggs are laid they should be replaced with false eggs or marbles available from bird suppliers. When the last egg is laid, then all the real eggs are put back into the nest and the false eggs removed. This is done so that all chicks hatch at about the same time and prevents the older chicks from trampling the younger ones. Most males will interfere with the nesting hen and therefore should be placed in a separate section of a partitioned cage.

There are 29 varieties of canaries today. They originated in the Canary Islands and have been bred in Europe since the early 1500s. The color and size variations were first seen in the early 1700s in France. The males are the most desirable because of their "singing" abilities. They can become finger-trained, however, they are not noted for their affection or talking ability. Canaries can be messy, since many seem to splatter their seeds out of their cage. When molting, the males do not "sing" as much. Some varieties are color-fed with "Flamen Oil" during the molting season. This oil is added to their drinking water and will help give the new feathers much added color.

Canary Varieties

American Singer: As the name implies, this variety was developed here in the late 1930s. It is a cross between a Roller and a Border Fancy. The males are the most popular canary because of their soft, harmonious song.

Description: At 5½ inches long from beak to the tip of the tail, this variety has a compact rounded appearance.

Border Fancy: The Border canary is the ideal type for the beginning breeder. It probably originated in England in the early 1800s.

Description: This canary is compact, slender, and has a clean-cut look. They are 5½ inches long from the head to the tip of the tail. They can be all yellow, all brown or a combination of the two.

Red Factor: This variety was originally obtained by crossing the wild canary with a brilliant vermilion Venezuelan hooded siskin. In order to further enhance the red coloring they can be color-fed.

Description: Since some are color-fed, there can be a variety of shades such as a frosted red, pastel pink, red-orange, rose-ivory, etc. They are about 6½ inches long from the head to the tip of the tail.

Norwich: It is generally accepted that this type was established in the 1600s in Norwich, England. They have a sturdy build and are hardy. Among canary fanciers they have a reputation as being rather clumsy.

Description: Its larger size and girth have earned the Norwich the nickname, "The John Bull of the Canary World." They are 6½ inches long from head to the tip of the tail. Some can be color-fed making numerous shades possible.

FINCHES

Common Name: Finch

Scientific Name: *Chloebia, Poephila, Zonaeginthus, Stizoptera, Lonchura, Amadina, Cardeuelis* and other genera

Country of Origin: Found in most areas of the world

Color: Varies with the species

Length: The body is three to eight inches long. The tails can be as long as 16 inches as seen in the giant whydahs.

Life Span: About five years depending on the variety.

Maturity: Over two months

Sex Determination: The male is usually brighter-colored or differently-colored than the female. In some varieties,, however, no color differences exist.

Cage Requirements: All finches enjoy flying, therefore the larger the cage the better. For a single pair the ideal size would be at least 36"L x 14"H x 10"W.

Diet: See Chapter 3.

Breeding Requirements

Cage: 36"L x 18"H x 12"W (for single pair)

Flight: 6'L x 6'H x 3'W (minimum)

Nest Box: Some finches will use small wooden boxes while others use small wicker baskets. Finches like to make their own nests out of materials such as sphagnum moss, dry grasses or pieces of coarse rope cut into three-inch strips.

Breeding Season: Year-round depending on the variety

Clutch Size: Three to seven eggs are laid that hatch in 12 to 14 days. The chicks become independent at three to four weeks. The eggs can be blue, green, white or other color depending on the variety.

Additional Information: Finches are sociable and, therefore, should be kept in pairs. Be careful when mixing the different varieties as some do not get along with one another. During the winter months they need added warmth. In some varieties the chicks have luminous patches in or alongside their mouths to help the parents feed them at night. Do not put too many pairs together in either a cage or a flight. Since finches are not chewers many non-toxic plants can be used in their flights.

These popular little birds are easy to maintain and are hardy. They do not demand a great deal of attention, but it's best to buy two birds because they like company. Some do have a pleasing "melody" while others vocalize with a "beeping" call. There is a tremendous variety of colors, shapes and sizes among finches from which to choose. Each species has its own personality and some can even become finger-trained.

Finch Varieties

Zebra Finch *(P. guttata)*: These birds are perky, hardy and pretentious. They make high pitched spurts of noise. They are the most popular of all the finches.

Description: The male has a white mask surrounded by a narrow black band below the eye; the tail is black-barred with white; the cheeks are a pale chestnut; the underparts are white with cinnamon flanks with white spots; the upper parts are ash gray; the beak orange; and the feet are salmon. The female is gray on the crown; plain buff below with a black and white barred tail and is brown on the upper parts. Their length is 4 to 4½ inches long from head to tip of tail.

Society or Bengalese Finch: *(P. domestica)* They have a squeaky little "melody" and will socialize with other varieties because they have a friendly nature. This variety is believed to have resulted from a cross between the striated and sharptailed finches bred by the Chinese centuries ago.

Description: The sexes are alike. They are found in varying shades of brown, some with white or cinnamon. Their length is four to 4½ inches long from head to tip of tail.

Lady Gouldian Finch: *(C. gouldiae)* This finch is often called the most beautiful bird in the world. They can be friendly. They come from a warm climate in Australia, therefore, it is important to keep them warm and dry during the winter months.

Description: The top and sides of the head are scarlet with a fine black band in both sexes; behind that band at the nape is a broader band of turquoise; chin and throat are black; breast is a deep purple; underparts are golden; back and wings are green; beak white with a red tip and the feet are pink. The female has a lilac chest. Their length is five to 5½ inches long from head to tip of the tail.

Paradise Whydah: *(S. paradisaea)* This graceful bird has a gentle disposition. It is hardy, lives long and gets along well with other finches. A larger cage is needed to accommodate its long tail.

Description: During the breeding season, the male's underparts are white; the head is black; the chest is chestnut and this color extends out to the nape, wings and tail. The beak is black and the long tail, which is seen only in males, is six to 14 inches long. The female is buff on the underparts; brown-streaked along the lower back and a black line extends along the side of the crown and behind the eye. When not in breeding plumage, the male usually resembles the female. The body length is six inches.

BUDGERIGAR

Common Name:	Parakeet, Budgie
Scientific Name:	*Melopsitticus undulatus*
Country of Origin:	Australia
Color:	Originally green with black barring on the wings and back.
Length:	Seven inches from head to the tip of the tail.
Life Span:	Eight to 15 years
Maturity:	Six to eight months
Sex Determination:	At about four months of age, the cere becomes blue in the male and brown or tan in the hen.
Cage Requirements:	12"L x 12"H x 14"W (minimum)
Diet:	See Chapter 3.

Breeding Requirements

Cage:	18"L x 12"H x 14"W (minimum)
Flight:	6'L x 6'H x 3'W (minimum)
Nest Box:	5"L x 5"W x 7"H with a concave bottom. Most budgies prefer no nesting material.
Breeding Season:	Year 'round. A good sign to watch for when the cere on the female swells or changes color.
Clutch Size:	Three to six white eggs. Young usually hatch at 16 to 18 days. Independence of the young ranges from four to five weeks.
Additional Information:	Budgies are usually good breeders and parents. Some may lay a second clutch even before the first chicks are out of the box. A maximum of three clutches per year is recommended in order to avoid health problems in both the parents and the chicks. If you have more than one pair together, sometimes a jealous female will make trouble. She could fight with another female with eggs, or even kill that female, destroy some eggs, or even kill the young. "English" budgies lay fewer eggs, but are equally good breeders. An understanding of genetics is important in order to achieve different color variations. Although

budgies do breed well in a flight, some people prefer to breed single pairs in a cage. In many states a small band must be placed on the chicks' leg for identification purposes. This banding is done when the young are three to five days old.

The budgie is the most numerous pet bird. They are hardy, not noisy and often will talk. Some males are known to have a large vocabulary and whistle short tunes. Occasionally you will see "English" budgies for sale in the pet stores. These birds are larger and make equally satisfactory pets as the more numerous variety. In their native Australia budgies are a migratory species and, therefore, remain good fliers. Some budgies have a "crest" and this looks like the feathers were parted down the middle of the head and are lying almost flat. There are many color variations to choose from. It is believed that John Gould was the first to bring the budgie to England in the 1800s.

The budgie was the first popular pet bird in the United States and remains a great favorite in America and the world over.

LOVEBIRDS

Common Name: Lovebird

Scientific Name: *Agapornis* (generic)

Country of Origin: All species are from countries extending from central through southern Africa and some islands off its western coast.

Color: The color will vary with the species. All have green feathering with various shades of red, blue, black, yellow or gray in the head and tail areas.

Length: Five to seven inches long from the head to the tip of the tail.

Life Span: Ten to 15 years

Maturity: Eight to 12 months

Sex Determination: Except for a few varieties, surgical sexing is the only reliable method.

Cage Requirements: 12"L x 12"H x 14"W (minimum)

Diet: See Chapter 3.

Breeding Requirements

Cage: 24"L x 18"H x 18"W (minimum)

Flight: 6'L x 6'H x 3'W (minimum)

Nest Box:	6"L x 6"W x 8"H. Palm fronds, various grasses, or even newspaper for nesting material is placed on the floor of the cage or flight since these birds like to build their own nest. Lovebirds will wet down this nesting material so have water readily available.
Breeding Season:	Year 'round depending upon variety.
Clutch Size:	Four to six white eggs are laid two days apart. The young hatch in 23 to 24 days and will be on their own at six to eight weeks of age.
Additional Information:	Lovebirds are hardy, sometimes noisy and aggressive. Do not mix the varieties as some do not get along with one another. The cross-breeding of varieties should be avoided since the chicks can be infertile. Some females can be aggressive to their mates, even killing them. Once a pair start to breed, they should continue producing numerous young. An understanding of genetics is important to achieve breeding success with the various color mutations.

Although lovebirds can be active and mischievous, they can also be loving pets. Some like to chew up the newspaper in their cage or maybe hide under the paper. They are hardy, inexpensive little birds and some have been known to talk. It is not uncommon to teach the pet lovebird some tricks such as pushing a miniature baby carriage, lying on its back, standing on its head or jumping through hoops. Some may be known to pick their feathers. It is not necessary to keep lovebirds in pairs unless desired. Single birds will be more affectionate and less noisy.

Lovebird Varieties

Peach-faced Lovebird: *(A. rosieicollis)*	This bird is probably the most familiar and most quarrelsome of all the lovebirds. They are smart and will learn tricks easily.
	Description: This is the largest of the lovebirds. The face and upper breast are rose-pink, the rump a bright blue, the tail is banded with orange and black and the rest of the body is green.
Fischer's Lovebird: *(A. fischeri)*	These birds usually have pleasing personalities. They are not aggressive and learn to do tricks easily.
	Description: Mostly green with some yellow on the underparts. Fischer's has a bright red beak

with a red-orange head. The rump is a dusky-blue and there is some blue in the flight and tail feathers. Total length is about 5½ inches.

Masked Lovebird:
(A. personata)

This bird is pleasing to look at and has a gentle personality.

Description: As the name indicates, it has a brownish-black head, a bright red beak and a white ring of bare skin (periopthalmic ring) around the eyes. There is some blue in the tail and flight feathers while the rest of the body is yellow-green.

COCKATIELS

Common Name:	Cockatiel
Scientific Name:	*Nymphicus hollandicus*
Country of Origin:	Australia
Color:	In their natural habitat, the wild cockatiel is predominantly grey.
Length:	Ten to 13 inches long from the top of the crest to the tip of the tail.
Life Span:	Fifteen to 25 years
Maturity:	Seven months to one year
Sex Determination:	See below
Cage Requirements:	18"L x 18"H x 16"W (minimum)
Diet:	See Chapter 3.

Breeding Requirements

Cage:	24"L x 24"H x 18"W (minimum)
Flight:	6'L x 6'H x 3'W (minimum)
Nest Box:	12"L x 12"W x 10"H with wood shavings as a bedding material.
Breeding Season:	Year 'round
Clutch Size:	Four to seven eggs laid two days apart. The young hatch in 18 to 21 days. The young birds are independent at seven to nine weeks.

Additional Information: These birds are usually good parents even when there are more than one pair housed together. A maximum of three clutches per year is recommended in order to avoid health problems in both the parents and chicks. The male and female sometimes share the sitting on the eggs and the feeding of the young. Occasionally one of the parents may feather-pick the young. Not much is known on why this occurs, but it is believed that the offending parent bird may want to breed again. An understanding of genetics is helpful when attempting to select for certain color varieties.

Cacatelho is a Portugese word meaning "little cockatoo." This is probably where the name cockatiel originated. In their native Australia they are called *Quarrion* and are nomadic. The cockatiel is a gentle and docile little bird. Males can become good talkers and whistlers but are more independent. Some females have been known to talk and they are more loving and quiet. They make wonderful pets.

We may never see a blue or green cockatiel. To create various colors, most birds have two basic pigments: yellow and black. The yellow pigments produce shades of yellow through red. The black pigment produces dull shades of yellow through browns to black. The cockatiel differs from other birds in its feather pigments. It lacks the modifiers of black pigments to produce blue coloration and yellow pigments for green coloration. All varieties have the same personality and temperament.

Cockatiel Varieties

Normal Grey: Males are various shades of grey with orange cheek patches and some white on the wings. The head is yellow and white including some of the crest feathers. Females tend to have grey heads, but retain the orange cheek patches. The underside of their wings and tails have either a faint yellow spotting or creamy yellow barring. All youngsters look like the female until their first molt at about seven months of age.

Lutino: These birds are all white; some have a yellow wash. Both male and female have the orange cheek patches. The beaks and feet are horn-colored and the eyes are a dark red. In a mature bird, the male will be all white on the underside of the wings and tail. The female will have a faint yellow barring on these areas.

Pied:	These cockatiels are mottled with spots. Pieds with more white feathering are called "Heavy Pieds" while the ones with more grey feathers are called "Light Pieds." These are the hardest to sex because there is no difference in the coloring.
Pearl:	The ends of almost all of the feathers are scalloped in white or yellow. Males will lose some of this scalloping after their first molt. By the time males are 18 months old they look like a normal gray cockatiel.
Cinnamon:	These birds are a light silvery-grey. Males usually have lighter facial areas.
Fallow:	These are the same as cinnamons but with red eyes.
Charcoal:	This is the newest variety to be developed. In both sexes the orange cheek patches are absent. The bird is a dull-colored charcoal with an all white wing patch since there are no yellow pigments. The males will have an all-white face when mature.

CONURES

Common Name:	Conure
Scientific Name:	*Aratinga, Nandayus, Pyrrhura, Enicognathus, Cyanoliseus*
Country of Origin:	Mexico and various countries in Central and South America.
Color:	Most are green with various shades of blue, red, orange, yellow or black.
Length:	From between nine to 18 inches long from head to tip of the tail.
Life Span:	Ten to 35 years, or more.
Maturity:	Depending on the variety, it can be from one to three years.
Sex Determination:	Surgical sexing is the only reliable method.
Cage Requirements:	18"L x 18"H x 18"W, depending on variety.
Diet:	See Chapter 3.

Breeding Requirements

Cage:	24″L x 18″H x 24″W (minimum)
Flight:	6′L x 6′H x 3′W (minimum)
Nest Box:	12″L x 12″W x 10″H for the smaller conures; 18″L x 18″W x 24″H for the larger ones. Peat moss and shavings are the preferred nesting materials.
Breeding Season:	March to August for most varieties. Jenday and Sun Conures: usually from October through June.
Clutch Size:	Four to seven white eggs are laid two to three days apart. The young hatch in 24 to 28 days and are independent at eight to 14 weeks of age.
Additional Information:	Some varieties will successfully breed with more than one pair to a flight or cage. Some varieties are known to break their eggs; therefore, it is best to remove the eggs immediately and place them in an incubator.

Conures are intelligent birds. They have a reputation for being very noisy and destructive; however, this does not apply to all individuals. Both sexes are known to talk, perform tricks, and are loving companions if acquired at a young age or if hand-fed. Conures are known as "miniature macaws" because of their strong resemblance to the larger birds.

Conure Varieties

Jenday *(A. jandaya):* These birds can be noisy, but are also extremely affectionate pets. When gently scratched, their feathers fluff up to make them resemble little balls.

Description: This bird has a yellow neck, head and chest. There can be some orange in the yellow. Some flight and tail feathers are blue, while the chest feathers are orange. The rest of the body is green. They are ten inches long from head to the tip of the tail.

Nanday *(N. nenday):* This variety is easy to obtain and inexpensive. Although they are not known for their talking ability, their personality is similar to the Jenday. They can be noisy.

Description: The beak and head is black while the upper chest is blue. Some parts of the wing and tail feathers are blue with green. The body is green with red thighs.

Petz's or Halfmoon
(A. canicularis):

This little conure is smart, will talk and do some tricks. It is sometimes called a "dwarf parrot" and is not usually expensive. They can be affectionate but noisy.

Description: They are about nine inches long and mostly green in color. There is a small amount of orange feathering above the nose. The upper part of the beak is a horn color while the lower beak is black.

Cherry Head
(A. erythrogenys):

If obtained at an early age they can make a charming and smart pet. Both male and female can talk and do some tricks. These birds are not usually expensive, but they are not always available.

Description: With an oversized, horn-colored beak, a large, almost all red head, a green, bulky body and slender tail, this conure appears top heavy. It measures about 13 inches long from head to the tip of the tail.

AFRICAN GREY PARROTS

Common Name:	African Grey
Scientific Name:	*Psittacus erithacus*
Country of Origin:	Various countries in central Africa such as Kenya, Uganda, Liberia, and some islands off the west coast of Africa.
Color:	Various shades of pastel grey feathers cover the body. The beak and feet are black, while the tail feathers are bright red.
Length:	Eleven to 13½ inches long from head to tip of the tail.
Life Span:	Forty or more years
Maturity:	Three years
Sex Determination:	Surgical sexing is the only reliable method.
Cage Requirements:	18"L x 24"H x 18"W (minimum)
Diet:	See Chapter 3.

Breeding Requirements

Cage:	6'L x 3'H x 3'W (minimum)
Flight:	8'L x 6'H x 3'W (minimum)
Nest Box:	18"L x 18"W x 24"H with a bedding of soaked peat moss and shavings.
Breeding Season:	Variable depending on each individual pair. Some will breed only once a year while others may breed as many as three times a year.
Clutch Size:	Two to four white eggs are laid every two to three days. The young hatch at 28 to 30 days and are independent at 12 to 14 weeks of age.
Additional Information:	Greys usually breed well with a single pair in a cage or flight. Some pairs will "hide" in their nest box during the day. When they are feeding young, they will accept new fruits and vegetables.

According to the *Guinness Book of World Records,* "Prudle", a male African grey was reported to have a vocabulary of nearly one thousand words. They are generally considered the best talking parrots and also have the unique ability to mimic sounds such as a doorbell, dripping faucet or other animal sounds. Hand-raised greys can begin talking as young as seven months of age. These birds may come to prefer only one person. They make an enjoyable "jungle sound" when relaxed. When frightened they produce a relentless "growl." All varieties have similar personalities and can talk.

African Grey Varieties

Congo *(P. e. erithacus):*	This grey is the largest at about 13½ inches long from the head to the tip of the tail. It is usually a lighter grey in color.
Ghana *(P. e. princeps):*	At about 12 inches, this grey is smaller than the Congo and it can be slightly darker grey in color.
Timneh *(P. e. timneh):*	The tail feathers on this grey are a maroon color. They are the smallest at 11 inches long and, unlike the nominate form, are a darker grey like the Ghana.

AMAZON PARROTS

Common Name:	Amazon
Scientific Name:	*Amazona* (Generic name)

Country of Origin:	Mexico and various countries in Central and South America.
Color:	Almost all Amazons are green with various shades of red, blue, orange or yellow. Most color differences are in the head areas.
Length:	Ten to 18 inches from the head to the tip of the tail.
Life Span:	Forty or more years.
Maturity:	Two years or more depending on variety.
Sex Determination:	Surgical sexing is the only reliable method.
Cage Requirements:	18″L x 24″H x 18″W (minimum)
Diet:	See Chapter 3.

Breeding Requirements

Cage:	6′L x 3′H x 3′W (minimum)
Flight:	8′L x 6′H x 4′W (minimum)
Nest Box:	12″L x 12″W x 18″H for the smaller Amazons; 14″L x 14″W x 24″H for the larger ones. Soaked peat moss and shavings are preferred for bedding.
Breeding Season:	Usually from March to July.
Clutch Size:	Two to four white eggs are laid every two to three days. The young hatch in 24 to 28 days. They become independent in eight to 14 weeks.
Additional Information:	Most Amazons breed readily, especially if they were raised in captivity or have been pets for a number of years. During the breeding season, some males may become very protective of their mates. They are usually good parents. The male may feed the female and then she will feed the young. Some Amazons may feather pick either themselves or one another during the breeding season. It is best to keep one pair per flight or cage.

For good reason these are among the most popular of the larger pet birds. They are often very loving and friendly, especially if purchased young. Older birds can be difficult to tame and are referred to as "broncos." Amazons can be very playful, so be sure to supply lots of toys for their enjoyment. Unfortunately, some are noisy during the early morning and evening hours.

Amazon Parrot Varieties

Yellow-Nape
(A. ochrocephala
auropalliata):

This bird is capable of learning a large vocabulary, and is usually curious and playful. During the breeding season, some males are known to become moody and may not talk even though there is no female present.

Description: They are almost all green, except for some yellow feathers at the nape and maybe above the nostrils. The beak is almost black and the feet are dark gray. They are about 14 inches long from head to tip of tail.

Double Yellow Head:
(A. o. ochrocephala)

The Yellow Head is the most common Amazon in the U.S. They may become good talkers, are playful, affectionate, but may also be unpredictable in their behavior.

Description: The most striking feature of this bird is the ample amount of yellow on its head. There is some orange and yellow at the bend of the wing and the thighs have some yellow feathers. The rest of the 14-inch body and tail are green. There are many varieties or subspecies of this bird.

Blue-Fronted:
(A. o. aestiva)

The Blue-Fronted Amazon can acquire an extensive vocabulary. They can be playful but noisy at times.

Description: It has a blue forehead and lores. Parts of the cheeks, crown and sometimes the upper breast, are yellow. The thighs are yellow and the bend of the wings have yellow and red feathers. The rest of the 14-inch body and tail are green.

Spectacled:
(A. a. albifrons)

Although this may be the smallest Amazon, it can be playful, affectionate and can talk, but does not usually develop an extensive vocabulary.

Description: This species has red, white and blue head coloration. Males will have red in their flight feathers while the female may have little or no red at all. The rest of this ten-inch bird is green.

Mexican Red-Head:
(A. viridigenalis)

This is another popular Amazon species. Although they are not known to be good talkers, they are affectionate and can be playful.

Description: A deep scarlet is the color of the lores, crown and forehead. There is some blue-lilac behind the eyes and the cheek feathers are green, as is the rest of the body. The beak is horn-colored. This Amazon is about 13 inches long from the head to the tip of the tail.

COCKATOOS

Common Name:	Cockatoo
Scientific Name:	*Cacatua, Probosciger, Calyptorhynchus, Callocephalon, Eolophus*
Country of Origin:	Australia, New Guinea, Indonesia, Moluccas, Philippines
Color:	The best known are all white with various shades of yellow, pink or orange usually in the crest. Other less common varieties can be various shades of black and grey with colors of pink, red, yellow and white either in the body, head or tail feathers.
Length:	Twelve to 28 inches from head to the tip of the tail.
Life Span:	Thirty years or more. (Among the longest-lived birds, a Greater Sulphur-Crested cockatoo was reported to have lived for over 100 years.)
Maturity:	Three years or more
Sex Determination:	In most of the white cockatoos, surgical sexing is recommended since eye color is not always accurate. With some of the black cockatoos, the sexes are differently colored especially in the body feathers.
Cage Requirements:	2'L x 3'H x 2'W (minimum)
Diet:	See Chapter 3.

Breeding Requirements

Cage:	6'L x 4'H x 4'W (minimum)
Flight:	8'L x 6'H x 4'W (minimum)
Nest Box:	18"L x 18"W x 28"H (minimum). Hollowed tree trunks, even garbage cans are used. Soaked peat moss and shavings are used for bedding. Some

varieties like to make their own nests out of branches, twigs and various other materials.

Breeding Season: Usually during the warmer months, however, in some of the warmer areas they may breed all year round.

Clutch Size: One to four white eggs are laid usually every two to three days apart. The young should hatch in 24 to 30 days, and become independent in 12 to 14 weeks.

Additional Information: Given time and some privacy, most cockatoos will breed. There are a few kinds, such as the Red-Vented and Goffin, that may be more difficult. In some of the varieties, both the male and female will sit the eggs and feed the young. Since some cockatoos are chewers, extra wood should be provided in the cage and nest box. Sometimes a thicker gauge wire may be needed for their cage or flight because they can chew through thinner wire. They can be very noisy at times, especially when breeding. Keep a careful eye on them when they have young because they can be neglectful about feeding. Try to make sure that the pair get along well together. In some instances the male will attack the female or it can be the reverse. In some cases the young should be taken away from the parents as soon as they are independent. Sometimes the father will be jealous of his son and attack the youngster. Since most cockatoos are territorial, they seem to do better when there is only one pair per flight or cage.

If obtained either very young or handfed, these birds can make exceptionally loving pets. Some males can be noisy, especially during the early morning and evening hours. Almost all cockatoos are natural chewers, therefore, they should be given branches or strips of wood to satisfy this habit. Some birds can become attached to one member of the family and no other. They can be mischievous one minute and sedate the next. All cockatoos are good fliers, hence, clipping their flight feathers may be advised under certain circumstances. The white cockatoos give off a fine powdery dust to which some people may be allergic. Frequent misting of the feathers on warm days will help keep this dust to a minimum. The uplifting of their crests is an emotional sign either when frightened, happy or just seeking some attention. All of the cockatoos can be moderate talkers.

Cockatoo Varieties

Greater Sulpher-Crested: The TV show "Baretta" with Fred the Cockatoo
(C. galerita) (a Triton subspecies) popularized this type of bird. They have warm, friendly natures. Although they can be noisy at times, this is usually overshadowed by the devotion they show their owners.

Description: At 19 inches long from head to tip of the tail, this type is one of the largest of the white cockatoos. The yellow crest feathers go up and forward when raised. There is some yellow on the cheek patches and the undersides of the tail and wings. The skin surrounding the eyes is white in the nominate form and pale blue in the Triton. The beak is almost black, while the feet are a dark grey.

Lesser Sulphur Crested: This type is usually not as noisy as some of the
(C. sulphurea) other cockatoos. They can learn to talk and are more active than the Greaters.

Description: The Lesser, at 12½ inches long, resembles a smaller version of the Greater. Most Lesser young do not acquire the black beak until they are about seven months old.

Umbrella *(C. alba):* The Umbrella can learn to talk, but can be very noisy. Some are playful and affectionate, while others are more sedate.

Description: They have long, broad white crest feathers that resemble an umbrella cut in half. When the crest is raised the feathers point backward. Almost all of the body is white with some dull yellow on the undersides of the tail and wings. *C. alba* is about 18 inches long, has a black beak and dark gray feet.

Moluccan: Although this bird can be noisy, it is usually gentle
(C. moluccensis) and loving, and can be taught to talk. The Moluccan is probably the most beautiful of the white cockatoos.

Description: The crest is similar to that of the Umbrella except that the feathers are salmon-pink in color. The underside of the tail feathers are pale orange, while the undersides of the wings are salmon. Various shades of pink-white to a deeper pink can be on the chest to belly areas. The beak and feet are almost black. They are about 20 inches long from head to tip of the tail.

Rose-Breasted: This beautiful cockatoo, also known by the native
(Eolophus roseicapillus) name, *Galah,* can be an affectionate pet and some
have developed a large vocabulary. They are usually not noisy and are very good fliers.

Description: At 15 inches long, they have a short pink-white crest. The body is a beautiful pastel to deep rose that extends upward to the face and nape areas. Various shades of soft gray cover the rest of the body. The beak is horn-colored and the feet are gray.

MACAWS

Common Name: Macaw

Scientific Name: *Ara, Anodorhynchus, Cyanopsitta*

Country of Origin: Mexico and various countries in Central and South America.

Color: Varies with the different species

Length: Twelve inches to 40 inches long from head to the tip of the tail.

Life Span: Twenty-five to 50 years or more.

Maturity: Approximately two years with the smaller macaws and about five years with the larger species.

Sex Determination: Surgical sexing is the only reliable method.

Cage Requirements: 18"L x 24"H x 18"W for small macaws and 5'L x 5'H x 5'W for larger macaws. Cages should be constructed of strong material such as wrought iron.

Diet: See Chapter 3.

Breeding Requirements

Cage: 8'L x 6'H x 3'W (minimum for small macaws)
8'L x 6'H x 6'W (minimum for larger macaws)

Nest Box: 12"L x 12"W x 18"H for smaller macaws; 2'H x 3'W x 4'L for the larger macaws. In addition to a wooden box, try a hollowed out tree trunk or a trash can with a large hole cut out for an entrance.

Nesting material should be soaked peat moss and shavings along with some twigs and branches.

Breeding Season: The smaller macaws tend to breed in late spring or early summer while the large species, depending on the climate, will breed year 'round.

Clutch Size: Small macaws: three to five white eggs laid one every two to three days. Young should hatch in 24 to 28 days becoming independent in 10 to 14 weeks.
Large Macaws: two to four white eggs laid one every two to three days apart. Young hatch in 28 to 32 days becoming independent in 12 to 16 weeks.

Additional Information: The small macaws are apt to breed more readily and are usually better parents. More time is necessary to get the larger birds into the breeding spirit. Also, the larger macaws, while nesting, should be closely watched since they may not sit on their eggs, feed the young chicks or may even feather pick them. Some may even crack their eggs and an incubator may be advisable to keep the parents away from them. The larger macaws may prefer their nest close to the ground. If possible, a nest box on the ground and one higher up could be provided to give them a choice. During the breeding season all macaws may become hostile to their owners or birds in adjacent cages or flights.

The best known and most often photographed varieties are the Scarlet, Blue and Gold, and Military macaws. They do require extra attention, but at the same time give back tremendous amounts of affection. Their vocabulary can become extensive and tricks are often easily learned. Because of their bulk and large stature they seem to prefer to climb and walk rather than fly around in small areas. Their powerful beaks can easily crack a Macadamia or Brazil nut. The smaller macaws require less attention, make good pets and can also learn to talk and do tricks. All macaws may like to chew, so supply plenty of wood and natural branches. Most macaws characteristically have a large featherless skin patch on their faces.

Macaw Varieties

Scarlet *(Ara macao):*   These intelligent, beautiful birds can be very affectionate toward and protective of their owners. They can also be unpredictable in their behavior at times.

Description: They are brilliant scarlet at the head, chest and wing areas. Blue, yellow, green and orange are the remaining colors in the wings. Some of their red tail feathers can be as long as 30 inches. The beak is horn-colored on the upper mandible and almost black on the lower. Length from head to the tail can be up to 40 inches.

Blue and Gold:
(Ara ararauna)

These birds, like the Scarlet macaw, are intelligent and can be very affectionate. They are also known to be mischievous.

Description: The forehead is green. The upper part of the body, wings and tail are a rich blue. From the side of the neck down the front to the lower body the feathers are a golden yellow. There is a black "bib" of feathers just below the lower beak. Both the upper and lower beak is black. They can be 34 inches long from the top of the head to the tip of the tail.

Hyacinth:
(Anodorhynchus hyacinthinus)

These are not commonly found as pets because they are difficult to obtain and are expensive. They can be very affectionate and gentle while at the same time learn to talk and do tricks.

Description: They have an oversized and powerful black beak and a beautiful cobalt blue body, wings and tail. There is some yellow skin surrounding the eye and lower beak. Their overall length is about 40 inches or more.

Noble *(Ara nobilis):*

They are the smallest and not as colorful as the other macaws, but make up for this with their personalities. They can learn words and phrases in a short time. The Noble can be a loving and gentle bird.

Description: These macaws are almost all green with some blue in the crown and some red at the bend of the wing. Some will have an all black beak, while others will have a silvery horn-colored upper beak. They have dark gray feet and can be 12 inches long from the head to the tip of the tail.

LORIES AND LORIKEETS

Common Name: Lory, Lorikeet

Scientific Name:	*Chalcopsitta, Eos, Pseudeos, Trichoglossus, Lorius, Phigys, Vini, Glossopsitta, Charmosyna, Oreopsittacus, Neopsittacus*
Country of Origin:	Australia, New Guinea, Solomon Islands, Indonesia, Celebes and other parts of the South Pacific.
Color:	Vary with the different kinds.
Length:	The lories can be from 9½ to 13 inches long from head to tip of tail. Lorikeets can be six to 11 inches long from head to tip of the tail.
Life Span:	Fifteen or more years depending on the species.
Maturity:	One to two years depending on the species.
Sex Determination:	Surgical sexing is the only reliable method.
Cage Requirements:	18″L x 18″H x 18″W (minimum for the smaller species); 24″L x 24″H x 18″W (minimum for the larger species)
Diet:	See Chapter 3.

Breeding Requirements

Cage:	2′L x 2′H x 2′W for the smaller varieties; 5′L x 3′H x 3′W for the larger species.
Flight:	6′L x 6′H x 3′W (minimum)
Nest Box:	12″L x 12″W x 18″H. Most lory boxes have a wire mesh (½″ x ½″) bottom rather than wood in order to avoid an accumulation of their messy, watery droppings. Below this wire is another wire mesh covered with small pieces of charcoal, grass and twigs to catch the droppings. Approximately three inches separate these two wire mesh pieces.
Breeding Season:	Depending on the climate, they can be bred almost any time of the year.
Clutch Size:	Two to five white eggs are laid every 48 hours. The young hatch in 23 to 28 days, becoming independent at about 10 to 14 weeks.
Additional Information:	These birds breed readily in captivity. They seem to prefer vegetation in and around their cage. Since they are not chewers this causes no problems. Their droppings are wet and runny. Con-

crete flooring is recommended as such floors can easily be washed clean.

Lories have rounded tails and lorikeets have pointed tails. They occur in a wide range of colors and some species even appear iridescent. Because of their comical and playful behavior they are considered by many as the "clowns" of the parrot world. They usually tame easily and seek the company of their owners if kept as a single pet in a cage. One of the major disadvantages of keeping these birds as pets is their tendency to squirt their droppings out of the cage and dirty the surrounding area. They have a brush-like tongue adapted for their natural diet of nectar, pollen, plant buds and insects. They frequently bathe and preen themselves.

Lory and Lorkieet Varieties

Blue Mountain Lorkieet: This is the most common of the lories. They can
(T. h. moluccanus) become very good companions because of their cheerful, comical and affectionate personality.

Description: The head is a rich violet-blue and the beak is a deep orange. The upper breast is scarlet with some red and yellow, while the lower body resembles the head. Usually there is a small yellow-green collar on the front of the neck. The back, tail and wings are various shades of green. There are approximately 21 different subspecies in this family, each varying in coloration. They are about 12 inches long from head to tip of tail.

Red Lory: They can have a harsh voice at times, but can also
(E. b. bornea) make good pets. They are cheerful and playful like the others.

Description: At 10 to 12 inches long, they are mostly red. The underside of the tail extending to the vent is blue. Some of the long flight feathers are black and red. The beak is orange and the feet are gray.

Blue-Streaked Lory: Like the others, they are cheerful and playful.
(E. reticulata)
Description: They have a purple-blue streak that extends from the corner of the eye downward and circles the upper neck area. There is a small amount of black and red in the wings; the tail is black. The rest of the body is red and its beak is red-orange. They are about 12 inches long from head to tip of tail.

Black-Capped Lory:
(L. lory)

Not only do these birds talk, but unlike the others, they can mimic sounds exceptionally well.

Description: The top of its head is purple-black. The back of the neck is blue and the blue extends downward to the lower body. The rest of the body feathers are red and the beak is yellow-orange. This lory is about 12 inches long from the top of the head to the tip of the tail.

MYNAHS

Common Name:	Mynah
Scientific Name:	*Gracula*
Country of Origin:	India, Java, Sumatra, Philippines and numerous islands in the surrounding areas.
Color:	The feathers are almost black with a small white patch in the wings. There is a patch of yellow skin extending from the cheek to near the back of the head. The beak is orange and the feet are a dull yellow.
Length:	Depending on the variety, they can be from 12 to 16 inches long from the top of the head to the tip of the tail.
Life Span:	Fifteen to 25 years.
Maturity:	One to two years.
Sex Determination:	Surgical sexing is the only reliable method.
Cage Requirements:	2½'L x 3'H x 24"W (minimum)
Diet:	See Chapter 3.

Breeding Requirements

Cage:	5'L x 3'H x 3'W (minimum)
Flight:	10'L x 6'H x 4'W (minimum)
Nest Box:	12"L x 12"W x 18"H with a bedding of shavings, twigs and dried grasses. A lory nest box may also be used.
Breeding Season:	Usually during spring and summer months.

Clutch Size: Two or three blue-green eggs with brown spots are laid 24 to 48 hours apart. The young should hatch in 21 to 31 days, becoming independent in 26 to 30 days.

Additional Information: Most mynahs do not breed readily in captivity. Some seem to prefer a hollowed out log rather than a box. The males may prefer to carry twigs and dried grasses into the nest box. Some birds are known to crack the eggs and even throw their young out of the nest. They seem to prefer vegetation in and around their cage or flight and since they are not chewers this causes no problems.

Mynahs are the unparalleled masters of the bird world when it comes to talking and mimicking sounds. Not only do they enunciate clearly, they are more apt to talk around strangers than are the parrots. Be careful of your vocabulary around them since it may be repeated by them at an embarrassing moment. They can become finger-trained and affectionate. One of their disadvantages is their messy droppings. Mynahs usually like to stay clean and enjoy bathing. Don't be surprised if you hear your doorbell ring and find no one there. It was probably your mynah imitating the sound.

The author wishes to thank Pat Coyle, Beverly Degen, Mrs. Fern Hubbell, Mary and Joe Lannom, Tony Silva, and Wayne Schulenburg for their contributions in the preparations of this section.

Appendix B

Security and Your Bird

Unfortunately, the increased popularity of birds has also created an increase in bird thefts. Most of the larger birds are quite valuable, easily moved, difficult to trace and easily sold, all of which has resulted in a lucrative black market.

As with all valuable possessions certain precautions should be taken to help prevent these thefts and insure positive proof of ownership should your bird be stolen and then recovered.

For Your Bird:

1. Don't let the world know you have birds.
2. Take close-up photographs of your bird—including distinguishing marks.
3. Record all distinguishing markings and color patterns. Also, note the particular vocabulary and any individual tricks your birds are able to perform.
4. Tattooing of the wing web is frequently used to identify males and females in breeding programs. Unfortunately, it is not yet a practical method for personally identifying pet birds.

For Your Home:

1. Follow the same recommendations that are used to prevent home burglaries. These include:
   a. dead bolts on all doors, locks or jambs on all windows and sturdy garage door fasteners,
   b. good lighting both inside and around the home. Timers work well to turn lights on at night if you are away from home.
2. Home alarm systems are now widely available and very effective.
3. Contact your local Crime Prevention Unit for more detailed advice on security.

Appendix C

The American Federation of Aviculture publishes a bi-monthly magazine called the *Watchbird.* Some articles may include up-to-date information on the care, breeding, diet, avian medicine and housing of all types of birds. It also contains articles on the breeding of rare and endangered species, where to buy birds and bird-related products and legislation affecting aviculture.
> The AFA
> P.O. Box 1568
> Redondo Beach, CA 92078

The Avicultural Society of America publiches a monthly bulletin with information concerning the care, breeding and feeding of all captive birds.
> Avicultural Society of America
> 1005 N. Eucalyptus
> Rialto, CA 92376

The African Lovebird Society publishes a monthly journal pertaining to the improvement and standardization of all species of lovebirds and their mutations.
> The African Lovebird Society
> P.O. Box 142
> San Marcos, CA 92069

The American Cockatiel Society publishes a bi-monthly bulletin on the care, breeding, exhibiting and genetics of cockatiels.
> The American Cockatiel Society
> 9812 Bois D'Arc Ct.
> Ft. Worth, TX 76216

The American Pheasant and Waterfowl Society publishes a monthly magazine with information on raising and care of ornamental waterfowl, pheasant, quail, doves, partridge and miscellaneous birds.
> The American Pheasant and Waterfowl Society
> Route 1
> Granton, WI 54436

In addition to these national organizations, there are numerous local bird clubs throughout the United States. For information on clubs in your area, see the club information section in *Bird World Magazine, American Cage Bird Magazine* or ask at your local bird pet shop.

Foreign Bird Organizations

The Avicultural Society of England was founded in 1894 and has an international membership that receives and contributes to *The Avicultural Magazine*, the oldest and most revered journal devoted to the study of wild birds in captivity. Write to:

The Hon. Secretary
The Avicultural Society of England
Windsor Forest Stud Mill Ride
Ascot, Berkshire, SL5 8LT
England

The Avicultural Society of Queensland caters to all birds both in captivity and in the wild. They publish a bi-monthly magazine on all aspects of aviculture and conservation.

The Avicultural Society of Queensland
Ray Garwood
19 Fahey's Road
Albany Creek, 4035 Qld.
Australia

The Feather Fancier, a Canadian organization, publishes a monthly newspaper for those interested in poultry, fancy and racing pigeons and pet birds.

Feather Fancier
R.R. 5
Forest, Ontario
Canada N0N 1J0

The British Columbia Avicultural Society publishes a monthly newsletter concerning all aspects of aviculture.

British Columbia Avicultural Society
C. Prior
11784 90th Avenue
Delta, BC
Canada V4C 3H6

The Golden Triangle Parrot Club caters to all psittacine birds in their monthly publication.

The Golden Triangle Parrot Club
Judy Weerheim
P.O. Box 1574, Station C
Kitchener, Ontario
Canada N2G 4P2

There are two additional societies in Australia that publish monthly journals concerning all aspects of aviculture.

Avicultural Society of Western Australia
18 Band Street
Lathlain, Western Australia 6100
Australia

Avicultural Society of Southern Australia
37 Ayre Street
South Plympton, S. Australia
Australia

The Singapore Avicultural Society publishes a monthly bulletin with articles on the care, breeding and feeding of all birds in captivity.
Singapore Avicultural Society
Mr. Patrick Tay
c/o 1st Floor, Gestetner House
Kallang Junction/Boon Keng Road
Singapore

Cage and Aviary Birds is a weekly newspaper concerning canaries, finches, parrots, breeding and much more. This is an excellent publication.
Cage and Aviary Birds
Surrey House, 1 Throwley Way
Sutton, Surrey SM1 4QQ
England

Note: These foreign organizations are open to membership for aviculturists throughout the world.

Appendix D

Magazines of Interest to Bird Owners

Bird World Magazine is published bi-monthly. It contains information on showing, caring for, housing and breeding birds.
Bird World
Box 70
North Hollywood, CA 91603

The *American Cage Bird Magazine* gives information monthly concerning canaries, budgies and other foreign birds. It also gives a listing of many local clubs throughout the United States.
American Cage Bird Magazine
3449 N. Western Avenue
Chicago, IL 60618

Bird Talk Magazine is published bi-monthly. It contains some articles on all aspects of bird life from caring for cage birds to bird life in the wild.
Bird Talk
P.O. Box 3940
San Clemente, CA 92672

The *Gazette* is published nine times a year containing articles from breeders, zoologists and conservationists on all types of birds.
Gazette
1155 E. 4780 S.
Salt Lake City, UT 84117

Appendix E

METRIC CONVERSION TABLE

Linear

1 millimeter	= 0.039 inch	1 inch	= 25.4 millimeters
1 meter	= 3.281 feet	1 foot	= 0.305 meter
1 meter	= 1.094 yards	1 yard	= 0.914 meter
1 kilometer	= 0.621 mile	1 mile	= 1.609 kilometers

Volume

1 liter	= 33.815 fluid ounces	1 fluid ounce	= 29.573 milliliters
1 liter	= 1.057 quarts	1 fluid ounce	= 0.03 liter
1 liter	= 0.264 gallon	1 pint	= 0.473 liter
		1 quart	= 0.946 liter
		1 U.S. gallon	= 3.785 liters
			= 0.83 British Imp. Gal.
		1 Brit. Imp. Gal.	= 4.546 liters
			= 1.2 U.S. Gallons

Mass

1 milligram	= 1/60 grain (Apoth)	1 grain (Apoth)	= 60 mg.
1 gram	= 0.035 ounce	1 ounce (Av.)	= 28.35 gm
1 kilogram	= 2.2 pounds	1 pound	= 0.454 kilogram (454 gm)
1 metric ton (1000 kg)	= 1.102 tons	1 ton (2000 lb)	= 0.907 metric ton (1000 kg)
1 mg/kg	= 0.454 mg/lb	1 mg/lb	= 2.2 mg/kg

Bibliography

The following reference material is listed by category as a helpful guide for additional reading.

Bird Information

Bates, H., Busenbark, R. and Vriends, Dr. Matthew M. *Parrots and Related Birds*. Third Edition, Neptune, New Jersey: T.F.H. Publications, Inc., 1978.

Bedford, The Duke of. *Parrots and Parrot-Like Birds*. Neptune, New Jersey: T.F.H. Publications, Inc., 1969.

Forshaw, J.M. and Cooper, W.T. *Parrots of the World*. Neptune, New Jersey: T.F.H. Publications, Inc., 1977.

Freud, A. *All About The Parrots*. New York: Howell Book House, 1980.

Hall, J. *Cockatiels . . . Care and Breeding*. Austin, Texas: Sweet Publishing Co., 1976.

La Rosa, D. *How To Build Everything You Need For Your Birds*. Simi, California: La Rosa Publishers, 1973.

The Parrots of South America. London, England: John Gifford Ltd., 1972.

Lories and Lorikeets—The Brush Tongued Parrots. Neptune, New Jersey: T.F.H. Publications, Inc., 1977.

Readers' Digest. *Complete Book of Australian Birds*. Sydney, Australia: Readers' Digest Services, PTY Ltd., 1976.

Restall, R.L. *Finches and Other Seed-Eating Birds*. London: Faber and Faber, 1975.

Rutgers, A. and Norris, K.A. *Encyclopedia of Aviculture. Vol. I: Cranes, Gamebirds, Waterfowl, Birds of Prey and Doves*. Poole and Dorset, England: Blandford Press, 1970.

Rutgers, A. and Norris, K.A. *Encyclopedia of Aviculture. Vol. II: Parrots, Budgies, Cukoos, Nightjars, Hummingbirds and Owls*. Poole and Dorset, England: Blandford Press, 1970.

Rutgers, A. and Norris, K.A. *Encyclopedia of Aviculture. Vol. III: Passeriformes of Africa, Australia, and America, Including Canaries, Zebra and Bengalese Finches*. Poole and Dorset, England: Blandford Press, 1977.

Roberts, C.H. *Encyclopedia of Cage and Aviary Birds.* New York: MacMillan Publishing Co., 1975.

Roberts, S. *Bird-Keeping and Bird Cages—A History.* New York: Drake Publishers, Inc., 1973.

Soderberg, P.M. *Waxbills, Weavers, and Whydahs.* Chicago: Audubon Publishing Company, 1963.

Speicher, Klaus. *Canary Varieties.* Neptune, New Jersey: T.F.H. Publications, 1979.

Bird Disease

Arnall, L. and Keymeyer, I.F. *Bird Diseases.* Neptune, New Jersey: T.F.H. Publications, Inc., 1975.

Association of Avian Veterinarians, "Proceedings of 1982 Annual Meeting." Atlanta, Georgia: Multiple Authors.

Fowler, M.E., D.V.M. *Cage Birds—Medicine and Surgery.* Unpublished Manuscript.

Fowler, M.E., D.V.M. *Plant Poisoning In Small Companion Animals.* St. Louis: Ralston Purina Co., 1981.

Fowler, M.E., D.V.M. *Zoo and Wild Animal Medicine.* Philadelphia, London, Ontario: W.B. Saunders, Co., 1978.

Hofstad, M.S. et al. *Diseases of Poultry.* 7th Edition. Ames, Iowa: Iowa State University Press, 1978.

Kirk, R.W., D.V.M. *Current Veterinary Therapy VI: Small Animal Practice.* Toronto: W.B. Saunders Co., 1977.

Kirk, R.W., D.V.M. *Current Veterinary Therapy VII: Small Animal Practice.* Toronto: W.B. Saunders Co., 1980.

McDonald, S.E., D.V.M. and Bayer, E.V., D.V.M., MPUM. "Psittacosis in Pet Birds." *California Veterinarian.* (April 1981): 6-17.

Olsen, D.E., D.V.M. and Dolphin, R.E., D.V.M. "Administering Therapeutic Agents to Cage Birds." UM/SAC (August, 1978), 1045-1050.

Petrak, M.L., D.V.M. *Diseases of Cage and Aviary Birds.* Philadelphia: Lea and Febiger Editions 1969 and 1982.

Steiner, C.V., D.V.M. and Davis, R.B., D.V.M., MS. *Cage Bird Medicine Selected Topics.* Ames, Iowa: Iowa State University Press, 1981.

Veterinary Clinics of North America, I. "Cage Birds." Multiple Authors, Toronto: W.B. Saunders Co., Vol. B, Number 2, (May 1973): 143-236.

Veterinary Clinics of North America, "Toxicology for the Small Animal Practitioner." Multiple Authors. Toronto: W.B. Saunders Co., Vol. 5, Number 4, (November 1973).

Bird Care

Axelson, D., D.V.M. *Caring For Your Pet Bird.* Toronto, Ontario: Canaviax Publications Ltd., 1982.

Gerstenfeld, S., V.M.D. *The Bird Care Book.* Reading, Massachusetts: Addison-Wesley Publishing Co., 1981.

Lafeber, T.J., D.V.M. *Tender Loving Care For Pet Birds.* Niles, Illinois: Dorothy Products Ltd., 1977.

Bird Breeding

Low, R. *Parrots, Their Care and Breeding.* Poole and Dorset: Blandford Press, 1980.

Nothoft, A. *Breeding Cockatiels.* Neptune, New Jersey: T.F.H. Publications, 1979.

Smith, R. *Breeding the Colorful Little Grass Parakeets.* Neptune, New Jersey: T.F.H. Publications, 1979.

Wild Birds

Dolensek, E.P., D.V.M. and Bell, J. *Help! A Step-By-Step Manual For The Care and Treatment of Oil Damaged Birds.* 2nd Edition. New York Zoological Society, 1978.

Johnson, S.A. *Care and Feeding of Injured and Orphaned Wildlife of San Diego.* Project Wildlife, Inc., 1978. Revised edition 1981 by Faulkner, M.A. and Grape, C.

Schultz, W.E. *How to Attract, House and Feed Birds.* New York: Collier Books, 1970.

Sunset Books. *Attracting Birds To Your Garden.* Editor: Sherry Gellner. Menlo Park, California: Lane Book, 1974.

Nutrition

Department of Agriculture. *Handbook of the Nutritional Contents of Food,* (U.S.D.A. Handbook #8). New York: Dover Publishing, 1975.

Lafeber, T.J., D.V.M. *Tender Loving Care For Pet Birds.* Niles, Illinois: Dorothy Products Ltd., 1977.

McDonald, P., Edwards, R.A. and Greenhalgh, J.F.D. *Animal Nutrition.* Second Edition, London and New York: Longman Group Ltd., 1973.

Miscellaneous

Anthony, C.P. *Textbook of Anatomy and Physiology.* St. Louis: The C.V. Mosby Company, 1967.

Kirk, R.W., D.V.M. *First Aid For Pets.* New York: Dutton, 1978.

McGinnis, T., D.V.M. *The Well Dog Book.* New York: Random House Inc. and Co-Published with The Bookworks, 1974.

General Index

Abscesses, 137, 146
Accidents, 121
Administering Drugs, 189-191
African Grey Parrot, 263, 264
African Grey Varieties, 264
African Lovebird Society, 278
Air Sac Mites, 137, 158
Air Sacs, 90
Air Sacculitis, 137
Allergies, 67, 137
Amazon Parrots, 264-67
  Blue Fronted, 266
  Double Yellow Head, 266
  Mexican Red Head, 266, 267
  Spectacled, 266
  Yellow-Nape, 266
American Cage Bird Magazine, 281
American Cockatiel Society, 278
American Federation of Aviculture, 278
American Pheasant and Water-fowl Society, 278
Amino Acids, 32
Anatomy, 83
Anesthesia, 90
Antibiotics, 142, 189, 190
Antidotes, 128
Appetite, Loss of, 103
Articular Gout, 149
Aspergillus, 137
Association of Avian Veterinarians, 167
Atria, 91
Attention Span, 225
Auditory Nerve, 86
Aviary, 63
Aviary, construction materials for, 198, 200
Aviary Construction, Wood in, 198
Aviary, Design for, 199

Aviary, Roofing for, 200
Avicultural Society of America, 278
Avicultural Society of England, 279
Avicultural Society of Queensland, 279
Avicultural Society of Southern Australia, 280
Avicultural Society of Western Australia, 280

Bacteriology, 176
Balance, 86
Basic Needs, 49
Bathing, 63, 72
Bathing Methods, 72
Bathing Solutions, 72
Behavior, Innovative, 224
Behavior, Learned, 224
Behavioral Changes, 103
Behavioral Patterns, 49
Behaviors, 224, 234
Behaviors to Teach a Bird, 227-230
  Eagle, 229
  Kiss, 227, 228
  Nod Head "Yes", 228, 229
  Potty Training, 230
  Shake Head "No", 229
  Waving, 227
Beak, 72, 74, 79, 88, 94
  Bleeding During Trimming, 78
  Care of, 74
  Deformities, 131
  Disorders, 131, 133
  Fractures, 133
  Functions, 72
  Growth, 74
  Trimming, 74, 131, 133
  Trimming Tools, 74, 78

Biological Value, 32
Bird Baths, 241, 242
Bird Organizations, Foreign, 279, 280
Bird Organizations, National, 278
Bird-Sitter, 54
Bird Talk Magazine, 281
Bird World Magazine, 281
Birds, Care in Handling, 88
Birds from Canada, Rules Concerning, 214
Birds in Training, Separating,
Birds in Training, Wing Trimming for, 50
Birds of Prey, 246
Birth Defects, 131
Biting, 218, 219
Bleeding, 116, 119, 133
Blood Clotting, 116, 146
Blood Feather, 68
Blood, Functions of, 91
Blood Loss, 91, 92
Blood Tests, 173
Blood Volume, 91
Bones, Broken, 119, 121
Bones, Make-up of, 88
Bones, Pneumatic, 88
Brain, 96
Brain Damage, 101
Branches, 59
Breeding, 193-209
Breeding Birds, Deformities in, 194
  Environmental Temperature for, 196
  Feeding and Watering, 196
  Housing for, 197-200
  Hygiene for, 197
  Inspection/Observation, 196
  Management of, 196, 197
  Social Contact with, 196

Treating Sickness in, 197
Breeding, Common Misconceptions About, 203
Breeding Failures, 208
Breeding Species, Choice of, 193, 194
Bridge, 232
Bridging Stimulus, 224, 225
British Columbia Avicultural Society, 279
Bronchi, 89
Brown Hypertrophy, 133
Budgerigar, 256, 257
"Bumblefoot," 146
Burns, 123, 124

Cage,
  as Security, 224
  Covering the, 183
  Covers, 59
  Design, 55, 57
  Location, 57, 59
  Paint, 57
  Paper, 57, 64
  Welded Wire, 198
Cage and Aviary Birds, 280
Canaries, 251-253
  American Singer, 252
  Border Fancy, 252
  Norwich, 253
  Red Factor, 253
Candida, 138, 141
Candling, 201
Capillaria, 159
Carbohydrates, 31
Carbon Dioxide, 89, 91
Cardiovascular System, 91
Cat Litter, 57
Cataracts, 85
Catching a Bird, 79
Cats, 52
Cells, 83, 96
Cere, 89
  Disorders, 133
  Inflammations of, 133
Chain Link, 198
Chewing, 60, 74
Chicks
  Deaths, 209
  Feeding, 204
  Feeding Frequency, 207

Housing, 204
Hygiene, 204
Chlortetracycline, 164
Choana, 89
Cleaning, 64
Clipping Wings, 234
Cloaca, 93, 94, 96
Cloaca Prolapse, 145
Clotting Defect, 146
Cockatiels, 259, 261
Cockatoos, 267-270
  Greater Sulphur Crested, 269
  Lesser Sulphur Crested, 269
  Moluccan, 269, 270
  Rose-Breasted, 270
  Umbrella, 269
Cod Liver Oil, 35
Columella, 86
Coloration, 67
Colds, 90, 136
Communication
  in Training, 217
  in Taming, 219
Computer Paper, 57
Concrete, 200
Conjunctiva, 85
Conjunctivitis, 134
Constipation, 108, 109, 143
Contamination, 64
Conures, 261-263
  Cherry Head, 263
  Jenday, 262
  Nanday, 262
  Petz's, 263
Convulsions, 124
Cornea, 85
Corneal Ulcers, 134
Cost of a Pet Bird, 23
"Creepers," 151
Crop, 93, 94
  Disorders, 141, 142
  Emptying Time, 207
  Impaction, 141
  Milk, 93
  Sour, 142
Cues in Training, 232
Culture and Sensitivity Tests, 138, 176
Cups, Food and Water, 60

Dehydration, 142, 185, 249

Department of Fish, Game, Wildlife Rehabilitation, 249
Diabetes, 96, 145, 146, 176
Diagnostic Testing, 173
Diarrhea, 108, 143
Diet, 150
Diets, San Diego Zoo's Recipe for, 45, 46, 47
Diet, Lory and Lorikeet, 45
Diet, Mynah Bird, 45
Diet, Parrot, 45
Digestion, 92
Digestive Disorders, 138
Digestive System, 92
Digestive System Parasites, 158-161
Digestive Tract, 93
Dirt Flooring, 200
Discipline, Emotional, 222, 223
Discipline, Physical, 222
Discipline Using a Squirt Bottle, 222, 223
Disinfectant Characteristics, Summary of, 65
Disinfectants, 64-66
Dogs, 52
Dosages of Medication, 189, 191
Doves, 93
Drafts, 136
Drainage, 200
Dried Corn, 57
Droppings, 94, 96
  Abnormal, 103, 107, 109
  Examining, 157
  Guide to Normal Number, 107
  Normal Appearance of, 107,
Drugs, 189

Ears, 86
Eating from the Hand, 220, 221
Eggs, 96
  Binding, 209
  Fertility, 201
  Hatching, 201
  Laying, 200
Elizabethan Collar, 154
Emergencies, 113, 115
Endangered Species, 214
Endocrine System, 101
Endoscope, 196
Endoscopy, 176, 180

ergy Requirements, 31, 92
teritis, 143
vironment, 49, 50, 64
vironmental Sounds, 53
coli, 143
phagus, 93
rogen, 96
amination, Complete, 168, 170
amination, Conducting an,
  04, 107
cessive Warmth, 183
ercise, 60, 150
porting, 193
es, 83, 85, 86
Disorders, 133-136
Lids, 85
Medication, 190
Tumors, 134

conry, 246, 247
ss, 31
ather Fancier, 279
athers
  Contour, 67
  Cysts, 149
  Damaged, 150
  Disorders, 150
  Down, 67
  Flight, 67
  Mites, 156
  Picking, 151, 152
  Picking, Causes and Solutions,
    152, 154
  Problems, 103
cal Exam, 176
cal Steroid Analysis, 196
ces (See: Droppings)
eders, 239, 241
  Placement of, 241
eding Stations, 239
eding Tables, 239
eding Utensils, 204
et, Stress on, 59
ches, 253-255
  Lady Gouldian, 255
  ociety or Bengalese, 255
  Zebra, 254, 255
icky Eater, Feeding the, 47, 48
as, 157
ght, 67, 88
ghts, Prefabricated, 198
oring Materials, 200

Florescein Dye, 134
Fluids, Amounts to Give, 185
Flying Exercise, 50
Foods
  Choice of, 29
  Intake, Changes in, 103, 107
  Medicating, 190
  Rewards, 223, 224
  for the Sick Bird, 185
Force Feeding, 133
Foreign Bodies, 142
Fractures, 121
Fruit, 43, 208
Fruit Juices, 37

Galvanized Wire, 198, 200
Gapeworms, 157
Gazette, 281
Giardia, 160
Gizzard, 93
Gizzard Disorders, 142
Glorified Reptiles, 67
Goiter, 137
Golden Triangle Parrot Club, 279
Gout, 149, 150
Gram Scale, 207
Grass Flooring, 200
Greens, 41, 43
Grit, 37
Grooming, 67, 68, 72
Growths, 146

Halfmoon, 263
Hand-Fed Birds, 217
Hand-Feeding, 185, 203, 204, 207,
  208
Hand-Feeding Recipes, 207
Hand-Raised Birds, 193
Health Certificates, 53, 54
Health, Signs of, 20
Healthy Bird, Appearance of, 67
Hearing, 86
Heart, 91
Heart, Anterior Chamber, 85
Heart Disease, 92
Heart Rates, 91
Heat Lamp, 183
Heating Pad, 183
Heatstroke, 124, 125
Hematoma, 146
Hepatitis, 145

Hernias, 149
Home Emergency Kit, 191
Hormones, 101
Hospital and Staff,
  Evaluating the, 168
Housing, 49
Housing, Indoor, 198
Housing, Site Selection for, 198
Humidity, 63, 204
Hypovitaminosis A, 138

Import Regulations, 212
Imports, 214
Incubation, 200, 201
Infection, 64
Injection, Medication by, 190
Injured Birds
  Caring for, 244
  Handling, 113, 243, 244
  Transporting, 113
Insulation Material, 200
Integument (Skin), 86, 88
Intelligence, 217
Intestinal Disorders, 143
Intestine, Large, 93
Intestine, Small, 93
Iodine, 35
Iris, 85
Isolation, 164, 166

Keratin, 68, 72, 74
Kidney, Biopsies, 150
Kidney Disease, 94, 96, 150
Kidneys, 54
Kitchen Foods, 238

Laboratory Tests, 173
Lacrimal Fluid, 85
Larynx, 89
Lead Poisoning, 57
Leg Bands, 123
Lens, 85
Lice, 156
Lipoma, 149
Liver, 93, 94
Liver Disorders, 145
Lories, 272-275
  Black-capped, 275
  Blue-streaked, 274
  Red, 274

Lorikeets, 272-275
  Blue Mountain, 274
Lovebirds, 257-259
  Fischer's, 258, 259
  Masked, 259
  Peach-faced, 258
Low, Rosemary, 49, 193
Lugol's Solution, 35
Lymphatic System, 92

Macaws, 270-272
  Blue and Gold, 272
  Hyacinth, 272
  Noble, 272
  Scarlet, 271-272
Malocclusion, 131
Marrow, 88
Mating, 96
Medications, 189
Medicines, Over-the-Counter, 185
Metabolism, 89
Metric Conversions, 282
Millet Spray, 220
Mimicry, 231
Mineral Oil, 141
Minerals, 35
Minerals, Essential in Bird
  Feeding, 38, 39
Minerals, Sources of, 35
Mites, 131
Molt
  Abnormal, 150, 151
  French, 151
  Special Care During, 68
Motion Sickness, 54
Mouth, Medication by, 190
Mucus Membranes, 94
Multiple Birds, 52
Musculoskeletal System, 88, 89
Mynahs, 275, 276

Nails, 74, 78
  Bleeding During Trimming, 78
  Tools for Trimming, 78
  Trimming, 78
Nasal Discharge, 133
Neck Bones, 88
Nerve Damage, 101
Nerves, 96
Nervous System, 96, 101
Nest Box Inspection, 197

Nest Boxes, 200
Nesting, 242
Nesting Materials, 242, 243
Neuroses, 151
Newcastle Disease, 20, 137, 164,
  165, 212, 215
Newly Acquired Bird, 25, 27
Newly-Hatched Chicks, 201, 203,
  204, 207
Newspaper, 57
Nictating Membrane, 85
Nose Medication, 190
Nostrils, 89
Nutrition, 29

Obesity, 137, 150
Observation, Sexing by, 196
Oil-Damaged Birds, 249, 250
Oil Damaged Birds,
  Cleaning Procedures, 250
Ophthalmic Medication, 249
Organs, 83
Ornithosis, 163
Orphaned Birds, 243
  Caring for, 244, 245
  Housing and Feeding, 245, 246
  Releasing, 246
Otoscope, 196
Ova, 96
Oval Window, 86
Ovary, 96
Oviduct, 96
Owning a Bird, Reasons to, 19
Oxygen, 89, 91
Oyster Shell, 35

Pacheco's Disease, 165
Pancreas, 93
Pancreatic Disorders, 145, 146
Panting, 86
Paper Towels, 57
Parasites, 154-161, 176
Parrots: Their Care and Breeding,
  49, 193
"Pasted Vent," 96
Pelleted Food, 43
Perches, 59, 60
Pet Bird
  Definition, 211
  Importing, 211, 212
  Ports of Entry for, 213

Phallus, 96
Pharynx, 89, 93
Physical Modification, 83
Physiology, 83
Pigeons, 93
Pin Feather, 68
Plaques in the Mouth, 94, 138
Playpen, 60
Pneumonia, 137
Poisoning, 125-130
  How to Prevent, 130
  Insecticide, 129
  Lead, 129
  Teflon, 129
Poisonous Plants, Common,
  126-128
Poisons, Common Household
Positive Relationship, 231
Positive Reward, 219, 220, 22
Post-Mortem Examination, 1
Post-Operative Care, 181
Poultry, 211, 212, 213, 215
Pox Infection, 139
Preening, 67, 68, 72
Professional Parrot Trainers,
Progesteron, 96
Protein Metabolism, 94
Proteins, 32
Proventriculus, 93
Proventriculus Disorders, 142
Psittacosis, 20, 137, 163, 164,
Psittacosis Symptoms in Hum
  164
Pulse, 91
Pupil, 85
Purchasing, 19, 20, 23
PVC Tubing, 59, 198

Quarantine, 54, 164, 165, 213
  Exceptions to, 213, 214
  Period of, 213
  Regulations, 211
Questions on Taming and
  Training, 232-235
Quick, 78

Radiographs, 121
Radiology, 177
Raptors, 246, 247
Record Keeping, 197
Records, 231

gurgitation, 139, 141, 187
primand, Verbal, 222, 224
productive Problems, 208
productive System, 96
spiration, 89
spiratory Infections, 134, 136,
38, 170
spiratory Problems, Common,
37
spiratory Rates, 91
spiratory System, 89, 90
spiratory System Disorders, 136
spiratory System Parasites,
57, 158
st, 185
straint, 79, 81
During Beak Trimming, 74
Methods of, 79, 81
tina, 85
ward, 232
dent Control, 197
of, Double, 200
undworms, 158
unners," 151

liva, 93
monella, 143
n Diego Zoo's Hand-Feeding
Formula, 207, 208
aly-Face Mite, 155
atic Nerve, 101
lera, 85
asonal Management, 197
curity Measures, 277
eds, 41, 208
zures, 124
micircular Canals, 86
x Determination, 194, 196
xing, Genetic, 156
xing, Surgical, 180, 194, 196
ock, 115, 116, 121, 123, 124,
143, 170
k Birds
Appearance of, 67
Handling, 113
Transporting, 53
kness, Signs of, 103
gapore Avicultural Society, 280
uses, 89
usitis, 136
us Infections, 133

Skin Medication, 190
Skin Parasites, 155-157
Skull, 88
Sleep, 185
Sleeping Conditions, 59
Smuggled Birds, 164, 166
Smuggling, 20, 215
Space Heater, 183
Spasms, 124
Species, Choice of, 20
Species, Number of, 19
Spleen, 92
Spraying, 63
Spraying, Precautions When,
129, 130
Stapes Bone, 86
Staying on the Hand, 225, 227
Sternum, 88
Stress, 25, 27, 136, 163, 185
Subcutaneous Emphysema, 149
Suet, 238
Sunflower Seed, 219, 220
Surgery, 180, 181
Survival, 67, 83, 96
Swallowing, Difficult, 94
Swellings, 146
Syrinx, 89

T-Stand, 60
Table Food, 43
Talking, 23, 230-232, 234, 235
Talking on Cue, 231, 232
Talking, Best Parrot for, 235
Taming, 217, 218, 219-223, 224, 225
Tapes, 231
Tapeworms, 159
Tattooing, 277
Temperament, 23
Temperature, 63, 249
Temperature, Body, 91
Temperature for Young Chicks,
204
Testicles, 96
Testosterone, 96
Tetracycline, 190
Therapy, 180
Thermometer, 183
Thyroid, 151
Thyroid Gland Function, 35
Ticks, 157
Tissue Biopsies, 176

Toenails, Trimming, 234
Toes, 88
Towel, Use in Restraint, 79, 81
Toys, 50, 60
Toys for Larger Parrots, 60, 63
Toys, Lead paint in, 63
Trachea, 89
Trainability, 23
Training, 217, 218, 219, 223-225
Training Sessions, 225
Training Sessions, Length of, 223
Training Sessions, Frequency of,
223
Trauma, 101, 134
Travel Crate, 53
Travel, Food During, 53
Travel Needs, 53
Travel Precautions, 53
Travel, Reservations for, 53
Travel With Birds,
By Car, 53
By Air, 53
By Bus or Train, 53
Treats, 219, 220
Trichomonas, 160, 161
Tube Feeding, 187, 188
Tube Feeding, Frequency of, 188
Tube Feeding Recipes, 188
Tube Feeding Technique, 187
Tumors, 137, 149, 176
Tympanic Membrane, 86

USDA-APHIS, 211-213, 214, 215
U.S. Customs Service, 214
U.S. Department of the Interior,
214
U.S. Public Health Service, 214
Urates, 94
Ureters, 93, 94
Uric Acid, 149
Urinalysis, 176
Urinary System, 94
Urine, 94
Uropygial Gland, 68 Uterus, 96

Vagina, 96
Vaporization, 190, 191
Vegetables, 41, 43, 208
Ventricles, 91
Veterinarian, Selecting a, 168
Veterinarians, 167-173

Veterinary Fees, 170, 173
Veterinary Visits—What to
  Bring, 173
Visceral Gout, 149
Vision, 83
Vital Signs, 91
Vitamin A Deficiency, 134, 136,
  138
Vitamin A Therapy, 139
Vitamin K, 116
Vitamin Supplements, 32, 35
Vitamins, 32

Vitamins, Essential in Bird
  Feeding, 36
Vitreous Chamber, 85

Warmth, 183
Watchbird, 278
Water, 37, 185
Water Intake, Changes in, 103, 107
Water Intake, Increased, 96
Water, Medicating, 190
Weaning, 208
Weather, 198

Weighing, 207, 208
Weight, Dosage by, 189
Whydah, Paradise, 255
Wild Birds, 50, 237-250
Wild Birds, Food Preferences
  237-239
Wild Birds, Supplementary F
  for, 237, 238
Wild Birds, Water for, 242
Wing Bones, 88
Wing Trimming, 68, 72, 234
Wood Shavings, 57